Pleasure Dome:
on reading modern poetry

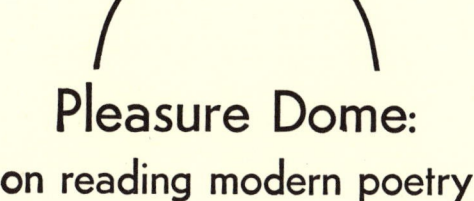

BOOKS BY LLOYD FRANKENBERG

The Red Kite
Pleasure Dome: on reading modern poetry

Pleasure Dome:
on reading modern poetry

by LLOYD FRANKENBERG

GORDIAN PRESS
New York
1968

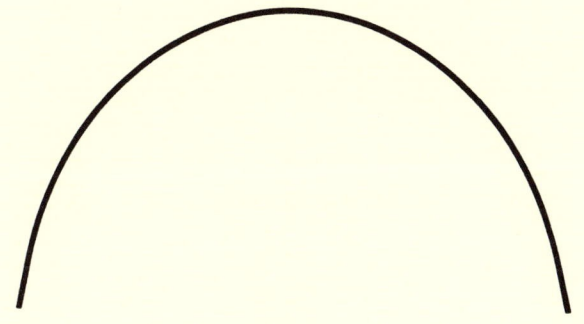

Originally Published 1949

Reprint 1968

Library of Congress Catalog Card Number 68-57701

Published by GORDIAN PRESS
By Arrangement

Selections quoted in this book are used by permission of the following:

BRANDT & BRANDT:

Collected Poems by E. E. Cummings. Copyright, 1923, 1925, 1926, 1931, 1935, 1938, by E. E. Cummings. Published by Harcourt, Brace & Company, Inc.

50 Poems, copyright, 1939, 1940, by E. E. Cummings. Published by Duell, Sloan & Pearce.

1 X 1, copyright, 1944, by E. E. Cummings. Published by Henry Holt & Company.

Santa Claus: A Morality, copyright, 1946, by E. E. Cummings. Published by Henry Holt & Company.

FABER AND FABER LIMITED:

Poems by W. H. Auden.

Another Time by W. H. Auden.

Collected Poems 1909–1935 by T. S. Eliot.

Selected Essays 1917–1932 by T. S. Eliot.

Murder in the Cathedral by T. S. Eliot.

The Family Reunion by T. S. Eliot.

Four Quartets by T. S. Eliot.

Selected Poems by Marianne Moore.

HARCOURT, BRACE & COMPANY, INC.:

Collected Poems 1909–1935 by T. S. Eliot. Copyright, 1936, by Harcourt, Brace & Company, Inc.

Selected Essays 1917–1932 by T. S. Eliot. Copyright, 1932, by Harcourt, Brace & Company, Inc.

Murder in the Cathedral by T. S. Eliot. Copyright, 1935, by Harcourt, Brace & Company, Inc.

The Family Reunion, copyright, 1939, by T. S. Eliot.

Four Quartets, copyright, 1943, by T. S. Eliot.

Lord Weary's Castle by Robert Lowell. Copyright, 1944, 1946, by Robert Lowell.

HARVARD UNIVERSITY PRESS:

The Use of Poetry and the Use of Criticism by T. S. Eliot. Copyright, 1933, by the President and Fellows of Harvard University.

HOUGHTON MIFFLIN COMPANY:

North & South by Elizabeth Bishop. Copyright, 1946, by Elizabeth Bishop.

ALFRED A. KNOPF, INC.:

Harmonium by Wallace Stevens. Copyright, 1923, 1931, by Alfred A. Knopf, Inc.

Ideas of Order, copyright, 1935, 1936, by Wallace Stevens.

The Man with the Blue Guitar, copyright, 1935, 1936, 1937, by Wallace Stevens.

Parts of a World, copyright, 1942, by Wallace Stevens.

Transport to Summer, copyright, 1942, 1947, by Wallace Stevens.

LITTLE, BROWN & COMPANY:

The Face is Familiar by Ogden Nash. Copyright, 1935, by Ogden Nash.

Many Long Years Ago, copyright, 1935, by Ogden Nash.

I'm a Stranger Here Myself, copyright, 1938, by Ogden Nash.

LIVERIGHT PUBLISHING CORPORATION:

Viva by E. E. Cummings. Copyright, 1931, by E. E. Cummings.

THE MACMILLAN COMPANY and MACMILLAN & CO., LTD., LONDON

The Charwoman's Daughter by James Stephens. Copyright, 1912, by The Macmillan Company.

The Crock of Gold by James Stephens. Copyright, 1912, by The Macmillan Company, 1940, by James Stephens.

The Demi-Gods by James Stephens. Copyright, 1914, by The Macmillan Company.

Songs from the Clay by James Stephens. Copyright, 1915, by The Macmillan Company.

for Loren
the first reader

"But given all the necessary mental faculties, birds sing only when they are in such a healthy condition that there is a surplus of energy."

— ENCYCLOPAEDIA BRITANNICA, XITH EDITION: "SONG"

Foreword

I HOPE to provide a bridge to modern poetry for readers like myself, brought up on prose.

The pleasures of music and the drama come to us through performance. Where can we go to hear poetry? We have nowhere to go but the books, the printed scores. In the absence of sustained public performance we have to be our own interpretive artists.

I have tried to give clues to the relationships between sound and meaning in the poems of living poets. Five poets are dealt with in detail; seven more briefly. They are chosen to illustrate the varieties of originality to be found in modern poetry. I have chosen only poets I like, but not the only poets I like.

To itemize my personal debts would make this book look more scholarly than it is meant to be. But I should like to thank, above all, U. T. and Joe Summers, at whose instigation it became a book.

Part One is expanded from an article, "Meaning in Modern Poetry," in the *Saturday Review of Literature,* which also published "The

Poetry of James Stephens." Additional portions of Part One appeared in *The Tiger's Eye,* under the title "Poetry and the Silent Reader." A preliminary version of "Cummings Times One" was published in the *Harvard Wake,* and the section as it now stands, in *Art and Action,* the tenth anniversary issue of *Twice a Year.* The chapters on Marianne Moore are from an article in the *Quarterly Review of Literature.* I wish to thank the editors of these publications, and of the *New York Times Book Review* for permitting me to incorporate passages from reviews.

And I should also like to thank, for having made freely available, for critical purposes, the copyright material credited to them on the copyright pages, Mr. James Laughlin and the New Directions Press; my own publishers, Houghton Mifflin Company; the Harvard University Press; Brandt & Brandt; Faber and Faber Limited; and Macmillan & Company, Ltd., of London.

Contents

Part One

MEANINGS IN MODERN POETRY

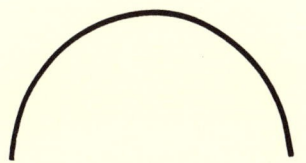

I

Poetry and the Silent Reader

MODERN POETRY is intelligible. Its forms and language may be personal but they are not inscrutable. Its pleasures are comparable to those of the other audible arts.

Why then do we have so much trouble with it, those of us who take the trouble? Why is the legend of its obscurity so prevalent? I think there are two reasons: one congenital, the other a by-product of our time.

The poetry of our own time is always more difficult than the poetry of other times. This is as true today as it was when Keats first published. The poetry of the past seems more familiar to us, whether we have read it or not. It has gone through so many critical hands, whose approval clings. Explicitly or implicitly it has given us whatever definition of poetry we may have.

With every significant new poet the definition changes. As I write, poems are being written that may expand the most comprehensive definition I could frame. Criticism tends always to lag behind creation. New work requires a more independent act of judgment. It cannot be judged entirely on the basis of standards taken from the past. To a degree depending on its originalities, the new imposes its own standards.

These difficulties are what might be called normal. From period to period they remain more or less constant; part of a natural resistance to change. But this is an age of revolutionary change. Why, at such an experimental time, should our resistance to the new poetry increase?

I believe the habit of silent reading is largely responsible. As an exclusive practice, it limits the ways in which we give our attention. We are inclined to attend partially or intermittently to what we read. Specialized forms of communication, designed to meet our shifting attention, tend to confirm us in it. The newspaper and the digest encourage us to look first for the salient feature, noting or dismissing its trailing details.

Our enjoyment of poetry is inhibited by this silent treatment. Not only contemporary, but past poetry as well, suffers. And since enjoyment is necessary to complete understanding, prose too is only superficially understood. As Buffon said, "The style is the man himself." The great style includes and conveys inflections. In prose or poetry, it conveys these to the inner ear: the ear that has had the prior experience of hearing and distinguishing between tones of voice.

Poetry is an art of the ear's discriminations: a heightening of the inflections of prose. Like music, its meanings are conveyed through sound. Sound forms part of its meaning. It does not always have to be read aloud; but it has to be read as if we were hearing it.

Unhappily today, our hearing of poetry is restricted. Often it has been restricted to an elocutionary tone of voice: the enthusiastic recitation that first gave us our aversion to poetry. If we are among those who have heard good readings – Robert Frost talking his poems, the Colums reciting, a recording of Eliot or Cummings, or of Joyce reading parts of *Finnegans Wake* – we keep these in our inner ear. Our enjoyment, when we read to ourselves, is that much fuller. We are still deprived of the fullest pleasure because these experiences are not continuous, nor varied enough. We are apt to mix styles of reading.

Not all poetry is intended to be chanted, with the tonal excitement of Vachel Lindsay's "The Congo" or G. K. Chesterton's "Lepanto." There are poems suitable, like concerti, for large audiences; and poems suitable for small, like chamber music. Always the sound, whether stressed or unstressed, is an integral part of the poem.

Differences in the styles of Chopin and of Stravinsky are clarified for us in the art of their interpreters. Lacking this intermediary art, the appreciation of music would be restricted to composers and to those experts who by glancing at the score may imagine the sound.

The symbols of poetry are more familiar to us than musical notation. But a voice no more accompanies a sheet of poetry than it does a sheet of music. It is this absence that accounts for many of our misconceptions.

II

The State of Meaning

One of the obstacles to the understanding of poetry, especially modern poetry, is a general misconception of "meaning" and "clarity." It is true that some meanings can be clearer than others. If I say, "I gave him an apple," the statement is clear, but it isn't clear about a great deal.

Prose is apt to go in the direction of this limited type of clarity. It tends to build up its complexities of meaning by addition, in a more or less continuous line. Fact succeeds fact. "I gave him an apple. He ate it."

Poetry tends to build up its meanings by multiplication. It is less concerned with facts as facts. If the eating of an apple occurs in a poem it is not likely to be passed on as a piece of informative gossip. It is more likely to be related to an emotion connected with the eating of apples. Fact is subordinated to imagination.

We have still not isolated poetry, because emotion and imagination enter of course into fiction. To this extent fiction tends in the direction of poetry. Poetry is a condensed form of imagination. This condensed form relies upon relationships that ply back and forth between the words, sounds, images and ideas.

By these means Marianne Moore's bird that "steels his form straight up," in the title poem of *What Are Years,* gains its specially dramatic significance:

> . . . He
> sees deep and is glad, who
>   accedes to mortality
> and in his imprisonment, rises
> upon himself as
> the sea in a chasm . . .
>
> . . . The very bird,
>   grown taller as he sings, steels
> his form straight up. Though he is
>   captive,
> his mighty singing
> says, satisfaction is a lowly
> thing, how pure a thing is joy.

The word "steels" is the crux of the poem. In its literal and figurative meanings the ideas of imprisonment and liberation meet. The bird, in his mighty singing, triumphs over captivity; he *becomes* the bars that confined him.

The symbols of imprisoned bird and enchasmed sea are integrally related to the form of the poem. Its rhythms rove with vinelike freedom from line to line in a profusion that is made possible by the underlying metric, one of the most exact to be found in all literature.

Wordsworth, in reaction to the poetic diction of his day, appropriated some of the language of prose. Marianne Moore is able to import its rhythms — any rhythm she wishes — and by means of her strict syllabic patterns subject them to a tension that unmistakably differentiates them from prose. Her poems are an expansion of the limits of poetry.

Poetry's clarity, then, is on a different level. The subsidiary and associational meanings of words, which are customarily slurred over in prose, contribute intensively to the total import of poetry. Rather than proceeding unilaterally, from the first word on, poetry's meanings are apt to start from somewhere in the middle and work both ways. That is why it requires rereading to become clear.

This characteristic varies from poem to poem. Some depend primarily on a simple melodic line, like Housman's:

> With rue my heart is laden
>   For golden friends I had,
> For many a rose-lipt maiden
>   And many a light-foot lad.

The idea here is easy to follow, although it shrinks with re-examination. This is not necessarily true of poems employing regular metres. But as the music of poetry becomes more variable, the subtlety of its interrelationships tends to increase, as in these lines from a sonnet of E. E. Cummings:

> what a proud dreamhorse pulling (smoothloomingly) through
> (stepp) this (ing) crazily seething of this
> raving city screamingly street wonderful
>
> flowers . . .

Poem and subject are one. The poem is a seeable, hearable, smellable city street. Into it a horse pulls a flowercart. His hoofbeats fall exactly as they do on the pavement, a heavy plod – " (stepp) " – for the first, a metallic click – " (ing) " – for the second. The horse comes right up beside us:

> o what a proud dreamhorse moving(whose feet
> almost walk air). now who stops. Smiles.he
>   stamps

The more one reads the poem the more meaning can be found in it. Beauty turns up unexpectedly anywhere. We perceive it, not by escaping the confusions and distractions of the present, but by observing them until their relationships fall into place.

Looking at the poem again, we may notice that the horse, "whose feet almost walk air," suggests Pegasus. The poem may be taken as an allegory, a modern allegory, of poetry.

Such interpretations will not be identical from person to person. Poetry is not above explanation, but around it. We find it convenient to make up simplifications: little stories or prose "ponies" of a poem, which translate its integrated meanings into the linear structures with which we are more familiar. These explanations, no matter how extended, can only *say* what, in the poem, is being *acted out.* They are successful if they return us to the poem more aware of what is going on in it. Their greatest success is to demonstrate their own comparative failure, by making us aware of what they have missed.

There is a point at which the meaning of a poem enters us fully, as if through the senses. Such an experience is one that may accurately be described as incommunicable, not because it is unrelated to what we ordinarily think of as experience, but because it is more complete.

There are two equally misleading attitudes toward this incommunicable quality. The first has often been called Philistine. Its contention is that no special quality resides in poetry. Figurative language, metrical arrangement, rhyme and other poetic devices merely provide elaborate distortions of the commonsense meanings of prose.

This frame of mind is not exclusive with us. But it seems to be peculiarly prevalent in the United States, perhaps in reaction to pedantic methods of teaching. We all tend to share it, consciously or not, intermittently or all the time. It constitutes our initial resistance to poetry of any sort.

The result is roughly analogous to what would happen in a nation raised on arithmetic, which resisted the dissemination of algebra. Higher mathematics, its commonsense attitude would hold, is merely an elaborate distortion of the concept "two plus two equals four."

We are able to appreciate the value of mathematics, even when we cannot follow all its steps. We realize that although higher mathematics may have many points of contact with arithmetic, it is able to solve problems not susceptible of solution in arithmetical terms. It does not replace arithmetic, any more than poetry could replace prose. But it demonstrates that the concept "two plus two equals four" is not true for all situations. The concept continues to have meaning; but its meaning has been shown to be limited.

Complementing the Philistine attitude is the cult of ineffability. This is where friends and defenders of poetry meet its best enemies. According to this attitude, meanings in poetry bear *no* relation to meanings in prose. Not only is it impossible to explain a poem; the very attempt destroys the poem.

It is true that analysis can only direct our attention to the various elements that go together to form the poem. If our attention is permanently directed to the parts rather than to the poem, our attention has been permanently misdirected. The poem is unique in the way its relationships, its meanings, coalesce. It is more than the sum of its parts. But to refuse analysis, to regard simply its "wholeness," its ineffability, leaves us with a very hazy notion of its nature.

III

Immediacy and Simultaneity

THE VERY PRECISE MEANS used by Cummings to reproduce a city street is typical of a tendency prevalent in modern poetry: the heightening of immediacy. "Immediacy" does not mean you "get it right off." It means that what you get, when you get it, is *presented*; it has the effect of happening right now. If you let it, it will come up very close, like the horse. The symbols become the experience they are symbolizing.

Immediacy has always been part of poetry. As impulse, it represents the constant feeling of poets. As result, it represents their developing technical means of carrying out this impulse. Until recently it has been more noticeable as an element of composition; as in Gerard Manley Hopkins' "Pied Beauty":

> Glory be to God for dappled things—
>   For skies of couple-colour as a brinded cow.

This is immediacy of detail. The second and succeeding lines present images that are the result of acute observation. This kind of immediacy demands the active participation of the reader. Rather than surrendering passively, say, to the mellifluous if somewhat cloying rhythms of a Swinburne, he must look with his mind's eye at what the poet has observed. His ear too must participate in the rhythms, which he cannot – as in the case of less varied measures – fore-hear.

In general, however, earlier poets used immediacy as an ingredient. The tendency in modern poetry, and all the arts, is to use it as an active principle working through the other elements of design. The intention is less to *represent* than it is to *enter.*

One of the most thoroughgoing examples of this tendency is a work that began as prose and moved in a direction that breaks down all formal distinctions. James Joyce's epic tragi-comedy begins, in *A Portrait of the Artist as a Young Man,* in a babyish style reproducing the age of its protagonist, Stephen Dedalus. The style alters and deepens as Stephen grows older. In *Ulysses* other characters live in his mind as they live in the imagination of an artist. In *Finnegans Wake* Stephen himself disappears, absorbed in the waters of the Liffey, which flows through dreams and through history just as the artist himself, fragmented, becomes one with his creation and with the world. The river of death is also the river of life.

Related to immediacy is another characteristic of modern art: simultaneity. Picasso, in some of his canvases, presents many sides (often including the insides) of an object or person at once. The visible world is not one-sided, two-dimensional; or even a series of faces, planes, or slices. But a strategic arrangement of such planes and slices can give us an experience of totality.

T. S. Eliot in *The Waste Land* draws together the sensations of a mundane present and of a mythological, classical or romantic past.

> Above the antique mantel was displayed
> As though a window gave upon the sylvan scene
> The change of Philomel, by the barbarous king
> So rudely forced; yet there the nightingale
> Filled all the desert with inviolable voice
> And still she cried, and still the world pursues,
> 'Jug Jug' to dirty ears.

This is an ironic compound of aggrandizement and belittlement. The dream of imperishable beauty, such as Ovid allegorized in *Metamorphoses* and Keats celebrated in his odes to the nightingale and the Grecian Urn, is brought together with man's grim insistence on "actuality": the nightingale's song is at times — especially after mating — a guttural croak reminding one of a chamberpot. Eliot's poetry interweaves the styles of past cultures in a manner expressive of the reliquary character of modern life, composed as it so largely is of fragments.

In Elizabeth Bishop's "Roosters" heroic and inglorious attributes of the domestic fowl are equally presented:

> The crown of red
> set on your little head
> is charged with all your fighting-blood.
>
> Yes, that excrescence
> makes a most virile presence,
> plus all that vulgar beauty of iridescence.

This treatment is appropriate to the poet's use of the rooster as a symbol. The same bird whose "uncontrolled, traditional cries" hatefully wake us from sleep, woke Peter from his triple denial; yet in that very act became the symbol of his forgiveness. Modern poetry is full of compound emotions, which often turn out to be the resolution of apparent antitheses.

A critic complained that the following passage from "The Atoll in the Mind," by Alex Comfort, was a succession of mixed metaphors, which should better have been similes:

> Out of what calms and pools the cool shell grows
> dumb teeth under clear waters, where no currents
> fracture the coral's porous horn
> grows up the mind's stone tree, the honeycomb,
> the plump brain coral breaking the pool's mirror,
> the ebony antler, the cold sugared fan.

Whatever metaphors there may be here, they are completely incidental and would certainly not be improved by turning them into similes. There is a new device at work. The arrangement throughout of words referring to shells, coral, and sea-forms indicates not only a visual resemblance between them and the structure of man, but a substantial identity. This, reinforced by the knowledge that all life originated in the sea, conveys a sensation of thoroughgoing relatedness. The poet does not say, "My body is (or is like) a shell." He presents a shell-body, body-shell configuration; a concentric relationship. The impulse is *like* that that goes into a simile, metaphor, or symbol, but the wavelength is different.

The danger in classifications is that we get to thinking things actually fit into them. When the discrepancy becomes too apparent, our reflex is to deny, not the classification, but the validity and very existence of the discordant item. Thus dissonance in modern music is imputed to ignorance of the rules of harmony.

When E. E. Cummings writes, "Spring is like a perhaps hand," he has not forgotten that "perhaps" is customarily an adverb. He has given it a double function: to describe precisely the tentative quality of spring and at the same time convey the elusive feelings it inspires. Such refreshings of language serve to remind us that parts of speech came into being before they were formularized. They are there to be used, altered or discarded in whatever way suits our requirements.

Few people would currycomb the hood of an automobile. But some of our routine ways of thinking about figures of speech are almost as outmoded. Similes, metaphors, symbols, along with metre and rhyme-scheme, are often regarded as if they existed not for use but somehow above and beyond it, like Platonic archetypes. They are taught as discrete entities, instead of processes. Processes change with people.

The form of a metaphor has not been determined for all time. Its function is to express a degree of relatedness merging on its less intense side with the simile, which presumes likeness. On its more intense side it merges with the symbol, which implies a configuration of relationships.

The history of figurative usage is complex, but its underlying intention is not. From the simplest pun to the structure of Dante's

Divine Comedy, its purpose is the catching of variable degrees of likeness between diverse elements. Some degree of this process is present in all language.

The poet restores purpose to our automatic usages. He invents new ones and elaborates the conventional fixtures to make them more consonant with his feelings, to infuse new life into otherwise trite devices. His desire is to recapture spontaneity; to reconstruct it; to construct a premeditated spontaneity: that totality of response in which sound, rhythm, sensation, emotion and thought — all the processes we think of and use as if they were separate — contribute intensively to each other, ceasing to exist as elements and becoming symbols of the whole man.

Part Two

JAMES STEPHENS, HIMSELF

I

The Prose

IT WAS THIRTY-SEVEN YEARS ago, from "a hole under a tree in the southeast of the field," that Meehawl MacMurrachu took a little crock of gold, the property of the Leprechauns of Gort na Cloca Mora. He was hunting his washboard, which they had stolen; but they did not consider this a fair exchange. Their anger at the Philosopher for directing Meehawl to their hiding-place motivated the plot of James Stephens' *The Crock of Gold* (1912).

In the end the crock was restored to its owners; not to say rightful owners, for they had filched it themselves. Stephens' fantasy too, lifted out of legend, has returned to its source. So thoroughly has it become part of its native domain that now it can be treated as folklore, and dug up again. In the musical comedy *Finian's Rainbow* the crock's removal to America caused a leprechaun to emigrate. That he migrated from a neighboring field was indicated by the song "How Are Things in Glocca Morra?"

James Stephens is remembered by those who heard him here twenty and more years ago as himself something of a visiting leprechaun. Today his books are classics; such accepted classics indeed that they are remembered with lazy warmth and seldom commented on. They so may count as neglected classics.

This is true not only of *The Crock of Gold* but of his other great fictions, *The Charwoman's Daughter, The Demi-Gods, Deirdre* and *In the Land of Youth*; of his collections of stories, gay, grim or macabre, in *Here Are Ladies* and *Etched in Moonlight*; and of his delicious *Irish Fairy Tales.* It is true equally of his ten books of verse, including *Collected Poems* (1926) and the subsequently published *Strict Joy* (1931) and *Kings and the Moon* (1938).

For James Stephens is first of all a poet. This has been the discovery of all the readers of his novels. Whether or not they have gone to the extreme of looking at his poems, the fact is plain to them. They know it, that is, in that large and loose and slightly benevolent way in which it is customary to employ the word "poetic."

The knowledge comes almost with a sense of exasperation and as a last resort. In an age that has cut the ground out from beneath all categories but still dotes on them, James Stephens defies classification. A great natural storyteller, he yet escapes the charge of being a novelist. His books develop action and reveal character, but so easily as to betray the fact that these are not their main concern. Their plots seem to be racks on which to display his philosophy. But the philosophy is itself too light and dazzling a thing to be held down by so weighty a word. So, it is concluded, he must be a poet.

Just what is it that is poetic about James Stephens' prose? If we could answer this, if we could catch prose in the act of being poetry, we might have a better notion of what poetry is and does when it is by itself.

He does not write "poetic prose." There is plenty of color to it but the hue is not predominantly purple. It is a supple prose, which distinguishes it from much fiction of the realistic school, and it seems to say naturally what it sets out to say. It could be that this comes from the habit of hearing. In the manuscript of his short story "Hunger" — written, as much of his work was, in a stenographer's notebook — the third paragraph originally began: "She had been married for ten years." The words are altered to read: "She was ten years married." This is not a change apt to occur to anyone who writes by eye.

The effect of one such instance is all but lost on the silent reader. But the cumulative effect is to make it uncomfortable to read James Stephens' prose in silence. It becomes urgent to share its pleasures. Who but a solitary drinker could keep to himself the description of that giant in the *Irish Fairy Tales* (1920), distracted from a foot race by a patch of blackberries? "He ate of these until he was no more than a sack of juice." Of course fairy tales are supposed to be delightful. And since we also suppose them to be written for children, there we are, deprived by our own categories.

But the delight gets over into other books, supposed to be for us. "Well the light of the world shone out of the lodger. He was like a sea breeze in a soap factory." (From *Here Are Ladies,* 1913.) The graces lie on every page: bubbles "based strongly in froth"; the riding of a horse, "that warm barrel." We come to discover that his prose is like poetry in that it means more when it is heard. There is an affinity in its meaning too.

The Charwoman's Daughter (1912, published in this country as *Mary, Mary*) relates the day-to-day occurrences of Mary Makebelieve and her mother. They live in the greatest conceivable poverty. What distinguishes them from the characters of, say, James Farrell is their having imagination. It is this that gives them, in their modest way, heroic proportions.

A hero meets an intolerable situation by changing it; and the Makebelieves change theirs as simply as breathing. Mary "knew every crack in the ceiling, and they were numerous and of strange shapes." At breakfast her mother

> . . . used to arrange . . . to have the room re-papered and the chimney swept and the rat-holes stopped up. . . . Her mother further arranged to have a Turkey carpet placed on the floor, although she admitted that oilcloth or linoleum was easier to clean, but they were not so nice to the feet or the eye.

The Makebelieves have their own values, which they impose on their surroundings. This attitude, more than the good fortune that overtakes them, is what makes them happy people. Not that their surroundings become rosy. Far from it; the struggle between fact and imagination is never-ending.

The matter-of-fact world is personified in the huge policeman who pays court to Mary.

> The policeman told her wonderful things. He informed her why the Phoenix Park was called the Phoenix Park. He did not believe there was a phoenix in the Zoological Gardens, although they probably had every kind of bird in the world there. It had never struck him, now he came to think of it, to look definitely for that bird, but he would do so the next time he went into the Gardens. . . . He rather inclined to the belief that the phoenix was extinct — that is, died out; and then, again, when he called to mind the singular habits with which this bird was credited, he conceived that it had never had but only a mythical existence — that is, it was a makebelieve bird, a kind of fairy tale.
> . . . He cited for Mary Makebelieve's incredulity the exact immensity of the Park in miles, in yards, and in acres, and the number of head of cattle which could be accommodated therein if it were to be utilized for grazing. . . .

So bizarre is his mentality that Mary is almost tricked by her imagination into accepting him. She credits him with fancies and feelings like her own; it is only when he violates these that she recognizes her mortal enemy.

Her kind is the young man continually hungry, who is only sad after a full meal, and whose spirits rise when food becomes again a topic worthy of spirited conversation.

> . . . He was no longer solid, space belonged to him also, it was in him and of him, and so there was a song in his heart. He was hungry and the friend of man again. Now everything was possible. The girl? Was she not by his side? The regeneration of Ireland and of Man? That could be done also; a little leisure and everything that can be thought can be done. . . .

In *The Crock of Gold* the struggle is shifted into the realm of speculative reality. The Philosopher, who rubs two facts together generating a Truth, represents the intellect of man. He is capable of the most astonishing feats, such as inferring where the earth's magic wealth is hidden. This is resented by its custodians, who have their revenge. MacMurrachu, the obtainer of the wealth, is afflicted with rheumatism and loss of sleep. His daughter, all innocence and beauty, is abducted and held in willing bondage to desire (the god Pan). And the Law intervenes.

The Law proposes to settle the matter by having the Philosopher up on an irrelevant charge of murder. The only hope for the Intellect of Man lies in invoking the old god of the imagination, Angus Óg. The god, with his retinue, descends from his mountain fastness; iron bars cannot prevail against him. Pan cannot prevail against him; he takes the daughter of MacMurrachu for himself. (At least, is MacMurrachu's consolation, "he's one of ourselves anyhow.") And the Philosopher's children having dug up and returned the pot of gold (since it was kept buried, nobody is the wiser), equilibrium is restored.

The Law – man's pitiful attempt to codify experience – is the villain of both pieces. But the policemen, while they fall under the shadow of its symbol, are also human. The one to whom the Philosopher gives himself up displays great reluctance.

> "A man as old as you are," said he, "oughtn't to be a fool. Go home now, I advise you, and don't say a word to anyone whether you did it or not. Tell me this now, was it found out, or are you only making a clean breast of it?"

Even the sergeant and his two bumbling aides, from whom the Philosopher has been spirited away, are convinced, when he voluntarily returns, that he can be no more guilty than themselves. Relieved of their sense of duty, they can for the first time meet him man to man.

For Kafka – the interminable patient – such a meeting would be a hideous twist giving impetus to the compulsive nature of the chase. To the sick fancy its very hopes are evidences to confirm its despair. The chase has more personality than the people.

The full imagination, while it looks squarely on the evil of the world, is not hopeless; for it can believe in the impossible. ("nothing except the impossible shall occur," says E. E. Cummings, a writer temperamentally related to Stephens.) Stephens, here and elsewhere, is conscious of the problem of guilt and the sense of being hunted physically or psychologically. But for him there is always a goal to the chase and that goal is a further revelation of human personality.

Here Are Ladies is a collection of stories about happy, sad or angry people, many of them husbands and wives. A man whose wife's death has freed him to pursue art in Paris finds his surroundings poisoned by the hatred he has concealed from her; he has murdered his imagination. A clerk throws up his job in anger, comes home to his nagging wife, and by the power he has released in himself wins back her love; their imagination has been reborn. The other stories deal with like themes.

In *The Demi-Gods* (1914) Patsy McCann and his daughter, who live by their wits (and their ass, who lives by *his*), meet their guardian angels on the road. Patsy is all for giving them the slip. "What," he asks, "would the priest say if he heard we were stravaiging the country with three big, buck angels, and they full of tricks maybe?" The angels are wise in the eternal verities but have much to learn on the practical side – how to make off with fowl, and the like. The divine imagination alone, it would seem, is not a sufficient guide for life in Ireland.

The cultural situation of Ireland is epitomized in the first story of the *Irish Fairy Tales.* Two mythologies meet when Finnian lays siege to Tuan Mac Cairill in order to convert him. He succeeds, but the triumph remains on both sides. For Tuan, consenting to give his history, reveals his mythical origin and successive changes into a stag, a boar, a hawk and a salmon; to all of which the good Abbott gives as hearty a faith as the faith he has required in return. There are (and this is a constant theme of Stephens') more than one imagination; but all have the quality, at the last, of recognizing each other.

Deirdre (1923) and *In The Land of Youth* (1924) are results of Stephens' studies in the old bardic tales of Ireland. His purpose, he announced, was to give modern Ireland "a new mythology to take the place of the threadbare mythology of Greece and Rome."

The latter book treats of a region more Irish than Ireland, the Shí of Connacht. This Land of Faery, into which the characters can be translated at stated seasons or moods, or by happy accident, is one of the countries of the mind. There are many such, and Stephens' genius is to reach many levels of interpretation, in turn or at once; often by means of the nest-of-boxes technique – a story within a story within a story. He uses this in several books, but most tellingly here.

Stephens' irony is not Cabell's – that what he is writing about is unreal – but quite the opposite. What goes on in these fabulous lands has its effect on the visible world. Nera beholds his companions brutally slaughtered by the hosts of the Shí. It is explained to him that when he returns from Faery he will find them alive and hearty. What he saw was a wish being fulfilled – "something happening which happened in the mind and did not happen anywhere else." But it is important to know what is going on in the Shí, for its wishes are powerful and will come about unless equally strong counter-wishes are made.

> ". . . A thing can be conceived and exercised in the mind, but when it has been so exercised in the mind that it really becomes real there, it then becomes real in every part of nature and in all the worlds where life is living."

This is psychologically and poetically sound. And the wishes are concerned more with violence than with sex; anticipating present-day psychiatry. Stephens proceeds from playfulness to insight, as in the diagnosis pronounced by the physician Fergne over the curious lethargy of Angus mac an Óg:

> "The boy is in love. That is all that's wrong with him."
>
> "But he always is in love," cried Boann; "love is his normal condition."
>
> "It is his normal condition to have love given to him," replied Fergne; "but this time some one is withholding love from him, and he is sick from desire and dissatisfaction."

Stephens had asked, in *The Demi-Gods:*

> . . . Is there actually a wolf in our neighbour? We see that which we are, and our eyes project on every side an image of ourselves; if we look with fear, that which we behold is frightful; if we look with love then the colours of heaven are repeated to us from the ditch and the dungeon. . . .

And in the fantasy, "Etched In Moonlight," from the book of that title (1928), he shows how the imagination, even in its distorted or clinical form, is realer than the facts. The man who believes he has committed a murder is acted upon by its guilt, though he tries to forget it. For "a trouble that is buried is not disposed of."

> Upon those having the gift of mental dismissal a revenge is taken. They grow inevitably irritable; and are subject to gusts of rage so unrelated to a present event that their contemporaries must look upon them as irresponsible.

When, years later, he discovers his delusion, the realization that he had had every intention of committing the crime is stronger than his accidental innocence. That very innocence becomes part of the mounting horror.

The same volume contains, among other fine stories, "Hunger." Few writers would have dared contemplate, much less have had the skill to make compelling, a story so unmitigated. It begins low and keeps going steadily lower, as if all the woe of the world were in it. His sureness of grasp comes from a poet's imagination; an identification with his material which is summed up in the words, "They were hunger."

Stephens' prose, then, is mainly concerned with the play between reality and imagination; in that sense it may be called a series of reflections on poetry; almost literary criticism. The distinctions of this criticism are brought to bear, not on other works of literature, but on the process itself that goes toward their making; the very act of creation. And these distinctions are such active and agile and lively performances that they refuse to lie down in the tame category, criticism.

So it is that his books are novels and not novels; criticism and not criticism. Like the characters themselves, his realistic allegories slip easily back and forth between the land of dust and the Land of Faery. As he himself, for the matter of that, slips easily back and forth between prose and poetry, and brings qualities of each into the other.

II

The Verse

THE IMAGINATION, as James Stephens shows us, is a great wanderer. It turns up unexpectedly anywhere; even here and now. But poetry is where the imagination is when it is at home. It is more *here,* in poetry; and more *now.*

In a double essay, *On Prose And Verse* (1928), Stephens explains how it was he came to write prose at all. A young writer, he says, will discover

> . . . that in the matter of mental and physical energy he is superhumanly endowed; so highly vitalized indeed that he is prepared to affront any mass or magnitude that can be presented to him: and he will inevitably arrive at the opinion that poetry alone cannot absorb the torrent that he actually is. He will turn hopefully to prose.

But from seeing how easily the work of the masters in prose could be bettered, the young man passes through a stage in which he recognizes the paucity of subjectmatter. The only things worth writing about, he concludes, are murder and philosophy.

> Of course there were some things that I did not know everything about. I knew, for instance, nothing about murder, and less than that about philosophy, and I did not know how to write prose.
>
> Nobody did know how to write prose. Nobody does now. Nobody ever will.
>
> If one were to assert that poetry is closer to speech than prose is we should, rightly, dislike and evade that malicious person, but we should be relieved that the statement had been made.
>
> Poetry is created in the whole phrase; is even, when the gods are benevolent, created in the entire verse. But prose must be invented from comma to comma.
>
> Everything that is in his nature helps the person who can write poetry to write it. Everything that can be conceived combines to prevent the writing of prose. . . . For the matter of poesy comes eagerly to its statement, but that which prose can serve is loath and reluctant; is without any spring or readiness; is void of good-will or good-humour; and of all else that is good. . . .
>
> In fact a writer of English might be forgiven, and might be somewhat petted and praised, if he should declare with rage, with resignation, that it is not possible to write prose at all.

An admirable conclusion for the writer of ten classics in prose; including *The Insurrection in Dublin* (1916), an excellent bystander's account of the happenings of the Easter Week uprising. But then he is the author of as many books of poetry. He has to be fair to them both. And he himself aids us in our search for their affinities and differences.

> This duty of universal self-identification is the same for the prose writer as for the poet. The distinction between them lies in the various tensions which these arts are competent to handle.

In the second part of the essay he goes on to talk more openly about poetry.

> It is not only that we cannot say what poetry is — we cannot say what anything is. . . . In fact reality (poetry) is incapable of expression or exposure, or definition.
>
> This incapacity is not because Reality is unknown to us. On the contrary, for there is nothing better known. There is nothing else known. . . . And when, by a chance, something of this quality of actual Being is caught into thought, we recognize it with delight and cry: this is poetry.

> We cannot say what poetry is, but we may adventure a speculation as to what it is not; and, by a negative definition, approach to something that has the appearance of the impossibly positive statement.
>
> Poetry is not action, nor passion, nor thought. It contains all of these, carelessly, as it were; but, in a true instance, when these qualities have been eliminated, there remains yet a quality, and that residue is poetry. Nor is it correct to say that a "residue" remains — an excess remains, and that excess is poetry.

And that excessive, violent and loving person, James Stephens, has been longest at home in poetry. His first book, *Insurrections* (1909), was a book of poems. And he has gone on writing them long after his last published work in prose.

Although poems of his are included in the anthologies, this side of his writing (which, more than a *side,* is really its center) has been comparatively neglected, especially of late. This may be due to the fact that in structure he does not visibly depart from the conventional. Rather like James Joyce, whose inventiveness went into his prose — and brought it closer to poetry — James Stephens for the most part uses regular metres and straight rhymes. In an age of poetry that has produced perhaps more technical originalities and a greater variety of individual forms than any other, critical interest has naturally tended to focus on these, pro or con. But in all the heated battles between "modernists" and "conservatives" the name of James Stephens is seldom brought up. For if he is not a radical, his position would give small comfort to the opposite camp. His introduction to *English Romantic Poets* (1935) writes a period to that epoch. He considers

> . . . that the official Classical and Romantic modes of poetry have reached their term: and that our day warrants the assumption that new values must be identified, and that a new method must be evolved for dealing with them. . . .

If the vogue has seemed to pass him by, it must be remembered that vogues bear no relation whatsoever to values, either affirmatively or negatively. By indicating some of the values that reside in James Stephens' poetry — those things that are, as Marianne Moore would say, "genuine" in it — we may be able to cast some light on what is valuable in poetry that presents greater initial difficulty. We may be able to use James Stephens, that is, as a touchstone.

The comparison with James Joyce is not so far-fetched as it may sound. True, their poetry is very different, though not opposed, in tone, mood and subjectmatter. And so, apparently, is their prose. Though who can identify, offhand, the following quotations? —

> . . . I'd love to have the whole place swimming in roses God of heaven there's nothing like nature the wild mountains then the sea and the waves rushing then the beautiful country with fields of oats and wheat and all kinds of things and all the fine cattle going about that would do your heart good to see . . . (1)

> . . . And Sorca Reilly to be trying to get him from me and Kate Finnegan with her bold eyes looking after him in the Chapel and him to be saying that along with me they were only a pair of old nanny goats and then we to be getting married and going home to my own little house with my man ah God be with me and him kissing me and laughing and frightening me with his goings on . . . (2)

> . . . It was a leg and an arm gripped then a swing for Fionn and out and away with him plop and flop for him down into chill deep death for him and up with a splutter . . . (3)

> . . . My great blue bedroom the air so quiet scarce a cloud in peace and silence I could have stayed up there for always only it's something fails us . . . (4)

I have picked passages the least telltale, and left out give-away punctuation, in order to stress the similarities of idea and rhythm between Molly Bloom's reverie in *Ulysses* (1) and the old woman muttering to herself on the road in *The Crock of Gold* (2); and between the *Irish Fairy Tales* (3) and *Finnegans Wake* (4). The differences are apparent enough: Joyce left Dublin and juggled with all the cultures of the world; Stephens, except for excursions, remained at home and confined himself largely to his native heritage. But both are interested in a present that is a palimpsest of the past; neither could, nor tried to, escape the infectious but inimitable speech-rhythms that were theirs by divine right of Irish birth; and Joyce once declared that, should *Finnegans Wake* be unfinished at the time of his death, there was one man in the world who might be able to complete it, and that man was James Stephens. (Both were born the same day and year in Dublin.)

It is partly his native speech-rhythms that make it unnecessary for Stephens to invent new forms. He can take whatever is ready to hand and by his power of song reanimate it. "The Centaurs" leaps with all the energy of its subject. (I quote from *Collected Poems,* 1926.)

> Playing upon the hill three centaurs were!
> They lifted each a hoof! They stared at me
> And stamped the dust!
>
> They stamped the dust! They snuffed upon
> the air!
> And all their movements had the fierce glee
> Of power, and pride, and lust!
>
> Of power and pride and lust! Then, with a
> shout,
> They tossed their heads, and wheeled, and
> galloped round,
> In furious brotherhood!
>
> In furious brotherhood! Around, about,
> They charged, they swerved, they leaped!
> Then, bound on bound,
> They raced into the wood!

The pace of this poem is set by its reversed refrain. Ordinarily a refrain, ending each stanza with the same line, induces a reminiscent pause. Here, by repeating the last line of each stanza at the beginning of the next, he lashes the rhythm. The poem ends at such breakneck speed that the centaurs have disappeared before we have had time to disbelieve in them. Since they have vanished, they must have been there.

The device is repeated in a number of poems. In "The Rivals" he reaches back an additional line:

I heard a bird at dawn
Singing sweetly on a tree,
That the dew was on the lawn,
And the wind was on the lea;
But I didn't listen to him,
For he didn't sing to me!

I didn't listen to him,
For he didn't sing to me
That the dew was on the lawn
And the wind was on the lea!
I was singing at the time,
Just as prettily as he!

I was singing all the time,
Just as prettily as he,
About the dew upon the lawn,
And the wind upon the lea!
So I didn't listen to him,
As he sang upon a tree!

The middle lines are repeated and the others so interwoven as to suggest a villanelle. But Stephens is more original than we might, at first glance, suppose. Looking more closely at the poem we observe that he has constructed a form in which the very arrangement of its lines expresses rivalry.

So, although Stephens gives the impression of working in traditional forms, he is far from orthodox. He does not mind, in "The Market," combining ballad metre and sonnet structure:

A man said to me at the fair
—If you have got a poet's tongue
Tumble up and chant the air
That the Stars of Morning sung:

—I'll pay you, if you sing it nice,
A penny-piece.—I answered flat,
—Sixpence is the proper price
For a ballad such as that.—

But he stared and wagged his head,
Growling as he passed along
— Sixpence! Why I'd see you dead
Before I pay that for a song. —

I saw him buy three pints of stout
With the sixpence — dirty lout!

And if Stephens had not told us, we should certainly take for contemporary his adaptations from Raftery, O'Rahilly and others of the Gaelic poets; such as "A Glass of Beer" (from O'Bruadair), which begins and closes:

The lanky hank of a she in the inn over there
Nearly killed me for asking the loan of a glass of beer;
. . . .
May she marry a ghost and bear him a kitten, and may
The High King of Glory permit her to get the mange.

No less scholarly and free are his adaptations from childhood, as in "Midnight":

And suddenly I wakened in a fright;
I thought I heard a movement in the room
But did not dare to look; I snuggled right
Down underneath the bedclothes — Then a boom,
And a tremendous voice said, *"Sit up, lad,
And let me see your face."* So up I sat,
Although I didn't want to — I was glad
I did though, for it was an angel that
Had called me, and he said, he'd come to know
Was I the boy who wouldn't say his prayers
Nor do his sums — and that I'd have to go
Straight down to hell because of such affairs:
. . . I said I'd be converted, and do good
If he would let me off — He said he would.

In all of these poems it is Stephens' identification with his material that gives them their force, or wit, or beauty, or truth. He identifies with everything he looks at, as in his often-quoted "Little Things"; as well as in "The Goat Paths," "The Snare," "The Lark," "To The Four Courts Please" and "What Tomas an Buile Said In A Pub." For him, everything in the universe is "The Voice Of God":

I bent again unto the ground
And I heard the quiet sound
Which the grasses make when they
Come up laughing from the clay.

— We are the voice of God! — they said;
Thereupon I bent my head
Down again that I might see
If they truly spoke to me.

But, around me, everywhere,
Grass and tree and mountain were
Thundering in mighty glee,
— We are the voice of deity! —

And I leaped from where I lay!
I danced upon the laughing clay!
And, to the rock that sang beside,
— We are the voice of God! — I cried.

Other poets may have identified with a greater variety of material, or with material in itself more elaborate; or they may, like Joyce, have extended the range and complexity of such identifications. But none exceeds Stephens in the vitality and genuineness of his.

As Stephens has said, this identification holds good for prose just as it does for poetry. But in poetry it is apt to be more localized, intense and unique. Certainly if it can be recognized in poetry, it can be recognized anywhere.

This genuineness of identification, then, may be the touchstone for which we have been looking. We do not perceive it as a *thing,* which we may take from one writer and apply, like a yardstick, to another. It is a *sensation,* which we obtain through an activity of the mind, of the whole person; through an act of the imagination corresponding somewhat to the original imaginative act of the artist. And when we have recognized this activity in one, we are more apt to recognize it in another; which is the acquisition of taste.

Taste is not infallible, like a measurement; which after all measures only sizes — that is, itself — and so, if it is done correctly, *cannot* go wrong. Taste is an activity which, like life, grows and develops with use; shrinks and withers away with non-use. And for the acquisition of taste in modern writing, there can be no more delightful an introduction, nor, I believe, any surer or more genuine a touchstone than the prose and poetry of James Stephens.

Part Three

TIME AND MR. ELIOT

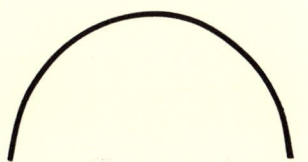

I

The Early Poems

Of T. S. Eliot's *Selected Essays* (1932), the earliest and still the most widely quoted is "Tradition and the Individual Talent." Dated 1917, the year that saw the publication of Eliot's first book of poems, *Prufrock and Other Observations,* the essay throws light not only on these early poems, which preceded it, but especially on the great works to follow, *The Waste Land* (1922) and *Four Quartets* (1943).

A continuously reappearing theme has had its first expression in the early poems. It is restated, in rather different terms, in the essay. Then what has been logically formulated is reapplied. By following the thread of this theme as it plies back and forth between Eliot's poetry and his criticism, it may be possible to see a little more clearly both the similarities and the differences between meanings in prose and meanings in poetry; where the two come together and overlap, and where they separate.

The theme, to state it broadly, is a concern with time. It becomes increasingly inclusive, so that in the end it may be said to contain everything Eliot has written. In "The Love Song of J. Alfred Prufrock" it appears primarily as a series of implied contrasts between time present and time past.

Time present is the year 1915 or shortly earlier, in a city whose emotional climate is Boston. Prufrock invites us to identify ourselves with him:

> Let us go then, you and I,
> When the evening is spread out against the sky
> Like a patient etherised upon a table;
> Let us go, through certain half-deserted streets,
> The muttering retreats
> Of restless nights in one-night cheap hotels
> And sawdust restaurants with oyster-shells . . .

From the dreary urban evening where nature and city soot, "the yellow fog" and "the yellow smoke," conspire damply, we enter a room where "women come and go / Talking of Michelangelo." The past survives in a name; culture is a conversation piece.

A note new to American poetry has been struck. Its tone is by now so familiar as to seem classic. Yet prior to Eliot the past, if introduced at all, served usually to redound to our credit. We were its automatic heirs; a recital of its glories was an indirect compliment to ourselves. At most, it might be referred to nostalgically; as in Poe's "the glories that were Greece / And the grandeurs that were Rome," which implied a criticism of contemporary civilization.

In "Prufrock" the attitude is reversed. A smug acceptance of the past has become the focal irony by which a criticism of the present is made explicit. The women who "come and go" are not awed by Michelangelo; they take him in their stride. But the present, epitomized by Prufrock, is a condition of acute social fright; since popularized by *The New Yorker:*

> And I have known the eyes already, known them all—
> The eyes that fix you in a formulated phrase . . .

The future will be a hideous prolongation of the present; of this very endless, tired and repetitive evening:

And indeed there will be time
For the yellow smoke that slides along the street,
Rubbing its back upon the window-panes;
There will be time, there will be time
To prepare a face to meet the faces that you meet;
There will be time to murder and create,
And time for all the works and days of hands
That lift and drop a question on your plate;
Time for you and time for me,
And time yet for a hundred indecisions,
And for a hundred visions and revisions,
Before the taking of a toast and tea.

Desiccation and indecision; these have absorbed and made indistinguishable even the acts of murder and creation. Everything is dead level. Not only the real but the imaginary has grown stale. Prufrock has "heard the mermaids singing, each to each." He does not think that they will sing to him. How shall he overmaster his timidity, his sense that time is running out? Shall he frighten all, by exposing his own fright to them? Shall he declare:

. . . 'I am Lazarus, come from the dead,
Come back to tell you all, I shall tell you all' . . . ?

For his timidity is at heart predatory:

I should have been a pair of ragged claws
Scuttling across the floors of silent seas.

But their defences, like his own, would be impervious to any line of attack he might adopt. They – as he – would merely say:

. . . 'That is not what I meant at all;
That is not it, at all.'

All significances are swallowed up in a general air of inconsequence. This is at once a symptom of the malady and a protection against recognizing it; a protection, moreover, that intensifies the malady. The present is the tomb of the past, as well as its murderer. The effect is underscored by three allusions: to the decapitated John the Baptist; to the resuscitated, but still death-bearing, Lazarus; and to that Prince of Indecision, Hamlet. The modern protagonist is "no prophet — and here's no great matter." John the Baptist was forerunner to a greater; Prufrock is not. He is not even, like Hamlet, making up his mind to some action, however delayed. Most nearly he is what he calls himself: Lazarus; a walking death.

The delicious rhythms and deliberate humor of "Prufrock" at first obscure, and finally liberate, its underlying horror. The sense of ghostly clashings between a dead past and an inert present is emphasized by something lying outside the poem proper, the six lines from Dante's *Inferno* that introduce it. These not only indicate the mood; they place the action of the poem, in the Eighth Pouch of the Eighth Circle of Hell, the Pouch of Fraudulent Counselors. Guido de Montefeltro is speaking to Dante. Both his name and his story relate to Eliot's title. The name has associations with rock and with a filter — by which liquids are "proved" — or a love-philtre or potion. The story concerns his putting his Church to the proof. Guido advised an evil pope how to deceive and destroy the pope's enemies, relying on his power to grant absolution. Since Guido's hope of absolution preceded his connivance, his repentance was not genuine and the promised absolution ineffectual. He says to Dante:

> "If I thought my reply were being made to one who would ever return to the world, this flame [his tongue, which is now his whole being; that is, his deceit has swallowed him up] would stand without quivering. But since no one ever returns alive from this abyss, if what I hear is true, I answer you without fear of ill fame."

So Prufrock, whose evil counsel is to himself, can speak freely only to himself, by way of soliloquy. Or — since fundamentally he considers all to be in similar plight — he can speak to anyone without fear of being understood; even to the reader of the poem. The reader will be similarly, and even more directly, implicated in *The Waste Land.*

The theme of "Portrait of a Lady" is again the dramatization of inaction. In a setting, as the title indicates, very Henry Jamesian, the

"I" of the poem pays a series of calls on a lady. The development of their relationship is monstrously arrested. We become aware of an irony in the use of three lines from Marlowe prefacing the poem:

> Thou hast committed—
> Fornication: but that was in another country,
> And besides, the wench is dead.

Active sin has been superseded by a deadlier one: acedia. The atmosphere is that

> . . . of Juliet's tomb
> Prepared for all the things to be said, or left unsaid.

If Prufrock, in the preceding poem, had a collar "mounting firmly to the chin," the visitor in "Portrait of a Lady" cannot walk up a flight of stairs without extreme effort:

> I mount the stairs and turn the handle of the door
> And feel as if I had mounted on my hands and knees.

Later, in "Rhapsody on a Windy Night," the lamp advises the anonymous nocturnal prowler:

> 'Four o'clock,
> Here is the number on the door.
> Memory!
> You have the key,
> The little lamp spreads a ring on the stair.
> Mount. . . .'

And in "The Boston Evening Transcript":

> When evening quickens faintly in the street,
> Wakening the appetites of life in some
> And to others bringing the *Boston Evening Transcript,*
> I mount the steps and ring the bell . . .

Another, usually paired, recurrence in these early poems is that of fog and smoke. In "Prufrock" it is "the yellow fog" and "the yellow smoke" of evening. "Portrait of a Lady" begins with the line, "Among the smoke and fog of a December afternoon." In "Preludes":

> The winter evening settles down
> With smell of steaks in passageways.
> Six o'clock.
> The burnt-out ends of smoky days.

"Morning at the Window" is characterized by "brown waves of fog." This reappears in *The Waste Land* (lines 60-61 and 206-7):

> Unreal City,
> Under the brown fog of a winter dawn . . .
> . . . .
> Unreal City
> Under the brown fog of a winter noon . . .

And a few lines later (215 and 220) evening is "the violet hour." "Yellow fog" suggests the presence of sulphur. Brown is a burnt, autumnal color. Whether Eliot intended these to reinforce an infernal association, we have dealt with enough of his recurrences to notice something about them. They all represent points of intersection. Fog is neither rain nor a clear day. Smoke is neither energy nor its absence. Morning and evening, Eliot's favorite settings, are neither day nor night. All are mixtures; like "the violet hour," a mixture of red and blue. And finally the "Unreal City" is the juncture of life and death; the city caught at moments when we are most aware of the impingement of time and eternity.

Such are the moments Eliot chooses for the hypnosis of his poetry; an hypnosis that is itself a condition in which the thoughts of the waking mind are mixed with intimations of the sleeping mind. This is the kind of assent to which Eliot was directly inviting us in the opening lines of "Prufrock":

> Let us go then, you and I,
> When the evening is spread out against the sky
> Like a patient etherised upon a table . . .

2

The intersections extend to the metre, language and style of the poems. "Prufrock" and "Portrait of a Lady" are written in a metre predominantly iambic. As the three lines quoted above illustrate, this metre is variously modulated and syncopated. The second line has a sweep that carries it almost to the point of being considered a three-foot line, with three, four and four syllables to the respective feet. The momentary resumption of insistent rhythm in "a patient etherised" accompanies an abrupt shift in imagery. "Evening" and "sky" are images congenial to traditional poetry. The "patient etherised" could only be modern. This particular evening is both.

The stanzas, of no set pattern, are halfway between stanzas and paragraphs. They combine lines of unexpectedly varying lengths, with something of the freedom of vers libre. Yet they are tightly constructed and rhymed, sometimes in couplets, sometimes alternately, and occasionally at irregular, judiciously placed intervals. Certain lines gain force from being unresolved:

> Streets that follow like a tedious argument
> Of insidious intent
> To lead you to an overwhelming question. . .
> Oh, do not ask, 'What is it?'
> Let us go and make our visit.

Here "question," prepared for by the preceding rhyme, is itself left in the air. Being unasked, it cannot be answered. By this means it is given an ironic emphasis, a deliberate pretentiousness, as if it had been capitalized. The patness of the succeeding rhyme, undoing this pretentiousness, underscores the irony. Eliot is a master of the nuances of rhythm and tone. They do exactly what he intends them to do. Here they prepare us, by a sudden back-tracking, for the subsequent development of Prufrock's character, a series of tentative advances and immediate withdrawals; for all his "visions and revisions."

The resulting style is one in which chaos struggles with a variety of "survivals of order." This mixed style, of the rhetorical and the colloquial, of tired Elizabethan, truncated heroic couplets, and light verse, is most effectively exhibited toward the end of "Prufrock":

> No! I am not Prince Hamlet, nor was meant to be;
> Am an attendant lord, one that will do
> To swell a progress, start a scene or two,
> Advise the prince; no doubt, an easy tool,
> Deferential, glad to be of use,
> Politic, cautious, and meticulous;
> Full of high sentence, but a bit obtuse;
> At times, indeed, almost ridiculous—
> Almost, at times, the Fool.
>
> I grow old . . . I grow old . . .
> I shall wear the bottoms of my trousers rolled.

This fine summation, suggesting that modern man has lost the quality of being a hero—that we are all in the condition of "attendant lords"—is the denouement of the poem. The climax, I feel, has occurred several lines previously, as an aside in the course of Prufrock's attempt to extract the essence of his "days and ways":

> It is impossible to say just what I mean!
> But as if a magic lantern threw the nerves in patterns on
> a screen . . .

The essential mystery, that escapes formulation, is something so deeply locked up inside him that he cannot express it. This mystery, he feels, is contained in the parts that go together to make him up; in his "nerves" rather than in himself as a whole person. He has more faith, then, in the very "formulations" he dreads than he has in the mystery. The latter, as rapidly as it is pursued by formulations, lodges itself in successively more remote areas of himself.

This intersection of the expressible and the inexpressible recurs as a separate strand of Eliot's general theme. In "Hamlet and His Problems" (1919) he writes:

> The intense feeling, ecstatic or terrible, without an object or exceeding its object, is something which every person of sensibility has known; it is doubtless a study to pathologists. It often occurs in adolescence; the ordinary person puts these feelings to sleep, or trims down his feeling to fit the business world; the artist keeps it alive by his ability to intensify the world to his emotions.

And in *The Use of Poetry and the Use of Criticism* (1933) he says of poetry (p. 155):

> It may make us from time to time a little more aware of the deeper, unnamed feelings which form the substratum of our being, to which we rarely penetrate; for our lives are mostly a constant evasion of ourselves, and an evasion of the visible and sensible world.

This may remind us of James Stephens':

> Something I can never find,
> Something lying on the ground
> In the bottom of my mind.

Prufrock's indecision, then, is the product of opposing forces. One is the desire to penetrate the impenetrable; to express the inexpressible. The other is his fear that, once penetrated, once expressed, it will prove as flat, stale and unprofitable as what can already be formulated about him.

To these intersections of time, metre, language and style, must be added the form of the poem. This is taken in part from Shakespearean soliloquy. But here, the aside's the thing. Rather than being set in the midst of a dramatic action, to serve as illumination and motivation, "Prufrock" infers its own play: a drama of inaction. In the sense of including what it leaves out, it more nearly approaches a dramatic monologue of Browning. Allusions to Browning are frequent in Eliot. "I grow old . . . I grow old . . . " suggests the ending of Browning's "A Toccata of Galuppi's": "I feel chilly and grown old." The same poem's "Dear dead women, with such hair, too" is parodied in the introduction of Eliot's "Burbank with a Baedeker: Bleistein with a Cigar":

Tra-la-la-la-la-la-laire — nil nisi divinum stabile est; caetera fumus — the gondola stopped, the old palace was there, how charming its grey and pink — goats and monkeys, with such hair too! — so the countess passed on until she came through the little park, where Niobe presented her with a cabinet, and so departed.

Browning's digressive tendency is the butt of this passage. Elsewhere Eliot has made skillful use of digression for his own purposes. And Browning's preoccupation with hair as a romantic symbol — especially amber, yellow or golden hair — is echoed by Eliot; in "Prufrock":

> Arms that are braceleted and white and bare
> (But in the lamplight, downed with light brown hair!)

and in "La Figlia Che Piange," who weaves the sunlight in her hair: "Her hair over her arms and her arms full of flowers." The image recurs in *The Waste Land* ("Your arms full, and your hair wet") and in the third movement of *Ash-Wednesday:*

> Blown hair is sweet, brown hair over the mouth blown,
> Lilac and brown hair . . .

But if Prufrock is not Prince Hamlet, neither would he be found in Browning's "Dramatis Personae." He shares neither the gustatory optimism nor the dark villainy that characterizes — one or the other — most of Browning's people. Prufrock is less "projected" than a Browning character. You do not feel that he was chosen primarily to display the poet's virtuosity at characterization and dramatic inference. He is more subjective, like the nameless hero of Tennyson's mono-drama *Maud.* Indeed, he has read that poem, especially the lines from Part II, section IV, stanza xiii:

> And I loathe the squares and streets,
> And the faces that one meets . . .

But Prufrock, preparing "a face to meet the faces that you meet," is more than a subjective device. Tennyson's tearful hero seems to be a part that Tennyson is playing. Prufrock, while he may to some extent be Eliot in disguise, is more deliberately conceived as an ironic commentary on the age. The age is a man turned inside out. A between-wars generation that adopted Prufrock's weary attitude, with or without the consciousness of its irony, testified to Eliot's acute perception of his age.

3

It is not surprising that a poet who, for all the "modernity" with which he was credited, had made such a study of traditional styles should be deeply concerned with tradition and his own place in it. And so we find, in "Tradition and the Individual Talent," Eliot exploring fully, if indirectly, the implications in his own poetry; both as to its use of the poetry of the past, and wherein it differs. At the outset he speaks of

> . . . our tendency to insist, when we praise a poet, upon those aspects of his work in which he least resembles any one else. In these aspects or parts of his work we pretend to find what is individual, what is the peculiar essence of the man. We dwell with satisfaction upon the poet's difference from his predecessors, especially his immediate predecessors; we endeavour to find something that can be isolated in order to be enjoyed. Whereas if we approach a poet without this prejudice we shall often find that not only the best, but the most individual parts of his work may be those in which the dead poets, his ancestors, assert their immortality most vigorously.

Eliot, then, may we infer? has had it as his conscious intention to continue the tradition of Dante, Shakespeare, Dryden, Tennyson and Browning — to name a few of his sources — by observing and dramatizing their ideas and feelings as they exert force in the modern world. If this force is exhibited largely ironically, the irony is not the result of a direct juxtaposition of prosaic present with poetic past. The irony is one that has always obtained, in varying degrees, between the idealized world of poetry and the so-called actual worlds of politics, business, science and family life. Since the ideas with which poetry concerns itself are taken, on the whole, even less seriously today by these actual worlds, the gap is greater. Consequently the irony is more acute.

Tradition, for Eliot, is not simple continuance or repetition. The essence of life is change; and tradition might be thought of as the product of this natural tendency, times an equally natural resistance to change. This is not quite the way Eliot thinks of it. He continues:

> Yet if the only form of tradition, of handing down, consisted in following the ways of the immediate generation before us in a blind or timid adherence to its successes, "tradition" should positively be discouraged. We have seen many such simple currents soon lost in the sand; and novelty is better than repetition. Tradition is a matter of much wider significance. It cannot be inherited, and if you want it you must obtain it by great labour.

The last clause perhaps casts an indirect light on the sense of effort, the "mounting of stairs," in so many of Eliot's poems. But this is incidental to the validity of his main conception, an extremely important and valuable one. It is developed by means of two interlocking propositions, the first having to do with "the historical sense,"

> . . . which we may call nearly indispensable to any one who would continue to be a poet beyond his twenty-fifth year; and the historical sense involves a perception, not only of the pastness of the past, but of its presence; the historical sense compels a man to write not merely with his own generation in his bones, but with a feeling that the whole of the literature of Europe from Homer and within it the whole of the literature of his own country has a simultaneous existence and composes a simultaneous order. This historical sense, which is a sense of the timeless as well as of the temporal and of the timeless and of the temporal together, is what makes a writer traditional. And it is at the same time what makes a writer most acutely conscious of his place in time, of his own contemporaneity.
>
> No poet, no artist of any art, has his complete meaning alone. His significance, his appreciation is the appreciation of his relation to the dead poets and artists. You cannot value him alone; you must set him, for contrast and comparison, among the dead. I mean this as a principle of aesthetic, not merely historical, criticism. The necessity that he shall conform, that he shall cohere, is not one-sided; what happens when a new work of art is created is something that happens simultaneously to all the works of art which preceded it.

The "historical sense," important in itself to an understanding of Eliot's poetry, is already leading us toward the statement of a second, related proposition; a proposition so crucial to Eliot's whole conception of tradition in poetry that he has repeated it in an essay written six years later, "The Function of Criticism":

> The existing monuments form an ideal order among themselves, which is modified by the introduction of the new (the really new) work of art among them. The existing order is complete before the new work arrives; for order to persist after the supervention of novelty, the *whole* existing order must be, if ever so slightly, altered; and so the relations, proportions, values, of each work of art toward the whole are readjusted; and this is conformity between the old and the new. Whoever has approved this idea of order, of the form of European, of English literature, will not find it preposterous that the past should be altered by the present as much as the present is directed by the past.

Such a conception outmodes all thought of a fixed order of tradition, in which "the existing monuments" take their static positions, and to which contemporary works can only hope, if they measure up, to be added. Eliot is profoundly aware of a continuous interaction between present and past. The latter only survives, in any meaningful way, in the minds of the living; by its active influence on the present. Conversely, to "learn from experience" is to change the past: to discover new meanings in it, rather than unconsciously to repeat its patterns.

The phrase, "an ideal order," possesses an ambiguity which Eliot, I feel, does not entirely resolve. This may be due partly to difficulties of language; especially the language of prose. To express so completely fluid a conception in concrete terms verges on the province of poetry. Only where the meanings of words act upon each other can so active a conception be adequately realized.

Eliot does seem, though, to be using "ideal" in its Platonic as well as its descriptive sense. "Ideal" can refer to ideas held in the mind; in his mind and in many other minds. Such ideas, like the people who hold them, are constantly changing; their "order" is a fluctuating one. To simplify our thinking about so involved a process we tend to limit our idea of "ideas" to their best available statements; such as, in this case, Eliot's.

"Ideal" can also refer to ideas existing above and independently of all minds. An "ideal order" formed by the existing monuments "among themselves" suggests a predilection on Eliot's part for this absolute, "realer" reality. At the same time he conceives of it as "slightly altering." There seem to be contradictory impulses here: to make dogma of insight, doctrine of hypothesis, while retaining the free play of insight and hypothesis. It is always difficult to counter dogma with insight; the insight hankers after an equivalent finality. Such an ambivalence may help to account for the drier of Eliot's ecclesiastical essays.

Certainly these twin conceptions of "historical sense" and "ideal order" do account, in large measure, for his subsequent development in the dual rôle of critic and poet. In his essays on Christopher Marlowe, Shakespeare and the other Elizabethans; Dante; Donne and the metaphysical poets; Marvell, Dryden, Blake, Swinburne, Arnold; Baudelaire; Wordsworth and Coleridge; Keats, Shelley and the rest, he is examining poets and critics largely in relation to their own time, with reference to the active influences from *their* past; such as that of Seneca on Shakespeare. In his own poetry, on the other hand, Eliot exhibits the active survival into the present of these poets, their ideas and feelings. He shows how, in large part, the present is *composed* of such elements from the past, acting upon each other.

In the process Eliot himself is catalytic agent. He says of the artist:

> What happens is a continual surrender of himself as he is at the moment to something which is more valuable. The progress of an artist is a continual self-sacrifice, a continual extinction of personality.

Something in Eliot corresponding to "the old Adam" regrets the change necessary to a *growth* of personality and prefers to call it *extinction*. This is a case where saying the opposite amounts to saying the same thing. However that is, his analogy of the poet as catalyst is the third significantly relevant conception in this essay:

> . . . When the two gases previously mentioned [oxygen and sulphur dioxide] are mixed in the presence of a filament of platinum, they form sulphurous acid. This combination takes place only if the platinum is present; nevertheless the newly formed acid contains no trace of platinum, and the platinum itself is apparently unaffected; has remained

inert, neutral and unchanged. The mind of the poet is the shred of platinum. It may partly or exclusively operate upon the experience of the man himself; but, the more perfect the artist, the more completely separate in him will be the man who suffers and the mind which creates; the more perfectly will the mind digest and transmute the passions which are its material.

4

The separation of artist and man, in the foregoing account, is all but complete. Again I feel that Eliot is pushing a valuable insight toward an impossibly absolute conclusion. But the image is helpful to think of in considering his unique interweaving of styles. In *Poems: 1920* this process has become more complex. What occurs is not simple juxtaposition, but, even more patently than before, the shock of ideas of one century turning into those of another.

"Gerontion," the most closely textured, is as its title indicates, concerned with old age. The poem is prefaced by a quotation from Shakespeare's *Measure for Measure*:

> Thou hast nor youth nor age
> But as it were an after dinner sleep
> Dreaming of both.

The poem is an old man's memories. Some of these, as F. O. Matthiessen[1] and others have shown, are taken almost verbatim from Henry Adams and Edward FitzGerald. This suggests that the composite old man's skepticism stands for the skepticism of an age, as Prufrock stands for its futility. His memories are most precise when they are negative, regretting adventures missed:

[1] F. O. Matthiessen, *The Achievement of T. S. Eliot* (Oxford, 1947; 2nd edition revised and enlarged). I am indebted to Matthiessen's book for help in identifying many of Eliot's allusions, and in translating epigraphs and lines from foreign tongues. E. M. Stephenson's *T. S. Eliot and the Lay Reader* (London: The Fortune Press, 1944); James Johnson Sweeney's paper on "East Coker" in *T. S. Eliot: A Selected Critique* (Rinehart and Co., 1948); and other sources to be noted, were also helpful in these connections.

> I was neither at the hot gates
> Nor fought in the warm rain
> Nor knee deep in the salt marsh, heaving a cutlass,
> Bitten by flies, fought.

What he remembers are images of decay and dispossession, corresponding to his present circumstances. The house he lives in is decayed; a rented house; he lives in the basement:

> The goat coughs at night, in the field overhead;
> Rocks, moss, stonecrop, iron, merds.

It is a halfway house to the grave. Its crumbling upper stories are heaped up over him, like the memories that pass in succession through his "dull head among windy spaces": Mr. Silvero, "who walked all night, in the next room"; Hakagawa, "bowing among the Titians"; Madame de Tornquist,

> . . . in the dark room
> Shifting the candles; Fräulein von Kulp
> Who turned in the hall, one hand on the door.

Their fragmentary significance for the reader reproduces the effect of an old man's failing memory. "Signs are taken for wonders." But these signs, their contours rubbed, blurred and obliterated, point now only to one significance, one wonder:

> The word within a word, unable to speak a word,
> Swaddled with darkness.

This phrase from a sermon of Lancelot Andrewes will recur, or be alluded to, in *Ash-Wednesday,* "Song for Simeon," *The Rock* and *Four Quartets.* The reference is to Christ, who as God was Logos, or the Word behind existence; yet being born as man, an infant, unable to speak. For the old man, Christ is also "the tiger" who "in the juvescence of the year" (a corrupt form of "juvenescence"?) "springs to devour." To approach death is to experience the first half of the cycle of rebirth, as exemplified by the seasons: destruction and renewal. The literal meanings of life have become husks:

. . . Think
Neither fear nor courage saves us. Unnatural vices
Are fathered by our heroism. Virtues
Are forced upon us by our impudent crimes.

But no higher significance has emerged. He is in the condition of a snake prematurely shedding its skin. He has lost his passions, the use of his senses and his faith in life, with nothing to replace them. The facts of his existence, the memories peopling his mind, are, like the characters in Thomas Kyd's tragedies, disintegrating,

. . . whirled
Beyond the circuit of the shuddering Bear
In fractured atoms.

5

The precise use of partial images, a mixture of the definite and the indefinite to reinforce a theme of disintegration, is characteristic of the first half of Eliot's development, culminating in the total destruction of *The Waste Land.* There are intimations, however, of the later more affirmative devotional poems. Such an intimation is the phrase, "the word within a word, unable to speak a word." Here he employs it to emphasize the speechlessness of inner experience. Like Prufrock, the old man is unable really to communicate. In *Ash-Wednesday* and the poems since, Eliot is more concerned with giving the incommunicable a voice.

The special hold of this phrase upon Eliot for over twenty years may be due to its triple significance. It has not only a theological application – the eternal imprisoned in the human – but a philosophic one as well. Plato's Ideas were conceived as archetypes pre-existing in a transcendent realm. Toward them the forms of nature continually aspired, themselves imperfect imitations, or mixtures of being (Idea) and non-being (matter) – the eternal imprisoned in the actual.

The philosophical conception antedated the theological and was to a large extent responsible for it, Christianity having incorporated neo-platonism, along with primitive rejuvenation rites ("Christ the tiger"; i.e., destroyer and renewer). Swinburne's complaint, "Thou hast conquered, O pale Galilean," might be reversed. Philosophically at least, it would appear to be the Platonists who annexed the Galilean.

The third application of "the word within a word" is poetic. Perhaps Plato's intentions were primarily allegorical. Then the poetic interpretation would be the oldest of all. Plato would be studying, not mind or nature, but the relations between them, the inner connections of poetry; as Aristotle investigated its outer connections, the structures of poetry. Ideas are imprisoned in things. A table is not just the physical object, or the materials that make it up. It also incorporates the thought and workmanship that have gone into it, and the uses to which it is put; to mention the most obvious of its human relationships. Without these relationships the table would have no significant existence. The physical object is then a symbol for its idea; a focal point for all its uses and values, actual or potential; including its suggestions of more perfect tables. An imaginary construction of these total potentialities suggests a Platonic Idea. The question of priority is irrelevant. All that can be observed is that the actual and the ideal flow out of each other. Like the mind and nature, they are reciprocal, neither being observable except in terms of the other. A consideration of these relations in particular instances, as in a poem, leads to an apprehension of total involvement, similar to the religious experience of a sense of oneness with the universe.

Read in this light, Plato's Ideas bear some resemblance to the symbols of French Symbolist poetry, which played an influential part in Eliot's development. Definitions of technical terms in poetry have to be fluid, since their meanings vary from poet to poet. A simile, a metaphor and a symbol, however, may be said to represent an ascending scale of intensities in the relationships felt to exist between apparently unrelated experiences. A simile implies likeness; a metaphor, likeness amounting to identity; and a symbol, a likeness or configuration of likenesses felt to be so strong that the originating term does not need to be stated.

Since they are historically developing processes rather than set forms, they tend to merge into each other. All are analogous to the pun, usually a fleeting likeness based solely on resemblance of sound. Coleridge's famous distinction between fancy and imagination was an elaborately metaphysical attempt to distinguish between such superficial, accidental resemblances and the more profound, underlying relationships. The distinction, while valuable, can also be misleading; for the accidental may lead to the profound. Joyce's multilingual puns are an instrument of insight, conveying the total relatedness of all experience.

Because of the general definition of a symbol as anything that stands for something else, the symbol derived from French Symbolist poetry, and ultimately from Edgar Allan Poe, has sometimes been referred to as if it were invariably a single term, a simple substitution; such as "Mammon" for "the world." In practice it is much less arbitrary. Usually it proceeds by indirection, in order to avoid too great emphasis on literal meanings. If a simile is *like* something else, and a metaphor *is* something else, the symbol proceeds *from* this "something else" without explicitly stating a comparison. Its relationships arise directly from its own powers of suggestion. It might be called "an emotion sealed into a phrase" – the phrase being anything from a word to the whole poem.

Eliot has made several adaptations of Symbolism.[1] An early poem, "Rhapsody on a Windy Night," displays it in dispersed form:

Half-past three,
The lamp sputtered,
The lamp muttered in the dark.
The lamp hummed:
'Regard the moon,
La lune ne garde aucune rancune,
She winks a feeble eye,
She smiles into corners.
She smooths the hair of the grass.
The moon has lost her memory.
A washed-out smallpox cracks her face,

[1] Edmund Wilson, in *Axel's Castle* (Scribner's, 1931) traces among others a connection between "Prufrock" and the poetry of Jules Laforgue.

Her hand twists a paper rose,
That smells of dust and eau de Cologne,
She is alone
With all the old nocturnal smells
That cross and cross across her brain.'

What is suggested here is an affinity between the mind and its surroundings. The mind's own emotions are placed within the natural objects it is contemplating; a refinement of the so-called "pathetic fallacy." Such a symbolic account is in one sense truer than a literal account.

The literal account might start: "I stood beside a lamp at three o'clock in the morning. The lamp and the moon above it affected me in the following ways." Something like this is what we expect of prose; yet it is a reconsidered account. It does not give an immediate perception of the experience, such as we have had before we started thinking about it.

To an infant, what happens happens everywhere. Later we come to separate ourselves from the experience. More and more literal-mindedly we inquire, "What has happened in me, and what has happened outside?" The whole experience is broken into fragments.

The poet and the artist are continually devising techniques to convey the "innocence" of experience, back past the sophistication of "thinking about it." Unless they are children or primitives, their attempts are themselves further refinements of that very thinking; but a corrective thinking, a "premeditated spontaneity," that relates itself back to emotions and sensations after having abstracted itself from them. The impulse is toward an integration that has been lost in the process of specializing. So Coleridge, originally a disciple of Hartley's "faculty" psychology, ultimately broke with it. The artist's attempt is to get beyond "faculties" to the living organism; to synthesize what has been analyzed; to present a whole experience.

This whole experience corresponds to "the Word within a word." It anticipates and eludes precise expression, being conveyed by nuances of rhythm, intimations of imagery, and the delicate equations of simile, metaphor and symbol. In a very real sense it is

. . . unable to speak a word,
Swaddled with darkness.

II

Sweeney and The Waste Land

From "Gerontion" on, Eliot begins to expand and elaborate his use of symbols. More and more they come to be composite symbols; intersection points where the crucial ideas of different ages and conditions of man meet. This is brought out in the Sweeney poems: "Sweeney Erect," "Mr. Eliot's Sunday Morning Service," "Sweeney Among the Nightingales," the unfinished *Sweeney Agonistes* and a reference to Sweeney in *The Waste Land.*

"Apeneck Sweeney," Eliot's most vigorous creation, has been taken to represent lower-class vulgarity; as contrasted with the over-refinement of J. Alfred Prufrock, that thinly lineal descendant of James, Tennyson and Dante. Eliot has indicated Sweeney's composite source, from the attributes of several South Boston Irishmen observed in his youth. The frame of reference may be even more inclusive. A Gaelic legend, of the same family from which Yeats and James Stephens have drawn for much of their material, has points of resemblance that seem more than coincidental.

The legend is *Buile Shuibne,* "The Frenzy of Sweeney." *Sweeney Agonistes* would be a fair translation. Eliot's title also carries an allusion to Milton's *Samson Agonistes.* An epigraph relates it as well to the pursuit of Orestes by the Furies: "You don't see them, you don't — but *I* see them: they are hunting me down, I must move on." This quotation from Aeschylus is coupled with another, from Saint John of the Cross: "Hence the soul cannot be possessed of the divine union, until it has divested itself of the love of created beings." Together, these suggest Eliot's interest in a connection between two forms of dispossession: mysticism and madness. Among other instances of the latter to which he refers, in the Sweeney and other poems, are the mad Hieronimo of Kyd's *Spanish Tragedy,* and *Hercules Furens* of Seneca.

If his examples of this literary type included Shuibne, he may have come across the story in J. G. O'Keefe's translation (London: published for the Irish Texts Society, 1913). More recently it has been used by Padraic Colum, in *The Frenzied Prince* (David McKay, 1943), as the framework for a retelling of other Irish legends. The original is summarized in Myles Dillon's *The Cycles of the Kings* (Oxford University Press, 1946); and in somewhat different form, with verse interpolations, in Kathleen Hoagland's *1000 Years of Irish Poetry* (Devin-Adair, 1947). Miss Hoagland, whose note I read after I had begun tracing the connection, suggests a point of contact, although leaving it undeveloped. "Apparently," she says on page 97, "the name Sweeney must have some association, at least to the poetic mind, with birds. See 'Sweeney Among the Nightingales,' by T. S. Eliot."

Shuibne (the Gaelic is also rendered Suibhne, Suibne or Suivne) was a seventh-century Irish prince, who went mad because of the curses put on him by Saint Ronan Finn. The holy man had proposed to build a church on Shuibne's territory. Shuibne proposed otherwise. Leaving his cloak in the hands of his wife, who tried to prevent him, he rushed out of his house and into the saint's presence naked. In that condition, the first curse ran, he was to wander the world.

In two of the Eliot poems Sweeney is presented naked. In "Sweeney Erect," while a female companion is "clawing at the pillow slip" in an epileptic fit,

Sweeney addressed full length to shave
  Broadbottomed, pink from nape to base,

. . . .

Tests the razor on his leg

In "Mr. Eliot's Sunday Morning Service," while divine worship is being elsewhere observed,

Sweeney shifts from ham to ham
Stirring the water in his bath.
The masters of the subtle schools
Are controversial, polymath.

Shuibne's anti-clericism was a more active affliction. He hurled Ronan's psalter into a lake, whence it was retrieved by an otter. Another cleric he slew for sprinkling him with holy water; and made a cast at Ronan too. The spear broke on the saint's bell, the shaft flying into the air. So the second curse was fulfilled during an ensuing battle when, maddened by the din of it, Shuibne "fled in a frenzy like a bird of the air." He was thenceforth to be found, from time to time, sitting in a yew; one of poetry's, and Eliot's, favorite trees.

Sweeney is "among" the nightingales. If not mad, he is surrounded by madness and, in *Sweeney Agonistes,* given to frenzied utterance. The correspondences are nowhere point-by-point, but suggest an interweaving of allusions. Thus the nightingales refer to Sweeney's companions of the evening, and also to the birds that

. . . sang within the bloody wood
When Agamemnon cried aloud,
And let their liquid siftings fall
To stain the stiff dishonoured shroud.

Whether or not, in the contemporary section of the poem, an actual murder is being plotted, Sweeney is assisting at the death of honor. He is modern man, cursed because of his rejection of faith and crazed by the resultant world-upheaval. As introduced into *The Waste Land,* he carries a weight of subtly shifting allusion; just as man carries all the past about with him:

But at my back from time to time I hear
The sound of horns and motors, which shall bring
Sweeney to Mrs. Porter in the spring.
O the moon shone bright on Mrs. Porter
And on her daughter
They wash their feet in soda water

Some of these allusions have been given by Eliot in his notes to the poem: the lines from Andrew Marvell's "To His Coy Mistress":

But at my back I always hear
Time's winged chariot hurrying near

and from Day's "Parliament of Bees":

When of the sudden, listening, you shall hear,
A noise of horns and hunting, which shall bring
Actaeon to Diana in the spring,
Where all shall see her naked skin.

Shuibne also, in one of his recurrent wanderings — sitting this time "on the summit of a tall ivy-branch," with a hag sitting in an adjacent tree — heard the sounds of hunting horns and the bellowing of stags. They recalled his former life to him; and he compared his present wild state with it.

The use of multiple allusion is typical of Eliot's practice, especially in *The Waste Land.* An at least quadruple cluster of attitude is implicit in the Sweeney symbol: (1) an originating Graeco-Roman myth; (2) its retelling in the Elizabethan and related periods; (3) the Irish myth and (4) the modern myth. These are not simply added to each other. They are multiplied together; or, better, they form the symbol very much as atoms contribute to a molecule. Neither analogy is perfect, since it is not quantities or particles that are coalescing, but attitudes of man toward experience.

The attitude conveyed by the Greek myth is a sense of balance between the visible world and the invisible forces that operate through it. If the gods are discovered through nature, nature is equally discovered through the gods. They are symbols of each other. The Romans and the Elizabethans, in their different ways, convey a sense of the balance between their worlds and antiquity. Through nature we are reminded of the ancient symbols; these are refreshed, or reincarnated, for us. A stronger sense of nostalgia is present; although – as Eliot has shown in his essay "What Is a Classic?" – such a quality was present to Greek mythology as well. Every age harks back to some vanished "Golden Age," and we hark back to them all.

The attitude of the Gaelic myth is rather different; more like our own in that it is a clash of cultures. Shuibne's madness is the outcome of a conflict between the ancient druidic culture and a recently imported Christianity. He cannot live the first, in comfort; nor can he, until the end of his life, accept the second. Instead he reverts to an impossibly primitive, almost purely animal existence. He is a symbol, then, of incorrigibility. Running through much of Irish myth is this sense of a basic incorrigibility in man; an atavistic survival underlying the clash of cultures.

What the sounds of hunting recall to Shuibne is not a vanished Golden Age, but his own recent life as a precariously cultivated prince. Throughout the saga he is fitfully recalled to the ties of family and tradition from which he has fled. Similarly the modern Sweeney is recalled by the horns of *his* culture; not of hunting, but of motors. What he is recalled *from,* and what he is recalled *to,* are equally ignoble. Not only man, but the culture, is equally incorrigible. Sweeney is recalled from the grossness of his nature to a parody of beauty. Like the nymphs of the Thames, Diana has departed. What is left for the moon to shine upon? The figures of an Australian ballad, "Mrs. Porter and her daughter" who "wash their feet in soda water."

All these attitudes are working on each other in the Sweeney symbol. The ignobility of modern culture extends into the past, stripping it of its alleged glories. For this reason, Eliot was first taken as a debunker. But his irony is multiple and reciprocating. The past is also operating on the present. A surviving sense of mystery and glory touches the ignobility, increasing both its humor and its pathos.

Anywhere we stop to analyze Eliot's poetry we find a similar process at work. Each symbol holds suspended within it the history of an idea or emotion. They are time-amalgams; ironic compounds of past, present and future. Their degrees of intensity and depth may vary, but always the centuries are moving about in them.

2

In *The Waste Land* Eliot developed his time-amalgams to their fullest potentiality. More deliberately than ever, he used as symbols phrases borrowed from poets of various periods, slightly altered as if by the corrosive action of time. The "emotion sealed into a phrase" is activated by its encounter with emotions generated in other ages. This parallels in an extraordinary manner his early conception of an "ideal order" constantly, if slightly, shifting.

The device of "creative borrowing," which Eliot has employed to a degree equaled only by Ezra Pound and Marianne Moore, and surpassed only by James Joyce, is clarified by certain remarks in his essay on Philip Massinger (1920):

> . . . One of the surest of tests is the way in which a poet borrows. Immature poets imitate; mature poets steal; bad poets deface what they take, and good poets make it into something better, or at least something different. The good poet welds his theft into a whole of feeling which is unique, utterly different from that from which it was torn; the bad poet throws it into something which has no cohesion. A good poet will usually borrow from authors remote in time, or alien in language, or diverse in interest.

So Eliot, who took over the device from his study, particularly, of the Elizabethans, applies it in a new way. The Elizabethans borrowed from each other or from the ancients, whom they used as models. Eliot's borrowing has a more deliberate intention as outright borrowing. His juxtapositions of familiar emotions release something new: an intensification of the sense of time. Increasingly he is coming to show — or attempting to catch the sensation — that "all time goes on everywhere at once." In leading up to this extreme, he has on the way elucidated whole epochs of feeling; an emotional history, or travelogue, of ideas.

Throughout his poetry the interweaving of styles, languages, lines from poems, serves the purpose of elaborating Eliot's sense of the present as a continuous flux between the past and the future, and between all time and eternity. It is not eclecticism, the heaping together of various and disparate cultures and philosophies. He catches the moment at which one thing is turning into another; an adaptation to poetry of principles laid down for sculpture in Lessing's *Laokoön.* The action portrayed — a movement of time — is more like that of sculpture or painting than it is like the actions ordinarily represented in writing.

The Waste Land is a mosaic of such intersections: past with present, life with death, day with night, male with female. Its style is expressive of the reliquary character of modern life. The main theme is related, as Eliot has indicated, to the Grail legends[1] and their connection, traced in Jessie L. Weston's *From Ritual to Romance,* with certain widely held, persistent tribal superstitions. The latter, collected in Frazer's *The Golden Bough,* are variations of an underlying belief that the infertility of a land is caused or accompanied by the death, maiming, or loss of potency of its king.

The Waste Land is contemporary civilization; by extension, any civilization, since what is implied is a recurring cycle. The injured king is divine authority. By renouncing it, man loses faith, the water that would make fertile his life and his culture.

The first section, "The Burial of the Dead," introduces us to the dead land. It begins with a double intersection: winter and summer; death and life:

> April is the cruellest month, breeding
> Lilacs out of the dead land, mixing
> Memory and desire, stirring
> Dull roots with spring rain.
> Winter kept us warm, covering
> Earth in forgetful snow, feeding
> A little life with dried tubers.

[1] Cleanth Brooks, in his chapter on *The Waste Land* in *Modern Poetry and the Tradition* (University of North Carolina Press, 1939) has brought out many of the symbolic correspondences with stages in the Grail legends.

It is the dead who are speaking. Inhabitants of the dead land, the present, they are also – by Eliot's first irony – the living. For them April – the transition from winter to summer; from death to rebirth – is cruel. Rejuvenation means to rebegin a cycle that has already ended in defeat. Their memories of this defeat are disjointed, as in "Gerontion." But here the fragments recorded are multilingual, racial, "a heap of broken images." The passage is a dramatization and expansion of two stanzas in an earlier poem, "Whispers of Immortality":

Webster was much possessed by death
And saw the skull beneath the skin;
And breastless creatures under ground
Leaned backward with a lipless grin.

Daffodil bulbs instead of balls
Stared from the sockets of the eyes!
He knew that thought clings round dead limbs
Tightening its lusts and luxuries.

The thoughts that cling round the dead in *The Waste Land* are their fitful memories of past forebodings; anticipations that led nowhere; lost childhood pleasures. These memories invade the present, with a change of tense that emphasizes it as a prolongation of the past; an historical present: "I read, much of the night, and go south in the winter."

What grows out of these memories? They lead only, in a vicious circle, to themselves; to fear and a nostalgic regret. "Under the shadow of this red rock" the narrator will show us

. . . something different from either
Your shadow at morning striding behind you
Or your shadow at evening rising to meet you;
I will show you fear in a handful of dust.

The first allusion is to *The Divine Comedy.* Dante, the only corporeal figure among the spirits in Purgatory, alone casts a shadow. We are, then, to be shown eternity; but through the medium of time:

"fear in a handful of dust." Here the allusion is to the Cumaean Sibyl in Petronius Arbiter's *Satyricon.* The passage in Latin, quoted as an epigraph to *The Waste Land,* is a speech of the drunken Trimalchio: "For I saw with my own eyes the celebrated Sibyl at Cumae, hanging in a bottle, and when her acolites said, 'What do you wish, O Sibyl?' she replied, 'I wish to die.'" The Sibyl had been granted eternal life, but forgot to ask for eternal youth. Withering away to dust, her implicit prophecy is that physical existence is eternal only as dust is eternal. This is close to the Christian idea of extinction – the "death" of physical desire – as the necessary prelude to spiritual rebirth.

A modern Sibyl, "Madame Sosostris, famous clairvoyante," now looks into the future by means of the Tarot Pack, the obscured and distorted wisdom of the past. She finds the future composed of reshuffled elements of the past: drownings, "situations," work, mystery. These resolve themselves into "crowds of people, walking round in a ring" – an aimlessness of the damned; Dante's Circles of the Inferno. The living and the dead, the future and the past, are one.

Her interpolation, "Those are pearls that were his eyes," will reappear in another context, and by association in several others. The pearls are the eyes of the King of Naples in *The Tempest,* presumed to be lost at sea; of a drowned Phoenician sailor; of the dead Fisher King of the legends: the glazed eyes of lack of faith. In the absence of faith, water, a symbol of fertility, becomes a symbol of death. A crowd "flows over" London Bridge. Intent upon the actual ("And each man fixed his eyes before his feet"), it too symbolizes death. The city – here London; elsewhere any city – is "Unreal." The poet, searching the crowd for the lost king, accosts a man named Stetson: any man; or, in the words of Baudelaire, "You, hypocritical reader, my likeness, my brother!" Baudelaire's preoccupation with evil represents man's consciousness of sin, prerequisite to remorse. Remorse or conscience, dogging man's heels, will dig up the corpse of the buried king, planted by each man in the garden of his soul. The thought is couched in a style echoing Webster, another student of evil. Eliot's implication is that what Webster projected melodramatically on the stage has validity for all of us in the privacy of our hearts.

The second section, "A Game of Chess," develops in terms of the moves of "pieces" and "pawns"; the upper and lower classes. Each section of the poem is itself an expanded metaphor or symbol of its theme. Thus the dead land, whose bones are phrase-fragments of the past, is now a checkerboard of such fragments, fitted together in an interlocking, timeless perspective. Life is the game played on this board. Since the King is in check, the moves are meaningless; the game is already lost.

The woman at the mirror, a Queen, spends her time like the Lady of Shalott, gazing at the reflection of life. What she sees are memories of departed glory: a Chair reminiscent of Cleopatra's barge; rococo furnishings suggesting Fragonard or Boucher; perfumes rivaling those of Keats' "Lamia." A subtle sense of corruption, reminding us of "an atmosphere of Juliet's tomb," deepens as the passage progresses:

> Above the antique mantel was displayed
> As though a window gave upon the sylvan scene
> The change of Philomel, by the barbarous king
> So rudely forced; yet there the nightingale
> Filled all the desert with inviolable voice
> And still she cried, and still the world pursues,
> 'Jug Jug' to dirty ears.

The allusions to Milton, Ovid and Keats (see page 13) contribute to the arrested motion of the scene. After the sumptuous introductory description, this is the first ironic compound of aggrandizement and belittlement. By a shift of focus — a reverse metamorphosis — the nightingale of mythology has been transformed into a raucous bird. Keats' urn of beauty is a jug of ugliness. And now the imagery changes, becoming broken and fearful:

> And other withered stumps of time
> Were told upon the walls; staring forms
> Leaned out, leaning, hushing the room enclosed.

This casts its irony back on the introduction. What started out so grandiloquently has come to "withered stumps." The development recalls a "trompe l'oeil" chromo of the woman at her dresser, a scene which on further inspection turns into a skull. The Queen, brushing out her hair, is, like a Medusa, staring herself to stone. She asks a shadowy "I" whether he is alive; whether there's anything in his head. But "I" is remembering the dead king: "Those are pearls that were his eyes." The moves of their lives are a set evasion of life:

> 'What shall we ever do?'
>   The hot water at ten.
> And if it rains, a closed car at four.
> And we shall play a game of chess,
> Pressing lidless eyes and waiting for a knock upon the door.

Like the Tarot pack, the imagery of chess suggests that reason has been supplanted by chance. We make game of the past. Its wisdom survives in a joke; the classic rhythms are syncopated:

> O O O O that Shakespeherian Rag—
> It's so elegant
> So intelligent

The relations between the sexes are also a series of moves in a losing game. While the Queen and "I" are playing out their lives in sterility, boredom and "nerves," Lil, of a lower social order, is expecting the return of her husband Albert, recently demobilized; a "pawn" in the game of war. A "kind friend" advises her to get the new set of teeth Albert had given her money for, when he went into the army four years ago. The teeth are another symbol of loss, related to "Those are pearls that were his eyes"; dice in a losing game. Without them, Lil may forfeit Albert to another woman; possibly the "friend." With them, she can only hope to continue the vicious circle of lust and decay. Her teeth have gone bad because of the pills she took for an abortion, since she had already had five children, and "nearly died of young George." Sensual desire leads only to its own destruction.

The "pawns" are in as bad case as the "pieces." Time is running out, as in a pub, before they can finish their drinks. (HURRY UP PLEASE ITS TIME) They may invite their friends in to have a "gammon" (even their food suggests a game of chance); but like the Queen and "I," they too are "waiting for a knock upon the door": "Good night, ladies, good night, sweet ladies, good night, good night."

Section III, "The Fire Sermon," is a vision of carnal desires in the light of the Buddha's Fire Sermon and Saint Augustine's *Confessions*. Common to the Eastern sage and Western saint is their conception of earthly desire as a consuming flame, experienced by each in youth, from which they were converted in middle age to an espousal of the "Middle Way" and asceticism.

The section opens with echoes of Spenser's "Prothalamion," which celebrated a courtly double marriage: "Sweet Thames, run softly, till I end my song." But the modern setting is a winter or late autumn scene; the "marriages" are mock, a series of betrayals. The Thames is associated with "the waters of Leman." Babylon, beside whose waters the Israelites lived in bondage, is the Biblical counterpart of a whore, or leman. Leman may refer also to a modern betrayal; being another name for the Lake of Geneva, beside which the League of Nations foundered.

The war, the season of fire from which Albert is returning; the dying season of the year; the summer of the Renaissance; all are to be succeeded by a period of drouth. "I," musing on the wreck of successive faiths —

> . . . upon the king my brother's wreck
> And on the king my father's death before him

— hears behind him, as Marvell heard the winged chariot of time, "The rattle of the bones, and chuckle spread from ear to ear." The dice of death are again suggested, the skull's toothless grin recalling Lil's mouth with its decayed teeth. What premonitions are there of rejuvenation?

> The sound of horns and motors, which shall bring
> Sweeney to Mrs. Porter in the spring.

Spring may not be far behind, but its hope is delusive. It will merely continue the cycle of futility and vulgarity. Where is the innocence of childhood?

Et O ces voix d'enfants, chantant dans la coupole!

Lost, altered, vanished; as the sisters Procne and Philomela, pursued by King Tereus, were turned into a swallow and a nightingale. Even their song is harsh:

Twit twit twit
Jug jug jug jug jug jug

For it is heard through the ears of Sweeney. In the myth, Tereus, as a hawk, continued to pursue the sisters. His modern counterpart, Sweeney, hunts down and vulgarizes beauty. Pursuing his origins, not in the gods, but in the beasts, he debases nature. Its very "innocence" becomes a symbol of bestiality.

This preamble leads to a series of tired seductions. Mr. Eugenides, the Smyrna merchant, invites "me" to a "weekend at the Metropole." The ambiguity of "me" — now either a woman or a homosexual — is resolved in the next episode, that of the typist and the "young man carbuncular." Here "I" becomes Tiresias, half man, half woman: the part of personality that is not sexual; that observes, with apprehension and disgust, the activities of its own sensual nature, as Tiresias struck the coupling snakes. What it observes is weariness, ignobility and lack of passion. The carnal delight is not only lacking in delight; there is a minimum of carnality in its performance. It has become routine, like the other performances in the lives of a typist and a "small house agent's clerk."

Now the Thames, in drifting snatches of song, brings echoes of other episodes: Elizabeth and Leicester in their barge, playing at love; a man and a girl supine on the floor of a canoe. Aimless lust succeeds aimless lust. These encompass the searcher after truth — Augustine, the Buddha, Eliot — all but distracting him from his course; as in *Ash-Wednesday* Eliot is to be distracted by fleeting glimpses of earth's beauty. The only salvation is through an act of Grace:

O Lord Thou pluckest me out

Section IV, "Death by Water," is the bare recital of the drowning of a Phoenician sailor. Eliot has translated it from the third stanza of an earlier poem, "Dans le Restaurant"; one of four he wrote in French. Since this poem bears on several recurrent themes, I have put it freely into English[1]:

IN THE RESTAURANT

The seedy waiter with nothing to do
But twiddle his fingers and breathe down my neck:
  "Where I come from it'll be the rainy season,
  With wind, bright sunshine, and rain;
  What they call the beggars' wash-day."
(Babbler, dribbler, with a round behind,
I ask you, at least, don't dribble in the soup.)
  "The drenched willows, and shoots on the brier—
  It's there, in a shower of rain, that one takes shelter.
I was seven, she was smaller.
  She was soaking wet, I gave her primroses."
The spots on his vest amount to thirty-eight.
  "I tickled her, to make her laugh.
  I experienced a moment of power and delight."

  How now, lecherous old boy, at that age . . .
"Sir, the fact is hard.
  There came along, to buffet us, a large dog;
  I was scared; I left her halfway.
  It's a pity."
      How now, you have your vulture!
Be off, and scrub the wrinkles of your face;
Wait—my fork; scratch your skull with it.
What right have you to pay for experiences like me?
Wait, there's ten cents; get yourself a bath.

Phlebas, the Phoenician, drowned a fortnight,
Forgot the cries of the gulls and the Cornish billow,
And the profits and the losses, and the cargo of tin;
An undersea current carried him a long way off,

[1] Leonard Unger translated part of this poem in his article "T. S. Eliot's Rose Garden: A Persistent Theme" in *T. S. Eliot: A Selected Critque* (Rinehart and Co., 1948).

> Passing him through the stages of his former life.
> Just think, this was a difficult fate;
> And yet he was once a handsome man, of considerable stature.

The incongruity of the waiter's slovenly appearance with his romantic story serves a double purpose. It emphasizes the irony of his life. And the spots counted by the diner (in French they *mount* to thirty-eight) emphasize the latter's boredom. The waiter, unexpectedly revealing himself, gets the kind of response feared by Prufrock.

In *The Waste Land* Eliot also uses a downpour to express a lost freshness of experience:

> Summer surprised us, coming over the Starnbergersee
> With a shower of rain . . .

And the impulse of love is a giving of flowers: "You gave me hyacinths first a year ago."

The name Phlebas is related to the Greek word φλέψ (phleps, phlebos), "blood-vessel"; a connecting link between all humanity. There is a universal quality to our experiences, whether we are an aged, rheumy waiter or a supercilious diner; whether we are alive today or plied the seas in the days of the great Phoenician trade-routes, inadvertent spreaders of culture. We are all navigators of our blood-vessels; capable of drowning in our sensations as the sailor was washed overboard. These sensations are themselves a recounting of past experiences. The waiter, drowning in his memories, is passing like the sailor through the stages of his age and youth.

In its context in *The Waste Land,* dissociated from the episode of the waiter, the Phlebas passage symbolizes another kind of drowning: baptism, the outward sign of religious conversion. The water of faith, in which one "drowns" from a mere physical existence, or materialistic conception of life, is the water which will again make fertile the waste land, restoring to it its king, no longer maimed, hanged or crucified, but whole and living.

The change of context indicates a continuous development in Eliot's poetry; implicit up to *The Waste Land,* explicit since. Many of the early poems are statements, by example, of human predicaments. In *The Waste Land* the predicament itself, as presented, contains an indication of its resolution. The very symbols of damnation are, by a change of focus, symbols of salvation. This insight, although couched in theological terms, has profound psychological validity. One limitation of Eliot's method, however, is already in evidence; not so much in the individual poems as in their cumulative effect; not so much in what he includes as in what he leaves out.

There are pleasures that are not disappointing. There are continuing experiences of joy. There are shared emotions of love that do not lead to disillusion and despair. These are not to be found in Eliot's poems. What love there is has never come to completion; the joys are all fled; the pleasures are remembered only after they have ceased. All is memory in absence, made doubly bitter if it is delight that is being remembered.

This is an emotional stacking of the cards; a loading of the dice. It lessens our confidence in Eliot's statement of the *general* human predicament. All experiences will undoubtedly end with death; that is a fixed human condition. Beyond that we may speculate; we may have faith; we cannot know. But in Eliot's poems this sense of death invades life; not as a spur to more productive activity, but as an inhibiting force. All his predicaments are fundamentally the same. They all share the neurotic pattern of the waiter.

For the waiter a feeling of power and delight is inevitably followed, as if in retribution, by its opposite, a proof of inadequacy. This is the significance of his memory of the childhood episode. He has been rehearsing it ever since; if not consciously, in the drowned parts of him. By implication all his subsequent life has been a re-enactment and confirmation of this early pattern. Years later he blurts out the story to a casual, uninterested diner. It has now become his justification for being an impotent, fumbling, dribbling old man.

Like Prufrock, he is a passive agent. His two positive acts — the giving of the flowers and the tickling of the little girl — come to nothing. Everything else happens to him from the outside, including his sensations. He happens to feel power and delight; they come to him like the dog, propelled by some *deus ex machina:* accident, or Fate. The dog happens to frighten him and he runs away. This turns out to be the pattern of his life. "It's a pity."

It is also his excuse. Because of it he now feels exempt from praise or blame. He didn't make the pattern; it was imposed on him, very much as an ugly life is imposed on the hero of James Farrell's *A World I Never Made.* Their conclusions are rather different, but the symptoms are similar. Where the latter reacts with rage, the waiter exhibits resignation. If he didn't make it, where did it come from, this arbitrary pattern? It is the cycle of parental authority: prohibition and punishment. In tickling the little girl he was overstepping an injunction no doubt connected with sex. This gave him an overwhelming sense of power; of getting back at, or evading, authority. His over-excitement betrayed an apprehension of guilt. He was emotionally prepared for the advent of the dog; for *anything* that would turn his feeling of power into a feeling of helplessness. The dog arrived with the timing of a rebuff; the prompt application of a parental precept.

This basic situation, the emotional conflict with his parents, follows him through life, disguised and overlaid by the more immediately vivid occurrence with the girl and dog. Like everything that will happen to him, the girl and the dog have been accidental; but the emotional cycle he has made of them is no accident. Now he perceives this cycle just enough to confirm it, as Prufrock rationalized his indecision. It has remained unresolved, self-confirming and self-perpetuating.

The poem, then, is not the interpretation but the accurate presentation, in depth, of a prevalent symptom. Here and elsewhere Eliot exhibits this cycle of power and helplessness with great perspicacity. As in any work of art, or as in life, we are free to make our own interpretations. Like life, the poem will be found to contain them. As Eliot said in the Preface to the 1928 edition of *The Sacred Wood:*

> We can only say that a poem, in some sense, has its own life; that its parts form something quite different from a body of neatly ordered biographical data; that the feeling, or emotion, or vision, resulting from the poem is something different from the feeling or emotion or vision in the mind of the poet.

In the diner's reaction — "How now, you have your vulture!" — Eliot is making the point that all who are human are heirs to the same weakness. He has not, as yet, expressly stated an explicitly religious intention. But from the subsequent development of his poetry, we realize that he will come to equate this weakness with the notion of original sin. There is to be no escape from the vicious circle except by renouncing the circle entirely. All human propensities are intrinsically evil, and are only to be redeemed by submission to a supernatural authority.

In the fifth section of *The Waste Land,* "What the Thunder Said," Eliot draws his themes together. After the inverted crucifixion of "Death by Water," this is the period of anguished waiting for an unbelieved-in Resurrection.

> After the torchlight red on sweaty faces
> After the frosty silence in the gardens
> After the agony in stony places
> The shouting and the crying
> Prison and palace and reverberation
> Of thunder of spring over distant mountains
> He who was living is now dead
> We who were living are now dying
> With a little patience

The present is an intersection time between death and rebirth. The Fisher King is maimed, the Phoenician sailor drowned; Christ has been crucified. Faith is all but dead; the fertility of the land has ceased:

> Here is no water but only rock
> Rock and no water and the sandy road
> The road winding above among the mountains
> Which are mountains of rock without water
> If there were water we should stop and drink
> Amongst the rock one cannot stop or think

In this blighted landscape, where there is not even silence, "But dry sterile thunder without rain," the immanence of Resurrection is nevertheless suggested:

> Who is the third who walks always beside you?
> When I count, there are only you and I together
> But when I look ahead up the white road

There is always another one walking beside you
Gliding wrapt in a brown mantle, hooded
I do not know whether a man or a woman
— But who is that on the other side of you?

This vision of the appearance of Christ to his disciples on the road to Emmaus is followed by a vision of the heavenly Jerusalem which above the destruction of the cities — Jerusalem Athens Alexandria Vienna London — "cracks and reforms and bursts in the violet air." Every war, the intersection point between a civilization that is dying and a new one already doomed, is accompanied by visions of a true and fertile culture; an unearthly glory. Such visions come to us in "the violet light" of nightfall; in "the violet air" announcing a storm. Through destruction, redemption is made possible. Our values are topsy-turvy:

And bats with baby faces in the violet light
Whistled, and beat their wings
And crawled head downward down a blackened wall
And upside down in air were towers
Tolling reminiscent bells, that kept the hours
And voices singing out of empty cisterns and exhausted wells.

The fragmented ending of *The Waste Land,* with its three claps of thunder speaking over the rubble of images, ideas and languages, corresponds in miniature to the form of the poem as a whole, with its fragments of epic, dramatic and lyric styles. The breakdown is complete and thoroughgoing. Yet in its utter disintegration and hopelessness lie the seeds of redemption and hope; the "peace that passeth understanding," represented in the formal Hindu ending: "Shantih shantih shantih."

Eliot no doubt intends to mean, in the light of his later poetry, that through the consciousness of guilt the soul is driven to knowledge of God; to a revelation of the forms which shall supersede this necessary earthly cycle. But the reader is not limited to this strictly theological interpretation. By a conscious knowledge of the cycle of birth, growth and decay, and a corresponding awareness of our own, superimposed, man-made patterns, we may learn to accept the former and to remedy the latter; to achieve a culture which is not self-defeating.

III

The Plays

THESE FRAGMENTS I have shored against my ruins," reads one of the last lines of *The Waste Land,* followed by the words of the mad Hieronimo: "Why then Ile fit you." If *The Waste Land* may be regarded, symbolically, as a total destruction of the world, Eliot has since set about rebuilding. Significantly, his first full-length venture in dramatic form, *The Rock,* written twelve years later (1934), was inspired to aid the rebuilding of a church.

The intervening years had been comparatively sparse of poems. "The Hollow Men" (1925) is a simplified lyric version of the despair of *The Waste Land.* Its fifth section attempts to fix with greater precision the moments at which the eternal intersects the temporal:

> Between the idea
> And the reality
> Between the motion
> And the act
> Falls the Shadow
>
> *For Thine is the Kingdom*

Between the conception
And the creation
Between the emotion
And the response
Falls the Shadow

Life is very long

Between the desire
And the spasm
Between the potency
And the existence
Between the essence
And the descent
Falls the Shadow

For Thine is the Kingdom

The succeeding Ariel Poems, one a year, are religious in theme: "Journey of the Magi" (1927), "A Song for Simeon" (1928), "Animula" (1929), "Marina" (1930); as well as the culminatingly devotional *Ash-Wednesday* (1930). He returned to more mundane considerations in "Triumphal March" (1931); later incorporated, with "Difficulties of a Statesman" (1932), in "Coriolan," a meditation on the hero and the mass in modern times. *Sweeney Agonistes* (1932) was his first experiment with dramatic verse. Subtitled "Fragments of an Aristophanic Melodrama," it rendered the theological paradox, death versus life, in terms of slang, with a music-hall setting.

Together these poems reflect a period, apparently, of meditation, prayer and theological research. Their interwoven phrases come less from Elizabethan or metaphysical sources; more from the sermons of Anglican divines like Lancelot Andrewes, who supplies the opening lines of "Journey of the Magi":

'A cold coming we had of it,
Just the worst time of the year
For a journey, and such a long journey:
The ways deep and the weather sharp,
The very dead of winter.'

From Symbolism Eliot is passing to symbolics. The "Word within a word, unable to speak a word," used formerly as a symbol of the inexpressible emotion, now refers more specifically to the mystery of the Incarnation.

During this time Eliot was writing the bulk of his theological essays, many of them collected in *For Lancelot Andrewes* (1928) and the volume that replaced it, *Essays Ancient and Modern* (1936). In these, and in "Thoughts After Lambeth" (1931; included in *Selected Essays*); in *After Strange Gods* (1934), and in his later *The Idea of a Christian Society* (1939) and *Notes Towards the Definition of Culture* (1949), insight is all but overwhelmed by orthodoxy. The dryness of their style testifies to a sense of obligation:

> Before attempting to remove the remains of his reputation to a last resting place in the dreary cemetery of literature, it is desirable to remind the reader of Andrewes' position in history.

Not that they are devoid of insight; nothing that Eliot has written is. But what insight there is is not free to develop. It is being used, very ably, to bolster up a theological structure.

In his first essay in *The Sacred Wood,* "The Perfect Critic," Eliot had poked mild fun at Coleridge's "metaphysical hare-and-hounds." He went on to develop, by negative example, a memorable criterion of insight:

> . . . His end does not always appear to be the return to the work of art with improved perception and intensified, because more conscious, enjoyment; his centre of interest changes, his feelings are impure. . . . It is one more instance of the pernicious effect of emotion.

Except for the revealing fallacy of the last sentence, this passage might well have been retained by Eliot in his *Selected Essays.* The irony of his having taken Coleridge to task, however, does not entirely escape Eliot. He breaks off a flight of speculation at the conclusion of *The Use of Poetry and the Use of Criticism* (1933) with the words: "The sad ghost of Coleridge beckons me from the wings."

Yet during this period the greatest of Eliot's critical studies were also to appear: "Homage to John Dryden," "Shakespeare and the Stoicism of Seneca"; especially "Dante." In these his end *is* "the return to the work of art with improved perception and intensified, because more conscious, enjoyment." It was a time, then, of the reassessment of all values, literary and religious alike; as if he were searching, in that tradition whose main current, he says, "does not at all flow invariably through the most distinguished reputations," for his own course.

This was to be, he announced in *For Lancelot Andrewes,* "classicist in literature, royalist in politics, and anglo-catholic in religion." The statement testifies to his orderly inclinations; although he qualified it, in *After Strange Gods,* by saying that he had not intended to imply a necessary connection between the three positions, "religious, political and literary."

If the effect of his theological preoccupation has been to dictate the subjectmatter of his later poems — and for some time, perhaps, to limit their quantity — much of the poetry so inspired transcends its theme. By nature poetry cannot be restricted to any one interpretation or intention, even that of its originator. As Eliot said in *The Use of Poetry and the Use of Criticism* (p. 130):

> . . . What a poem means is as much what it means to others as what it means to the author; and indeed, in the course of time a poet may become merely a reader in respect to his own works, forgetting his original meaning — or without forgetting, merely changing.

The Rock, however, written in collaboration with Martin Browne, who supplied the scenario while Eliot provided the words, offers few examples of such transcendence. Eliot has included its Choruses in his *Collected Poems: 1909–1935.* They are preponderantly dutiful; evidence of the struggle to rise to a worthwhile occasion, or to write down to it. Their occasional ironies are weary, underlined parodies of his own style: "What does the world say, does the whole world stray in high-powered cars on a by-pass way?"

Yet in them, as in the rather slight "Landscapes" (1934–35) of the period, may be found the beginnings of themes later to be expertly woven into the texture of *Four Quartets.* In "New Hampshire" the "children's voices" and the "apple-tree" (recalling *"O ces voix d'enfants"*); and in "Cape Ann" the "O quick quick quick, quick hear the song-sparrow," are all anticipations. So is the first Chorus from *The Rock,* with its grand, if rather bare and repetitious, rhetoric:

The Eagle soars in the summit of Heaven,
The Hunter with his dogs pursues his circuit,
O perpetual revolution of configured stars,
O perpetual recurrence of determined seasons,
O world of spring and autumn, birth and dying!
The endless cycle of idea and action,
Endless invention, endless experiment,
Brings knowledge of motion, but not of stillness;
Knowledge of speech, but not of silence;
Knowledge of words, and ignorance of the Word.

The Rock was designed as a pageant. It is merely a criticism of the form, then, to say that in it the elements of theological disputation and dramatic action war against each other. They are not fully resolved in *Murder in the Cathedral,* which followed a year later (1935). But the latter is more play than pageant. Its action is largely intellectual, and its language, with some exceptions, in the dry, sermonizing accents of Lancelot Andrewes:

They know and do not know, what it is to act or suffer.
They know and do not know, that acting is suffering
And suffering is action. . . .

This language is, however, appropriate to its theme. The thought is dramatically broken up by the successive arrival of four Tempters, each holding forth progressively more persuasive reasons for Thomas Becket to compromise his position. The Fourth Tempter offers him not so much a compromise as a base motive — his own hope of martyrdom — for acting in the way he has determined to act.

Thus the ideas, including the most subtle, arrive climactically; and this constitutes the action of the play. The Four Tempters, repulsed, become the Four Assassins of Becket.

There are two structural weaknesses. The women of the Chorus, commenting on the action, are in reality aloof from it:

For us, the poor, there is no action,
But only to wait and to witness.

They underscore the aloofness of Becket himself, preoccupied with preserving the salvation of his soul. This is what has chiefly motivated his return to the archbishopric at an inauspicious time. It motivates his resistance to three of the temptations: to curry favor with the King; with the corrupt Bishops; or with the Barons. We do not feel that he has entirely escaped, although he recognizes, the fourth temptation: to curry favor with his Lord.

The second weakness is the scene in which the Four Assassins turn to the audience and justify their deed. Their speeches are parodies of modern "genteel" Englishmen of vaguely liberal pretensions haranguing an election crowd: "You are Englishmen, and therefore you believe in fair play . . . your sympathies are all with the under dog." Perhaps Eliot intended this scene to be a "temptation of the audience." But it is violently out of key, marring the dignity of the play sustained up to this point; like the sudden irruption of a scene from Auden's *The Dog Beneath the Skin,* which it suggests.

For many years Eliot had been elaborating his theories on the construction of verse plays for modern audiences. As early as 1919 he was speculating, in " 'Rhetoric' and Poetic Drama," on an appropriate language:

> At the present time there is a manifest preference for the "conversational" in poetry — the style of "direct speech," opposed to the "oratorical" and the rhetorical; but if rhetoric is any convention of writing inappropriately applied, this conversational style can and does become a rhetoric — or what is supposed to be a conversational style, for it is often as remote from polite discourse as well could be.

And in "The Possibility of a Poetic Drama" (1920), on the appropriate form:

> . . . The Elizabethan drama was aimed at a public which wanted *entertainment* of a crude sort, but would *stand* a good deal of poetry; our problem should be to take a form of entertainment, and subject it to the process which would leave it a form of art. Perhaps the music-hall comedian is the best material.

And in his tribute to "Marie Lloyd" (1923), a music-hall entertainer of the period, on the problem of different levels of expression corresponding to the classes of society:

> . . . The middle classes, in England as elsewhere, under democracy, are morally dependent upon the aristocracy, and the aristocracy are subordinate to the middle class, which is gradually absorbing and destroy-

ing them. The lower class still exists; but perhaps it will not exist for long. In the music-hall comedians they find the expression and dignity of their own lives; and this is not found in the most elaborate and expensive revue.

Taken together, these form the basis for his experiment in *Sweeney Agonistes* with a style, form and language suitable for the music hall. But they suggest, as well, why he may have left it fragmentary. His dissatisfaction may have been with what he sensed would have, at best, a limited appeal. He wanted something capable of reaching a wide audience. In "A Dialogue on Dramatic Poetry" (1928) he ranged over the field of dramatic verse, from Aeschylus to modern times. One of his characters says:

> . . . The tendency, at any rate, of prose drama is to emphasize the ephemeral and superficial; if we want to get at the permanent and universal we tend to express ourselves in verse.

After a mention of the ballet, as a dance form concerned "with the permanent and universal," another character relates it to liturgy:

> . . . I say that the consummation of the drama, the perfect and ideal drama, is to be found in the ceremony of the Mass. I say . . . that drama springs from religious liturgy, and that it cannot afford to depart far from religious liturgy.

The most recent and significant statement occurs toward the end of *The Use of Poetry and the Use of Criticism:*

> . . . The most useful poetry, socially, would be one which could cut across all the present stratifications of public taste — stratifications which are perhaps a sign of social disintegration. The ideal medium for poetry, to my mind, and the most direct means of social 'usefulness' for poetry, is the theatre. In a play of Shakespeare you get several levels of significance. For the simplest auditors there is the plot, for the more thoughtful the character and conflict of character, for the more literary the words and phrasing, for the more musically sensitive the rhythm, and for auditors of greater sensitiveness and understanding a meaning which reveals itself gradually. And I do not believe that the classification of audience is so clear-cut as this; but rather that the sensitiveness of every auditor is acted upon by all these elements at once, though in different degrees of consciousness. At none of these levels is the auditor bothered by the presence of that which he does not understand, or by

> the presence of that in which he is not interested. I may make my meaning a little clearer by a simple instance. I once designed, and drafted a couple of scenes, of a verse play. My intention was to have one character whose sensibility and intelligence should be on the plane of the most sensitive and intelligent members of the audience; his speeches should be addressed to them as much as to the other personages in the play—or rather, should be addressed to the latter, who were to be material, literal-minded and visionless, with the consciousness of being overheard by the former. There was to be an understanding between this protagonist and a small number of the audience, while the rest of the audience would share the responses of the other characters in the play. Perhaps this is all too deliberate, but one must experiment as one can.

This apology for *Sweeney Agonistes* must be extended to include *Murder in the Cathedral.* For its disunity is due to the deliberate contrivance of the Choruses and justifying speeches. Eliot allowed his sense of "stratifications" so to invade his design that it destroys the central intention. Perhaps one difficulty is that, in this case, so much critical speculation has preceded performance. Creation does not seem to flow as naturally out of criticism as criticism out of creation.

2

The Family Reunion (1939) is more interesting, but in some ways less successful, than *Murder in the Cathedral.* Instead of portraying an ecclesiastical personage of whom other-worldly speculation is to be expected, it attempts to present such speculation on the part of worldly characters.

The scene is an English country house, Wishwood. The three sisters and two brothers-in-law of Amy, Dowager Lady Monchensey, have gathered to celebrate her birthday. Also present is Amy's companion Mary, a distant relative "getting on for thirty." Amy's three sons are expected. Lord Harry, eldest and heir, has been away for eight years. He has married, instead of Mary (his mother's choice), an unsuitable woman with whom he has traveled about the world. A year ago his wife was swept overboard, like Phlebas, from an ocean liner.

Aunt Agatha, the Cassandra of the play, is given speeches that parallel themes in the *Four Quartets;* of which "Burnt Norton" had already been published. It will be painful, she says, for Harry to return to Wishwood:

> I mean painful, because everything is irrevocable,
> Because the past is irremediable,
> Because the future can only be built
> Upon the real past. . . .
> Harry must often have remembered Wishwood —
> The nursery tea, the school holiday,
> The daring feats on the old pony,
> And thought to creep back through the little door. . . .
> The man who returns will have to meet
> The boy who left. . . .
> When the loop in time comes — and it does not come
>   for everybody —
> The hidden is revealed, and the spectres show themselves.

As Gerald, one of the brothers-in-law, remarks, "You seem to be wanting to give us all the hump." Her speech and his reply indicate two of the four "levels of response." Gerald's lines, typical of the prosaic characters, are in a loose, colloquially flat variant of blank verse. In contrast, the speeches of Agatha, Harry and occasionally Mary are pitched somewhat higher. At moments of greater intensity, both levels are correspondingly heightened. Agatha's runic chant is typical of the top level:

> Thus with most careful devotion
> Thus with precise attention
> To detail, interfering preparation
> Of that which is already prepared
> Men tighten the knot of confusion

This is clearly, by its idiom as well as by the fact that the others do not respond, a withdrawal-soliloquy, reminiscent of O'Neill's device to project unspoken thoughts and moods. The prosaic characters at moments of stress join together in a Chorus; a group soliloquy on a light-verse plane, usually expressing their communal boredom and bewilderment:

Why do we feel embarrassed, impatient, fretful, ill at ease,
Assembled like amateur actors who have not been assigned
their parts?

Harry's first concern upon arrival is with the drawing of the curtains. How can they bear to sit in a blaze of light for all the world to see? "Do you like to be stared at by eyes through a window? . . . Can't you see them?" he asks; and continues in a vein reminiscent of Orestes:

. . . *You* don't see them, but I see them,
And they see me. This is the first time that I have seen
them.
In the Java Straits, in the Sunda Sea, . . .
There were a thousand places where I might have met
them!
Why here? why here?
Many happy returns of the day, mother.
Aunt Ivy, Aunt Violet, Uncle Gerald, Uncle Charles.
Agatha.

They exchange embarrassed commonplaces. At Wishwood, his mother assures him, nothing has been changed. How can she say that, asks Harry: "You all look so withered and young." As for him, great changes have taken place, impossible to explain to people who

. . . have gone through life
in sleep,
Never woken to the nightmare. I tell you, life would be
unendurable
If you were wide awake. You do not know
The noxious smell untraceable in the drains . . .
. . . I am the old house
With the noxious smell and the sorrow before morning,
In which all past is present, all degradation
Is unredeemable. . . .

This repetition of Agatha's theme is related, in his succeeding speech, to that of Madame Sosostris:

The sudden solitude in a crowded desert
In a thick smoke, many creatures moving
Without direction, for no direction
Leads anywhere but round and round in that vapour—

The world is the Inferno. We are reminded too of Prufrock's "patient etherised upon a table" and his "It is impossible to say just what I mean":

> The partial anaesthesia of suffering without feeling
> And partial observation of one's own automatism
> While the slow stain sinks deeper through the skin . . .
> . . . I talk in general terms
> Because the particular has no language.

Harry now makes his revelation:

> It was only reversing the senseless direction
> For a momentary rest on the burning wheel
> That cloudless night in the mid-Atlantic
> When I pushed her over.

The others, except for Agatha, react with shocked unbelief. Harry must have worried himself into this diseased fancy. "Your conscience can be clear," says Charles. Harry answers:

> It goes a good deal deeper
> Than what people call their conscience; it is just the cancer
> That eats away the self. I knew how you would take it.
> First of all, you isolate the single event
> As something so dreadful that it couldn't have happened,
> Because you could not bear it. So you must believe
> That I suffer from delusions. It is not my conscience,
> Not my mind, that is diseased, but the world I have to live in.

He retires to dress for dinner. The others, in dismay, telephone Dr. Warburton, the family physician; consult Harry's valet. It is the latter's opinion that her Ladyship's death, while it may have been suicide, was accidental; she drank rather heavily. Systematic doubt is thus cast on the manner of her death; even Harry has said:

> I expected to find her when I went back to the cabin.
> Later, I became excited, I think I made enquiries . . .

Mary, who would like to leave Wishwood now that Harry has returned, encounters him while arranging flowers. He is distracted and rude, but insists on talking to her. He recalls the hollow tree, their hiding-place and one recollection of childhood freedom. He confronts her with his bleak despair. Why should he have returned here; here of all places, where "they" are always present?

> Here and here and here — wherever I am not looking,
> Always flickering at the corner of my eye,
> Almost whispering just out of earshot —
> And inside too, in the nightly panic
> Of dreaming dissolution. You do not know,
> You cannot know, you cannot understand.

Mary is convinced his troubles are in himself. "You attach yourself to loathing," she says, "As others do to loving." He is almost swayed by her attraction; by the news she brings him "Of a door that opens at the end of a corridor." They go into a mutual trance reminiscent of the beginning of *The Waste Land:*

> . . . Is the cold spring
> Is the spring not an evil time, that excites us with lying
> voices?

At this moment the Eumenides reveal themselves to Harry, in the embrasure of the window. He realizes that Mary is "of no use" to him; he must fight the Furies. These do not represent remorse, apparently; they have been pursuing him for the last eight years.

With Dr. Warburton he gets into a metaphysical and cross-purpose discussion of health and disease, crime and punishment:

> For what you call restoration to health
> Is only incubation of another malady.

To which Warburton replies:

> We call it health when we find no symptom
> Of illness. Health is a relative term.

This anticipates "East Coker": "The wounded surgeon plies the steel. . . . Our only health is the disease."

After dinner Warburton advises Harry that his mother is quite ill. Any serious shock may have fatal consequences. But Harry is preoccupied and inattentive. He wishes the doctor to tell him about his father, separated from Amy when Harry was young. Warburton supplies a clue: "There was never the slightest suspicion of scandal."

News comes by a police sergeant that one of Harry's brothers, John, has been injured in a motor accident. Harry at first thinks the sergeant has come to arrest him. Later he makes light of the accident:

> A brief vacation from the kind of consciousness
> That John enjoys, can't make very much difference
> To him or to anyone else. If he was ever really conscious,
> I should be glad for him to have a breathing spell:
> But John's ordinary day isn't much more than breathing.

Leaving his aunts Ivy and Violet quite properly shocked, Harry leads his mother off to her room. A trunk call comes through from Arthur, the third brother, saying he has been detained in London. It develops that Arthur has also been involved in an accident, brought about by his reckless speeding, and has made an ass of himself in the manner of an Evelyn Waugh character. He thought the police chasing him were merely having a game with him. Backing into a shop window on Ebury Street, he explained "I thought it was all open country about here."

Harry, determined to discover the family curse, questions Agatha about his father. Agatha, who has spent

> . . . thirty years of solitude,
> Alone, among women, in a women's college,
> Trying not to dislike women,

reluctantly and obliquely reveals what happened when she, a younger sister, had been invited from college to alleviate Amy's boredom, those first years at Wishwood:

> . . . I remember
> A summer day of unusual heat
> For this cold country.

Harry too has remembered a day "of unusual heat." The repetition is puzzling, since the day Harry remembers is the day news came of his father's death in a distant land; while Agatha's memory is of an earlier year and a very different occurrence. After it she found Harry's father plotting the murder of his wife. Agatha dissuaded him. Harry was to be born in three months; she felt a bond between herself and her sister's unborn child. Compelled in his turn, now, by this strange bond, Harry declares:

> Perhaps my life has only been a dream
> Dreamt through me by the minds of others. Perhaps
> I only dreamt I pushed her.

The doubt cast on the murder of his wife is now complete, even to himself. Agatha replies:

> So I had supposed. What of it?
> What we have written is not a story of detection,
> Of crime and punishment, but of sin and expiation.
> It is possible that you have not known what sin
> You shall expiate, or whose, or why. It is certain
> That the knowledge of it must precede the expiation.
> It is possible that sin may strain and struggle
> In its dark instinctive birth, to come to consciousness
> And so find expurgation. It is possible
> You are the consciousness of your unhappy family,
> Its bird sent flying through the purgatorial flame.

At this revelation Harry feels "happy for a moment, as if I had come home." To him it is like an end. And a beginning, Agatha reminds him; anticipating still another theme of *Four Quartets.* A runic chant, begun by Agatha, links *The Waste Land* and *Four Quartets* through its symbol of the "garden":

> I only looked through the little door
> When the sun was shining on the rose-garden:
> And heard in the distance tiny voices
> And then a black raven flew over. . . .

The intervening years, the chant continues, have been for them both like a concrete corridor; a circular desert; the stone passages

Of an immense and empty hospital
Pervaded by a smell of disinfectant,
Looking straight ahead, passing barred windows.
Up and down. Until the chain breaks.

Harry repeats:

The chain breaks,
The wheel stops, and the noise of machinery,
And the desert is cleared, under the judicial sun
Of the final eye, and the awful evacuation
Cleanses.
I was not there, you were not there, only our phantasms
And what did not happen is as true as what did happen,
O my dear, and you walked through the little door
And I ran to meet you in the rose-garden.

AGATHA

This is the next moment. This is the beginning.
We do not pass twice through the same door
Or return to the door through which we did not pass.

The rose-garden, suggesting Eden and lost innocence, also suggests the womb. But whether Harry is re-enacting the rôle of his father, or feels himself to be the child Agatha should have had, as well as what connection either of these has with the "family curse," is left dark. The "curse" is felt more by association with *Genesis* and Aeschylus than by any development of the immediate circumstances.

Agatha tells him he has a long journey. "Not yet!" he exclaims. This is the first time he has been free from "the ring of ghosts with joined hands, from the pursuers." At this, the Eumenides again appear. But now, without fear, he accepts them; willing to follow wherever they may lead.

To Amy, who feels that Agatha is driving her son away, as previously his father, Harry's parting speeches are rather messianic:

I do not know the words in which to explain it —
That is what makes it harder. You must just believe me,
Until I come again.

Where he is going is "still unsettled":

I have not yet had the precise directions.
Where does one go from a world of insanity?
Somewhere on the other side of despair.
To the worship in the desert, the thirst and deprivation . . .

Apparently his "expiation" will consist in a resumption of traveling. All Amy's hopes for Wishwood have come to nothing. Everyone is leaving her; Mary too, who asks Agatha:

. . . I suppose it is much too late
Now, to try to get a fellowship?

Distractedly Amy announces that Harry is leaving "to become a missionary." This "false note," with the futile responses of the Uncles and Aunts, recalls the out-of-key scene of the Four Tempters. It is an echo of the ribaldry in *Sweeney Agonistes:*

SWEENEY: I'll carry you off
To a cannibal isle.
DORIS: You'll be the cannibal!
SWEENEY: You'll be the missionary!
You'll be my little seven stone missionary!
I'll gobble you up. I'll be the cannibal.

Later in that scene, Sweeney had confided:

I knew a man once did a girl in
Any man might do a girl in
Any man has to, needs to, wants to
Once in a lifetime, do a girl in.

Harry, besides doing in his wife — either outrightly or by making her life so miserable that she threw herself, or allowed herself to fall, into the sea – completes the action of the play by doing in his mother. Amy, as he has been warned, does not survive his departure. He is released, apparently, from moral responsibility by the Christian platitude uttered by Agatha:

> . . . Love compels cruelty
> To those who do not understand love.

This love, like Becket's, is a higher, spiritual love: a preoccupation with his own salvation. Such love can afford to be ruthless. It needs to justify it no human feeling for a dead wife, a girl who has waited years for him, or his mother. They exist as backdrops to his exploration of his soul; to his discovery of "sin and expiation."

I have given the plot in some detail because I think *The Family Reunion* is central to a reappraisal of Eliot. A poet is to be judged by his best, rather than his poorest, performances. But *The Family Reunion* exhibits the failure of Eliot's ideas to translate into action. The symbols of his poetry, his time-amalgams, are not sufficient to a play, which must deal with people. The various levels of response hardly amalgamate; they are more divisive than unifying. After his callous remarks about his injured brother, Harry says:

> It's only when they see nothing
> That people can always show the suitable emotions –
> And so far as they feel at all, their emotions are suitable.
> They don't understand what it is to be awake,
> To be living on several planes at once
> Though one cannot speak with several voices at once.
> I have all of the rightminded feeling about John
> That you consider appropriate. Only, that's not the language
> That I choose to be talking. I will not talk yours.

There is little evidence that Harry has "rightminded feeling" about anyone. His inability to express the several planes on which he lives indicates that they are at cross purposes. As with the categories "matter" and "spirit," there is no organic connection between them. They exist independently, each negating the other.

Many of the symbols suggest a deliberately Freudian interpretation. Certainly there seems to be a consciously sexual meaning to "rose-garden." But by transferring Harry's incestuous feelings from his mother to his aunt, Eliot has discarded one of the more productive insights of Freudian analysis — its perception that emotional patterns can be traced back to the interrelation of child and parents — and retained a less desirable feature — its insistence on sex as *the* emotional motivation.

Eliot is concerned, as he states in his essay on Dante, with "the high dream" — the *vision* — as distinct from what he considers "the low dream" of modern times. Perhaps *The Family Reunion* constitutes his answer to Freud; an attempt to restore what he feels is a lost truth of Greek drama; the fulfillment of a destiny rather than the confirmation of a psychological pattern. But the destiny, as he develops it, has little human relevance. He seems to be propounding, with the "family curse," the theory of a "family unconscious" — a modification of Jung's "racial unconscious." The blood relationship has skipped a beat; possibly to indicate that this is a spiritual more than a physical linkage. But if he does consider the two planes as separate and distinct, why insist on a "family curse" at all? It appears to be the desire to retain two mutually contradictory planes of existence at once; like an "ideal order" which is "slightly shifting."

The basic ambiguity is revealed, I think, in Agatha's lines:

> What we have written is not a tale of detection,
> Of crime and punishment, but of sin and expiation.

Sin is no action but an attitude, a way of regarding action. In his desire to isolate it Eliot has left out, or at least rendered inoperative, the crime and punishment. His reluctance to establish whether Harry did or did not push his wife overboard evaporates the plot. In contrast to the "realism" he deplores on the stage — action without attitude — Eliot has written a play of attitude without action; a supernatural explanation of facts that are not given. The effect of evoking the supernatural is thus strikingly complementary to the effect of invoking economic determinism.

A great play or an epic, as Eliot the critic well knows, is composed of action with a definite attitude. But a poem, lyric or didactic, may be written out of attitude alone. *The Family Reunion* is chiefly of interest, then, in the context of Eliot's poetry. Not that it should be regarded as a poem rather than a play. As Eliot has demonstrated, in "A Dialogue on Dramatic Poetry" and elsewhere, you cannot separate "the poetry" from "the play." If *The Family Reunion* suffers as a play, it suffers equally as a poem; although there is memorable poetry in it, lines of great beauty and distinction. Its principal value is in the light it throws on Eliot's recurrent, subtly altering themes as they have been developed, twenty years apart, in the two peaks of his performance, *The Waste Land* and *Four Quartets*.

IV

Four Quartets

In "The Music of Poetry," an address at the University of Glasgow subsequently published in *Partisan Review* (November-December, 1942), Eliot develops two points of special relevance to the *Four Quartets*. In contrast to his speculations on verse drama, these follow the composition of all or most of the Quartets. The first concerns a "cyclical movement" in the language of poetry:

> . . . At some periods, the task is to explore the musical possibilities of an established convention of the relation of the idiom of verse to that of speech; at other periods, the task is to catch up with the changes in colloquial speech. The poet who did most for the English language is Shakespeare: and he carried out, in one short lifetime, the task of two poets. . . . During the first, he was slowly adapting his form to colloquial speech; so that by the time he wrote *Antony and Cleopatra* he had devised a medium in which everything that any dramatic character might have to say, whether high or low, 'poetical' or 'prosaic,' could be said

with naturalness and beauty. Having got to this point, he began to elaborate. The first period — of the poet who began with *Venus and Adonis,* but who had already, in *Love's Labour's Lost,* begun to see what he had to do — is from artificiality to simplicity, from stiffness to suppleness. The later plays move from simplicity towards elaboration.

Eliot's most original effects have been gained chiefly by his juxtapositions of the elaborate and the colloquial. He has been least convincing when he descends to the *merely* colloquial, as in the prose dialogue of *The Rock,* the speeches of the Four Assassins in *Murder in the Cathedral,* and of the valet in *The Family Reunion:*

> . . . You mean them ghosts, Miss!
> I wondered when his Lordship would get round to seeing them —
> And so you've seen them too! They must have given you a turn!
> They did me, at first. You soon get used to them.
> Of course, I knew they was to do with his Lordship,
> And not with me, so I could see them cheerful-like,
> In a manner of speaking. There's no harm in *them,*
> I'll take my oath. Will that be all, Miss?

This gift of prescience to a member of the "lower order" seems gratuitous, in the nature of a tip. It is too patent an attempt to tie together the different "levels of response." Rather than increasing, it decreases the Eumenides' credibility, by treating them with unseemly levity.

Such failures of key do not intrude upon the Quartets. There the levels of response have become simply four levels of intensity. They interact rather than condescend. The musical elaboration is consistent throughout, both as regards language and form. In "The Music of Poetry" Eliot says:

> . . . I think that a poet may gain much from the study of music: how much technical knowledge of musical form is desirable I do not know, for I have not that technical knowledge myself. But I believe that the

> properties in which music concerns the poet most nearly, are the sense of rhythm and the sense of structure. . . . The use of recurrent themes is as natural to poetry as to music. There are possibilities for verse which bear some analogy to the development of a theme by different groups of instruments; there are possibilities of transitions in a poem comparable to the different movements of a symphony or a quartet; there are possibilities of contrapuntal arrangement of subject-matter.

It is evident from Eliot's choice of Quartets for his title that he had four instruments or "voices" in mind, each to introduce or develop recurrent themes. As in the later string quartets of Beethoven, one of his inspirational sources, these themes are simply, almost tersely introduced, their subsequent development moving toward ever greater complexity. Eliot warns against "working too closely to musical analogies." The correspondences with Beethoven are general rather than specific, the greatest being a prevailing mood of high seriousness with religious overtones.

While Beethoven employed a variable number of movements, Eliot divides each of his poems into five. These are further divided into contrasting or complementary sections, whose changes of key and tempo often introduce forms related to dance movements. There is a sketchy resemblance to Sonata Form in his introductory movements, which usually begin with a brief Exposition of related themes, a longer Development, enlarging on one or both of these themes, and a very brief Recapitulation. From a musical standpoint the design might be considered rudimentary; but for poetry it is about as complex as could be managed without recourse to set forms.

In contrast to Beethoven's, each of which is an individual work, all four of Eliot's Quartets are organically interrelated. Each develops a different aspect of an underlying grand theme. The concluding movement of the fourth Quartet, "Little Gidding," weaves together all the important strands of this theme, to form a coda or finale to the entire group.

Their autobiographical content is indicated in the titles. As F. O. Matthiessen has observed:

> . . . "Burnt Norton" . . . borrows its title from a Gloucestershire manor near which Eliot has stayed. The titles of the other three quartets indicate more intimate relationships: East Coker, in Somerset, is where the Eliot family lived until its emigration in the mid-seventeenth century to

the New England coast; the Dry Salvages, a group of rocks off Cape Ann, mark the part of that coast which the poet knew best as a boy; Little Gidding, the seat of the religious community which Nicholas Ferrar established and with which the names of George Herbert and Crashaw are associated, is a shrine for the devout Anglican.

* * *

"Burnt Norton" opens with a statement of the grand theme: time and eternity. This has been led up to by all of Eliot's preceding poetry:

> Time present and time past
> Are both perhaps present in time future,
> And time future contained in time past.
> If all time is eternally present
> All time is unredeemable.

The dry expository tone is characteristic of this first of the four voices of the Quartets. It is the mind, or intellect, that is speaking. Its speech, didactic verse, is one level of intensity removed from prose; a bass under the other voices. No extraneous graces of ornamentation interrupt the clear and ordered rendering, by this instrument, of the intellectual content of the poems. The poetry is in the clarity and arrangement — the "ordonnance," in Lancelot Andrewes' term — of the ideas being communicated. These ideas form the base upon which the structure is built.

The theme thus enunciated — the interpenetration of time and its consequently unredeemable quality — is one, as we have seen, subsequently employed in *The Family Reunion,* which "Burnt Norton" anticipated by some four years. A countersubject is immediately introduced:

> What might have been is an abstraction
> Remaining a perpetual possibility
> Only in a world of speculation.
> What might have been and what has been
> Point to one end, which is always present.

Just as time past, present and future point to one end, which is timeless; so both the actual and the imaginable point to the unimaginable. Now a different voice develops a series of variations on these related themes.

> Footfalls echo in the memory
> Down the passage which we did not take
> Toward the door we never opened
> Into the rose-garden. My words echo
> Thus, in your mind.
>   But to what purpose
> Disturbing the dust on a bowl of rose-leaves
> I do not know.

"Footfalls," the first noun that is not an abstraction, signals the change. Where the Didactic Voice conveyed ideas, the Lyric Voice is translating them into emotions. It is the heart that is speaking. Its language is full of images. Its speech is distinguished by a singing tone and a greater intensity of rhythm. Later these rhythms are to be elaborated in more formal patterns.

Here the Lyric Voice is playing back the original themes in a series of modulations resembling changes of key: a progression through past, present and future. A nostalgic memory, not only of "what has been" but of "what might have been" ("the door we never opened / Into the rose-garden"), is exactly equivalent to an imaginary present, exemplified by the symbols of a poem: "My words echo / Thus, in your mind." A subsidiary theme, later to be developed in detail, has been introduced: the problem of communication; the attempt of words to reach the incommunicable. And the future, too, is similarly nostalgic. Looked at from the point of view of the interpenetrability of time, it too becomes a memory. A poem is the evocation of these phantoms; but "to what purpose?"

>   Other echoes
> Inhabit the garden. Shall we follow?

A third voice is being introduced, the Narrative Voice. Its concern is with events. It is mainly the senses that are speaking. Their speech, in a running rhythm, combines images — the residues of sensations — into a sequence of action. The verbs are all active:

> Quick, said the bird, find them, find them,
> Round the corner. Through the first gate,
> Into our first world, shall we follow
> The deception of the thrush? Into our first world.

This voice speaks now of certain "presences" of childhood, which recall Wordsworth's lines:

> There was a time when mountain, grove and stream,
> The earth, and every common sight,
> To me did seem
> Appareled in celestial light,
> The glory and the freshness of a dream.

The theme of "lost innocence" has haunted Christian thinking. For Wordsworth the intuitive perceptions of childhood argued a more direct relationship between the temporal and the timeless. In Eliot the "presences" are ghostly; they have a quality of foreboding precursive of the Eumenides in *The Family Reunion:*

> There they were, dignified, invisible,
> Moving without pressure, over the dead leaves,
> In the autumn heat, through the vibrant air,
> And the bird called, in response to
> The unheard music hidden in the shrubbery,
> And the unseen eyebeam crossed, for the roses
> Had the look of flowers that are looked at.

A fourth voice is blending with the Narrative Voice: the Apocalyptic. It is the spirit or soul that is speaking. Its incantatory speech is in the form of symbols. These symbols are images with a greater weight of meaning than the experience of the senses alone could have left in them; images with an other-worldly, non-physical import. This prophetic voice will be encountered in runic chants similar to, but more highly evolved than, those in *The Family Reunion.* It is concerned with what Eliot will call, in later Quartets, "the intersection of the timeless moment"; a prescience of the supernatural.

Here the voice is no more than intimated:

> There they were as our guests, accepted and accepting.
> So we moved, and they, in a formal pattern,
> Along the empty alley, into the box circle,
> To look down into the drained pool.
> Dry the pool, dry concrete, brown edged,
> And the pool was filled with water out of sunlight,
> And the lotos rose, quietly, quietly,
> The surface glittered out of heart of light,
> And they were behind us, reflected in the pool.
> Then a cloud passed, and the pool was empty.
> Go, said the bird, for the leaves were full of children,
> Hidden excitedly, containing laughter.
> Go, go, go, said the bird: human kind
> Cannot bear very much reality.

The last phrase has also concluded a speech of Thomas Becket. And the "heart of light" recalls a moment of ecstasy recorded in *The Waste Land:*

> —Yet when we came back, late, from the Hyacinth garden,
> Your arms full, and your hair wet, I could not
> Speak, and my eyes failed, I was neither
> Living nor dead, and I knew nothing,
> Looking into the heart of light, the silence.

In the Quartets such moments, although they are all we have to indicate a higher plane of existence, are nevertheless mere hints and guesses; "distraction fits." Eliot will sum them up in the fifth movement of "The Dry Salvages," where the Didactic Voice says :

> . . . But to apprehend
> The point of intersection of the timeless
> With time, is an occupation for the saint—
> No occupation either, but something given
> And taken, in a lifetime's death in love,

Ardour and selflessness and self-surrender.
For most of us, there is only the unattended
Moment, the moment in and out of time,
The distraction fit, lost in a shaft of sunlight,
The wild thyme unseen, or the winter lightning
Or the waterfall, or music heard so deeply
That it is not heard at all, but you are the music
While the music lasts. These are only hints and guesses,
Hints followed by guesses; and the rest
Is prayer, observance, discipline, thought and action.
The hint half guessed, the gift half understood, is Incarnation.

These then are the four voices of the Quartets: Didactic, Lyric, Narrative and Apocalyptic. Like instruments, they are only occasionally heard separately; although in each movement or its subsidiary parts, one or another may predominate. Movement II of "Burnt Norton" –

Garlic and sapphires in the mud
Clot the bedded axle-tree.

– begins with a duet between the Lyric and Apocalyptic Voices, recounting analogies between the motion of the stars, the motion of life on earth, and the "dance along the artery." In the second half, the Didactic Voice joins in the theme:

At the still point of the turning world. Neither flesh nor
    fleshless;
Neither from nor towards; at the still point, there the dance
    is,
But neither arrest nor movement. And do not call it fixity,
Where past and future are gathered. . . .

The "still point" corresponds to the "intersection of the timeless moment." Time is conceived as a wheel, an "axle-tree," of which the motionless center is eternity. By analogy, this corresponds to an emotional center of calm with which to meet the flux of life:

The inner freedom from the practical desire,
The release from action and suffering, release from the inner
And the outer compulsion, yet surrounded
By a grace of sense, a white light still and moving. . . .

In the third movement the present is thought of as intersecting the past and the future: "a place of disaffection." It is neither day nor night:

. . . Only a flicker
Over the strained time-ridden faces
Distracted from distraction by distraction
Filled with fancies and empty of meaning
Tumid apathy with no concentration
Men and bits of paper, whirled by the cold wind
That blows before and after time. . . .

This reminds us of "Gerontion." "Not here," it concludes, "Not here the darkness, in this twittering world." For the true darkness, the mystic's "dark night of the soul," we must descend, as if into death, into "abstention from movement." Now a lyric (IV) recounts the sensation of death:

Time and the bell have buried the day,
The black cloud carries the sun away.
Will the sunflower turn to us, will the clematis
Stray down, bend to us; tendril and spray
Clutch and cling?

In the concluding movement (V) the theme of communication is resumed. The Didactic Voice asserts that meaning comes only out of a pattern:

. . . Only by the form, the pattern,
Can words or music reach
The stillness, as a Chinese jar still
Moves perpetually in its stillness.

Not the stillness of the violin, while the note lasts,
Not that only, but the co-existence,
Or say that the end precedes the beginning,
And the end and the beginning were always there
Before the beginning and after the end.
And all is always now. . . .

The theme has been struck which will initiate "East Coker": "In my beginning is my end." "Burnt Norton" has been a general meditation on time and eternity, and the incidental problem of communicating the sense of the "intersection of the timeless moment," "the still point." In the process

. . . Words strain
Crack and sometimes break, under the burden,
Under the tension, slip, slide, perish,
Decay with imprecision, will not stay in place,
Will not stay still. . . .

The second half of Movement V is a coda to this Quartet. The Didactic and Apocalyptic Voices, in unison, sum up, concluding that the chief value of life is in its moments of ecstasy and illumination:

Sudden in a shaft of sunlight
Even while the dust moves
There rises the hidden laughter
Of children in the foliage
Quick now, here, now, always—
Ridiculous the waste sad time
Stretching before and after.

2

"East Coker," written some five years later, is concerned more specifically with time in the historical sense, as it affects the poet, his family and the world. It begins with Spengler's proposition, that the fall of a civilization is implicit in its rise:

In my beginning is my end. In succession
Houses rise and fall, crumble, are extended,
Are removed, destroyed, restored, or in their place
Is an open field, or a factory, or a by-pass.

The structure of each Quartet follows a very similar pattern of movements, with individual variations in the dominance of one or another voice, or combination of voices. Now the Narrative Voice expatiates in a tense similar to the historical present:

. . . Now the light falls
Across the open field, leaving the deep lane
Shuttered with branches, dark in the afternoon,
Where you lean against a bank while a van passes,
And the deep lane insists on the direction
Into the village, in the electric heat
Hypnotised. . . .

In such a distraction fit the poet sees, as if forming in a fairy ring, figures of an earlier day

. . . dancing around the bonfire
The association of man and woman
In daunsinge, signifying matrimonie—
A dignified and commodious sacrament.
Two and two, necessarye coniunction,
Holding eche other by the hand or the arm
Whiche betokeneth concorde. . . .

As a poem's meaning arises from its formal pattern, so life is given meaning by order, typified by the "concorde" of dancing. The "commodious sacraments" repeated the cycles of the "seasons and the constellations." The archaic language is taken from the writings of one of Eliot's ancestors. For the order he has been envisioning is that of an earlier time:

Dawn points, and another day
Prepares for heat and silence. Out at sea the dawn wind

Wrinkles and slides. I am here
Or there, or elsewhere. In my beginning.

In the second movement, the disorder of the present is invoked by the Apocalyptic Voice. The present is a November season of storm, destruction and war:

Thunder rolled by the rolling stars
Simulates triumphal cars
Deployed in constellated wars

All is

Whirled in a vortex that shall bring
The world to that destructive fire
Which burns before the ice-cap reigns.

This recalls both "Gerontion" and the Sweeney of *The Waste Land.* The Didactic Voice now comments:

That was a way of putting it — not very satisfactory:
A periphrastic study in a worn-out poetical fashion,
Leaving one still with the intolerable wrestle
With words and meanings. . . .

Where is the promised serenity of autumn, of old age? Did the elders deceive us, or were they themselves deceived? Experience is not the best teacher, for what it teaches us is a pattern, and the pattern is constantly changing:

And every moment is a new and shocking
Valuation of all we have been. We are only undeceived
Of that which, deceiving, could no longer harm.

"History has many cunning passages," said the old man in "Gerontion": "deceives with whispering ambitions," gives too late or too soon. The pattern of the past, says "East Coker," is dead:

The houses are all gone under the sea.

The dancers are all gone under the hill.

Movement III, the most ambitiously orchestrated so far, resumes this theme of death, suggesting an equation between the darkness of physical death and the spiritual darkness of our time:

O dark dark dark. They all go into the dark,
The vacant interstellar spaces, the vacant into the vacant . . .

All the voices alternate and combine on the theme. The Narrative Voice speaks in an epic style, recalling the massive linked similes of Vergil:

. . . As, in a theatre,
The lights are extinguished, for the scene to be changed
With a hollow rumble of wings, with a movement of darkness on
darkness,
And we know that the hills and the trees, the distant panorama
And the bold imposing façade are all being rolled away—
Or as, when an underground train, in the tube, stops too long
between stations
And the conversation rises and slowly fades into silence
And you see behind every face the mental emptiness deepen
Leaving only the growing terror of nothing to think about;
Or when, under ether, the mind is conscious but conscious of
nothing—

Here the past is conveyed by the form, and the present by its subjectmatter. The combination releases a sense of the timeless; of underlying patterns existing through the ages. The similes lead, by analogy, to the mystic's experience of dispossession:

In order to arrive at what you are not
You must go through the way in which you are not.

This paradox is further elaborated in Movement IV, the most formal and balanced of the lyrics, beginning:

The wounded surgeon plies the steel
That questions the distempered part;
Beneath the bleeding hands we feel
The sharp compassion of the healer's art
Resolving the enigma of the fever chart.

An analogy with the Crucifixion is made plain by the terminal line: "Again, in spite of that, we call this Friday good." But for those who do not subscribe to Eliot's belief, the analogy remains faithful to its originating term. It is by the observation of our own processes that we become competent to assist each other. This is dramatically exemplified in the practice of psychiatry. Thus Eliot's theological paradox may be reversed and reapplied to life. The significance of Christ, in such a context, is his humanizing of the idea of God; a stage in the progressive elimination of absolute authority.

In Movement V, Eliot returns to the theme of communication, recounting his own development as a poet. This has led him to that "middle of the journey" from which Dante began his difficult exploration:

So here I am, in the middle way, having had twenty years —
Twenty years largely wasted, the years of *l'entre deux guerres* —
Trying to use words, and every attempt
Is a wholly new start, and a different kind of failure
Because one has only learnt to get the better of words
For the thing one no longer has to say, or the way in which
One is no longer disposed to say it. And so each venture
Is a new beginning, a raid on the inarticulate
With shabby equipment always deteriorating
In the general mess of imprecision of feeling . . .

In the second half of this movement, the coda to the Quartet, Eliot brings together echoes of his own early poems ("Prufrock" and "A Cooking Egg") and of Tennyson's "Ulysses," to draw a personal and universal moral reversing the conclusion of "Burnt Norton":

. . . Not the intense moment
Isolated, with no before and after,
But a lifetime burning in every moment . . .

There is a time for the evening under starlight,
A time for the evening under lamplight
(The evening with the photograph album). . . .

Old men ought to be explorers
Here and there does not matter
We must be still and still moving
Into another intensity
For a further union, a deeper communion
Through the dark cold and the empty desolation,
The wave cry, the wind cry, the vast waters
Of the petrel and the porpoise. In my end is my beginning.

The Quartet has come full circle. That which was its object of despair – "In my beginning is my end" – is now its object of hope.

3

"The Dry Salvages," the third Quartet, considers the intersection of the timeless and the temporal geographically, in terms of an analogy with land and water. The great river that flows through our continent and through our lives "is within us"; the sea "is all about us." We are the perpetual navigators of our lives.

We cannot think of a time that is oceanless
Or of an ocean not littered with wastage
Or of a future that is not liable
Like the past, to have no destination.

The form of this second movement is a variant of Arnaut Daniel's sestina. It rhymes the respective lines of each of the six six-line stanzas, instead of employing the same ending-words in varying order, and omits the three-line summing-up. Perhaps this is a deliberate reflection of the modern temper, which is to avoid the conclusive in favor of the continuous. It is relevant to the thought of "The Dry Salvages," that the attitudes with which we meet experience change. The river, from being considered a "sullen god," is now a mere vehicle for commerce, or an obstacle to be circumvented by bridges. Becoming familiar, experience loses its primitive terrors. But just as moments of happiness and illumination are retained in memory, so too "the agony abides." It is like "the ragged rock in the restless waters":

> Waves wash over it, fogs conceal it;
> On a halcyon day it is merely a monument,
> In navigable weather it is always a seamark
> To lay a course by: but in the sombre season
> Or the sudden fury, is what it always was.

While it remains constant, we are continually changing:

> 'Fare forward, you who think that you are voyaging;
> You are not those who saw the harbour
> Receding, or those who will disembark . . .'

This advice of Krishna indicates an underlying attitude toward life, whose every moment may be the moment of death; not to "think of the fruit of action":

> Not fare well,
> But fare forward, voyagers.

In the lyric fourth movement, the Queen of Heaven, who watches over sailors, is invoked as a symbol of eternal time. She is "Figlia del suo figlio": "daughter of her own son." And in V, the temporal and ephemeral "fruit of action" is exemplified in communication as it is commonly practised:

> To communicate with Mars, converse with spirits,
> To report the behaviour of the sea monster,
> Describe the horoscope . . .
> . . . dissect
> The recurrent image into pre-conscious terrors—
> To explore the womb, or tomb, or dreams; all these are usual
> Pastimes and drugs, and features of the press . . .
>
> . . . But to apprehend
> The point of intersection of the timeless
> With time, is an occupation for the saint . . .

4

In the concluding Quartet, "Little Gidding," this point is located in time and space. Just as midwinter spring is an intimation of the real spring, so our temporal experiences are precursive of the eternal:

> Here, the intersection of the timeless moment
> Is England and nowhere. Never and always.

In the most sustained and complexly organized section of the Quartets, the seventy-two lines which make up the second part of Movement II, Eliot follows his master Dante, blending all four voices, all levels of intensity:

> In the uncertain hour before the morning
>   Near the ending of interminable night
>   At the recurrent end of the unending
> After the dark dove with the flickering tongue
>   Had passed below the horizon of his homing
>   While the dead leaves still rattled on like tin
> Over the asphalt where no other sound was
>   Between three districts whence the smoke arose
>   I met one walking, loitering and hurried
> As if blown towards me like the metal leaves
>   Before the urban dawn wind unresisting.

The figure encountered is a composite of Dante and other masters who have been Eliot's literary and spiritual guides. The time is an intersection time of past and present, actual and imaginary; at once Dante's region of the damned and the hell of wartime England after an air-raid. The imaginary has become the real. The style too is composite; a variant of Dante's *terza rima,* using occasional half-rhymes and assonantal endings in place of the regular rhyme-pattern of the original. The final locking line of Dante's usage is omitted.

The familiar stranger reveals to Eliot the torments reserved for old age: "the cold friction of expiring sense"; "the conscious impotence of rage / At human folly";

'. . . the rending pain of re-enactment
Of all that you have done, and been; the shame
Of motives late revealed . . .
From wrong to wrong the exasperated spirit
Proceeds, unless restored by that refining fire
Where you must move in measure, like a dancer.'
The day was breaking. In the disfigured street
He left me, with a kind of valediction,
And faded on the blowing of the horn.

The "refining fire" alluded to by the ghostly air-raid warden is elucidated in the beautiful short lyric that forms Movement IV:

The dove descending breaks the air
With flame of incandescent terror
Of which the tongues declare
The one discharge from sin and error.
The only hope, or else despair
Lies in the choice of pyre or pyre—
To be redeemed from fire by fire.

Who then devised the torment? Love.
Love is the unfamiliar Name
Behind the hands that wove
The intolerable shirt of flame
Which human power cannot remove.
We only live, only suspire
Consumed by either fire or fire.

The conception of evil as misdirected love is central to Dante and to Christian thinking generally. It is the attempt to resolve the paradox of an all-powerful, all-merciful God who yet allows evil to exist. If it has proved cumbersome as a theological conception, it nevertheless expresses an insight into human emotions. Aggressive traits, leading toward the extinction of others, and repressive traits, leading toward the extinction of the self, are equally misdirections of energy; short-circuitings of personality. Again Eliot's theological analogy may be reversed, and the poem transcend its intentions.

The final movement concludes "Little Gidding" and draws together all the significant themes of the preceding Quartets: the interpenetrability of time, the cyclical movement of history, the geographical analogy, the communication of the incommunicable, the "concorde" of dancing, the garden, the children's voices, the intersection of time and eternity.

> What we call the beginning is often the end
> And to make an end is to make a beginning.
> The end is where we start from. And every phrase
> And sentence that is right (where every word is at home,
> Taking its place to support the others,
> The word neither diffident nor ostentatious,
> An easy commerce of the old and the new,
> The common word exact without vulgarity,
> The formal word precise but not pedantic,
> The complete consort dancing together)
> Every phrase and every sentence is an end and a beginning,
> Every poem an epitaph. . . .
>
> . . . .
>
> We shall not cease from exploration
> And the end of all our exploring
> Will be to arrive where we started
> And know the place for the first time.
> Through the unknown, remembered gate
> When the last of earth left to discover
> Is that which was the beginning;
> At the source of the longest river
> The voice of the hidden waterfall
> And the children in the apple-tree
> Not known, because not looked for
> But heard, half-heard, in the stillness
> Between two waves of the sea.
> Quick now, here, now, always—
> A condition of complete simplicity
> (Costing not less than everything)

And all shall be well and
All manner of thing shall be well
When the tongues of flame are in-folded
Into the crowned knot of fire
And the fire and the rose are one.

In *Four Quartets* Eliot has brought his intersections to their most highly developed, fully conscious form. This form, a refinement of that of *The Waste Land,* includes but is not the didactic, the narrative, the lyric and the prophetic. Within it ideas, images and symbols move in a musical pattern, a "complete consort," with an almost mathematical interweaving of themes.

This inclusive form, only exceeded by Joyce, is Eliot's major achievement. Where he has attempted to express his ideas didactically alone, as in *The Rock* and in his theological essays, or dramatically alone, as in *The Family Reunion,* his powers have been hampered. While he has always employed narrative elements, these — as in the Sweeney poems — suggest actions rather than convey a story; indicate traits rather than present a person. This intimative quality — apt to confuse the direction of a play, its necessary clear line of action — is the chief virtue of his poems.

He is more interested in ideas than in people. But his ideas too have been restricted in range by his preoccupations. One is conscious of a deep strain of melancholy exceeding the evidence. This impression comes not alone from his recording of sorrow, or of the bitterness of missed delights, but from his expression of the very quality of delight, which invariably includes an apprehension of its loss.

In developing the thesis that it is man's guilt that drives the soul toward God, Eliot has retained a remote, arbitrary notion of the "spiritual" and a correspondingly arbitrary notion of guilt, which he equates with man's very existence. Such a conception of sin — the compulsive insistence on regarding evil as a mysteriously immaterial, all-pervasive entity or essence — has the effect of placing an ominous sense of taboo upon *all* experience. Under such a cloud it is of supremely little consequence whether a specific act was a crime or not, or even whether it was committed.

But this sense of taboo does generally prevail in our civilization. In exposing it, even in succumbing to it, Eliot has made luminous the last pitch of human unhappiness. If what he has reached seems more a means of consolation than an effective method of salvation, one cannot fail to respect the intensity, integrity and devotion of his art. And if he continues to explore the vapors and the fogs, the miasmas and the grimpens, one can no longer say that he is exploring a purely private myth. In his own way, Eliot continues to express the age.

Part Four

MARIANNE MOORE'S
IMAGINARY GARDEN

I

"The Mind is an Enchanting Thing"

On a street like any other, at an ordinary address, there is an enchanted house. When you go in, at noon on the sunniest of days, it's like walking into the light. The house is all windows.

It's when you look out the windows that the enchanting thing happens. Instead of looking out, you've gone through. You are in a garden. In the garden are flowers and birds, toads, monkeys and elephants, unicorns, clocks, walking-sticks and trees hung with cherries, thoughts, plums and nectarines. When you look at them, another strange thing takes place.

It isn't that you've never seen them quite like this before. It's something different about your way of seeing and hearing. You can still hear the birdsong, you hear it very well. But you hear something else. You hear what the bird is hearing to make him sing that way. You can feel his heart beat.

Only Marianne Moore could write a poem about the mind and fill it with thoughts that glow like buried treasure just brought to light. Her mind, like the poem in her latest book *Nevertheless* (1944), "is an enchanting thing."

Part of the enchantment is music: "Like Gieseking playing Scarlatti." Part is observation:

like the apteryx-awl
  as a beak, or the
kiwi's rain-shawl
    of haired feathers, the mind
    feeling its way as though blind,
walks along with its eyes on the ground.

These are what they are because of "memory's ear" and "memory's eye," a gyroscopic activity of thought "trued by regnant certainty," her "conscientious inconsistency" and that candor that

. . . tears off the veil; tears
  the temptation, the
mist the heart wears,
    from its eyes, — if the heart
    has a face; it takes apart
dejection. . . .

Over all plays light: "like the dove- / neck animated by / sun." Literally and figuratively, light is the source of her enchantment. What she sees provides symbols for the unseen, the inner vision. If the sun seems to figure more than the moon, the day-side more than the dream-side, in her meticulously conscious art, it is because her poetry dreams with its eyes open and weaves its spell out of the visible, the tangible, the intelligible; a wide-awake magic; proof that a passionate intelligence can be haunting.

This sunlike quality rays out from every line, every phrase,

  like the glaze on a
katydid-wing
    subdivided by sun
    till the nettings are legion.

In her poetry the appearances of things — the way they greet the eyes and ears; what they feel like to the touch; their characteristic impact — come to us in a blaze of reincarnation. No detail is too incidental: "the crow-blue mussel-shells"; "the lion's ferocious chrysanthemum head"; "the blades of the oars moving together like the feet of water-spiders"; elephants "with their fog-coloured skin and strictly practical appendages" ("black earth preceded by a tendril?"); the swan "with swart blind look askance"; the plumet basilisk, "when captured, stiff and somewhat heavy, like fresh putty on the hand"; the frigate pelican, for whom "the feeling in a hand, in fins, is in his unbent downbent crafty oar." He glides

> a hundred feet or quivers about
> as charred paper behaves.

And the butterfly — "pawing like a horse," "trampling the air as it trampled the flowers" and "diminishing like wreckage on the sea" — blows through the poem "Half Deity" in *What Are Years* (1941) to prove that "They that have wings must not have weights."

"Nine Nectarines and Other Porcelain" in *Selected Poems* (1935) projects the scene on a "much-mended plate" where, "from manifold small boughs,"

> a bat is winging. It
> is a moonlight scene, bringing
>
> the animal so near, its eyes
> are separate from the face — mere
> delicately drawn gray discs, out from
> itself in space.

The compliments paid to other arts boomerang on her own: in "Smooth Gnarled Crape Myrtle" (*What Are Years*):

> It was artifice saw,
> on a patch-box pigeon-egg, room for
> fervent script, and wrote as with a bird's claw

and in "Walking-Sticks and Paper-Weights and Water Marks":

. . . It must have been an able workman,
humorous and self-possessed,
a liker of solidity,

who gave this greenish Waterford
glass weight with the summit curled down toward
itself as the
glass grew, the look of tempered sword-
steel; of three-ore-d
fishscale-burnished antimony-
lead-and-tin smoky water-drop type-metal
smoothness emery-armored
against rust.

Her illuminations strike inward as well as outward, and invariably "dramatize a / meaning always missed / by the externalist." From appearance to significance, in her poems, is not a distance but, like those figures that as we look at them turn from convex to concave, a change in our own perspective. They are contained in each other; so interwoven as to be impossible to separate.

In some poems image and idea alternate, each fulfilling each. In "Virginia Britannica" ("England's Old Dominion"), the history of all dominion is inferred from nature:

. . . Like strangler figs choking
a banyan, not an explorer, no impe-
rialist, not one
of us, in taking what we
pleased — in colonizing as the
saying is — has been
a synonym for mercy.

The title poem of *Nevertheless* is a complete example:

you've seen a strawberry
that's had a struggle; yet
was, where the fragments met,

a hedgehog or a star-
fish for the multitude
of seeds. What better food

than apple-seeds — the fruit
within the fruit — locked in
like counter-curved twin

hazel-nuts? Frost that kills
the little rubber-plant-
leaves of kok-saghyz-stalks, can't

harm the roots; they still grow
in frozen ground. Once where
there was a prickly-pear-

leaf clinging to barbed wire,
a root shot down to grow
in earth two feet below;

as carrots form mandrakes
or a ram's-horn root sometimes. Victory won't come

to me unless I go
to it; a grape-tendril
ties a knot in knots till

knotted thirty times — so
the bound twig that's under-
gone and over-gone, can't stir.

The weak overcomes its
menace, the strong over-
comes itself. What is there

like fortitude! What sap
went through that little thread
to make the cherry red!

Image and idea fit so intimately (like "counter-curved twin hazelnuts") that they exchange characteristics. After a succession of images, in each of which the idea is held suspended, its explicit statement — "Victory won't come / to me unless I go / to it" — has the confirmatory force of another image. We can visualize it, as plainly as the "strawberry / that's had a struggle." The "grape-tendril" ties another knot in the idea. "The weak overcomes its / menace" continues to bind in the imagery. And the final cherry hangs from its stem, the completed globe of both.

There are some poems that are little essays in verse, like the famous "Poetry" and like "Picking and Choosing":

Literature is a phase of life. If
one is afraid of it, the situation is irremediable; if
one approaches it familiarly
what one says of it is worthless. Words are constructive
when they are true; the opaque allusion — the simulated flight

upward —accomplishes nothing.

This is a poem that must really worry the critic; it out-critics him. Indicating his proper courage, respect and insight, it goes on by means of thumbnail criticisms of its own to exemplify the fearless fairness that should be his:

. . . . Why cloud the fact
that Shaw is self-conscious in the field of sentiment but
is otherwise re-
warding; that James is all that has been
said of him if feeling is profound? . . .

Citing Gordon Craig and Burke as examples, it sums up the attitude necessary to good criticism in the phrase *summa diligentia* ("with the utmost of picking and choosing"), which a schoolboy mistranslated to have Caesar crossing the Alps "on the top of a *diligence*." This is a nice twist, to summon up, in the same breath with his highest requirement, the critic's deepest fear.

> . . . . . We are not daft about the meaning, but this
> familiarity
> with wrong meanings puzzles one. Humming-
> bug, the candles are not wired for electricity.
> Small dog, going over the lawn, nipping the linen and saying
>
> that you have a badger—remember Xenophon;
> only the most rudimentary sort of behaviour is necessary
> to put us on the scent; 'a right good
> salvo of barks,' a few 'strong wrinkles' puckering the
> skin between the ears, are all we ask.

This is the sort of poem responsible for the opinion that Marianne Moore is really an essayist in disguise. What a tribute to essayists! What is implied is a belief that ideas are better expressed in prose. Such is usually the case; but Miss Moore is an exception to many rules. Ideas are generally better expressed in prose because so few writers are able to think with that "heightened consciousness" of which she speaks in "The Past is the Present":

> If external action is effete
> and rhyme is outmoded,
> I shall revert to you,
> Habakkuk, as on a recent occasion I was goaded
> into doing by XY, who was speaking of unrhymed verse.
> This man said—I think that I repeat
> his identical words:
> 'Hebrew poetry is
> prose with a sort of heightened consciousness.' Ecstasy affords
> the occasion and expediency determines the form.

Her ideas crystallize to the point of concreteness, of object-imagery, in the presence of "ecstasy," which is used here so precisely. This is the third element—more a dimension than an ingredient—of her poetry; the emotion interpenetrating appearance and significance.

In ordinary thinking, "emotion" has limiting connotations, just as "intellect" has. The two are frequently considered mutually exclusive. There are not many writers who can be comfortable with their emotions without relaxing their minds. If, on the other hand, they wish to bring themselves to the point of thinking, this act requires so vigorous a focussing of attention that it shuts out the warmer areas.

But for Marianne Moore thinking is not so strenuous an occupation. It is as natural to her as breathing; she might almost be said to do it "without thinking."

If this asks, on the part of the reader, "a few 'strong wrinkles' puckering the skin between the ears," and on the part of the critic " 'a right good salvo of barks' " (as well as the wrinkles), it is because we are being put on the scent, as in all poetry of the highest order, of something unique. This is an unusual recombination of the elements, which have tended to become separated in our thinking, of sensation, thought and emotion.

Much has been said and written about a split in modern man between his head and his heart. Perhaps the split is not so much a dichotomy as a triptych; an inclination to stress, at the expense of the other two, one or another of these components: to be "intellectual" to the neglect of his feelings and sensations, the very sources of his intellect; to be sensual, circumscribing his emotions and his mind and ultimately the experiences of his senses, which come to resemble mechanical exercises without human value or personal meaning; to be swayed by gusts of feeling, like modern masses persuaded to act against their own self-interest.

His hope of development lies in that kind of integration of which Marianne Moore's poetry is a living symbol. Her mind, her senses, her emotions are not separate functions but extensions of each other. The more she thinks, the more she perceives; the more she perceives, the more she feels. It is the vicious circle reversed.

"Like Gieseking playing Scarlatti," her poems re-create an originating emotion, giving it substance, texture and meaning. And again like Gieseking, who is noted for his "in-playing," her feeling is pervasive rather than excessively showy. It does not often resort to what has been called "the lyric cry."

As she says, "The Student"

. . . . . . is too reclusive for
some things to seem to touch
him, not because he
has no feeling but because he has so much.

In her poetry, especially in the earlier books, emotion tends to be implied rather than stated; involved in the whole context rather than sparked out. The climaxes are inside the poems; not so much built up to as built around; inlaid; and come to us often as after-images.

In "The Jerboa" –

. . . Abroad seeking food, or at home
in its burrow, the Sahara field-mouse
has a shining silver house

of sand. O rest and
joy, the boundless sand,
the stupendous sand-spout,
no water, no palm-trees, no ivory bed,
tiny cactus; but one would not be he
who has nothing but plenty.

– a specific expression of emotion returns us immediately to the thought. They suffuse each other. "Marriage" – by intention a play of ironies, a series of contrasts between inward feeling and outward convention – affords passages that can be isolated; by lifting out of context the experience of Eve:

Below the incandescent stars
below the incandescent fruit,
the strange experience of beauty;
its existence is too much;
it tears one to pieces
and each fresh wave of consciousness
is poison.
'See her, see her in this common world',
the central flaw
in that first crystal-fine experiment,

this amalgamation which can never be more
than an interesting impossibility,
describing it
as 'that strange paradise
unlike flesh, stones,
gold or stately buildings,
the choicest piece of my life:
the heart rising
in its estate of peace
as a boat rises
with the rising of the water';

or Adam's perturbation:

Plagued by the nightingale
in the new leaves,
with its silence —
not its silence but its silences,
he says of it:
'It clothes me with a shirt of fire'.
'He dares not clap his hands
to make it go on
lest it should fly off;
if he does nothing, it will sleep;
if he cries out, it will not understand'.
Unnerved by the nightingale
and dazzled by the apple,
impelled by 'the illusion of a fire
effectual to extinguish fire',
compared with which
the shining of thc carth
is but a deformity — a fire
'as bright as broad
as long as life itself',
he stumbles over marriage,
'a very trivial object indeed'

Besides their intrinsic interest, such passages are prefigurative of the intensity and fullness of expression in the more recent development of her poetry.

II

The View

THE ENCHANTING and enchanted mind defines imagination. And it is her imagination that defines the mind of Marianne Moore; an imagination articulated by fact. Like the "apteryx-awl" and the kiwi's "rain-shawl," it "walks along with its eyes on the ground."

This is a modest comparison, but an apt one. The kiwi is a flightless bird; its wings serve as protection against the elements but do not tempt it from its habitat, its source of sustenance. So the mind's function is not to fly away from life, but to observe it.

Marianne Moore called the first book of hers to be published in this country, *Observations* (1924). These are always her point of departure. Active rather than contemplative, observation is for her a motion of the mind corresponding to what is being observed. Wherever our attention dwells in her poems, we are made aware of exquisite correspondences.

Anyone who has even idly watched seagulls will appreciate the drifting alternations in "Part of a Novel, Part of a Poem, Part of a Play" — the opening poem of her second book, *Selected Poems:*

One by one, in two's, in three's, the seagulls keep
  flying back and forth over the town clock,
or sailing around the lighthouse without moving the wings—
rising steadily with a slight
  quiver of the body . . .

The first line has a sparsity of rhythm, as we notice one, then another and others of the small details in the sky that turn out to be gulls. The second line rocks back and forth with their motion, a motion at once contrasted and defined by the plumb forthrightness of "the town clock." The third line is dramatically undramatic; it can be read almost without accent, just as the gulls in the distance glide for a time without perceptible effort; until as we watch them "rising steadily," one after another gives that "slight / quiver" that makes the break between the fourth and fifth lines.

We see that the correspondences are both external and internal. They convey not only the scene — the gulls, the clock, the lighthouse, the high sky — as graphically as a moving camera might record it. They convey as well a characteristic manner of perceiving these items. It is a natural way of perceiving; yet there is a raptness, an intent absorption with the scene, which we come to recognize as peculiar to Marianne Moore. Whatever her eyes rest upon is taken in, not only clearly as a whole but microscopically as to detail.

Often the allusiveness is richer and the correspondences play in several directions; as in these lines from "The Jerboa":

By fifths and sevenths,
in leaps of two lengths,
  like the uneven notes
  of the Bedouin flute, it stops its gleaning
    on little wheel castors, and makes fern-seed
    foot-prints with kangaroo speed.

Its leaps should be set
to the flageolet;
  pillar body erect
  on a three-cornered smooth-working Chippendale
    claw — propped on hind legs, and tail as third toe,
    between leaps to its burrow.

The small rodent of northern Africa ("the Sahara field-mouse" as she has called it) is related to its setting. Its rhythms are "like the uneven notes of the Bedouin flute." But the correspondences go deeper, into the very framework of the poem.

The rhymed couplets that begin and end each stanza – some regular; others rhyming an *on-* with an *off*-beat – re-create the double jump of the animal. The intervening section in each stanza suggests the poise of the jerboa gathering itself for the next spring.

This springy verse-form has been preparing us, through the preceding twenty-five stanzas, for the three "leaps" (in the second, seventh and twelfth lines of this passage) that bring the jerboa home. They no longer need to be "set to the flageolet"; they have been fitted to an even more delicate instrument, Marianne Moore's recorder, which simultaneously reproduces music and image.

Such correspondences are acts of translation between the senses, intensifying experience. Animals, primitives and children, we are told, tend to react with the whole creature. As we come to specialize the functions of our senses, we split up experience. These multiple experiences, in turn, partition us.

Through art such as this, with its demands upon the attention of the whole person, we are restored, not to a state of nature, but to that totality of experience which is the sign of organic development. It is a reintegration on a higher level of consciousness, to which the intervening specialization, the "loss of innocence," has contributed. To the extent that this is true, there is less cause to hark back to some "lost paradise" of savage or non-human behavior. We need no more regret not being a jerboa than the jerboa need regret not being human.

Marianne Moore's is not a poetry of nostalgic return. It "tears off the veil," the "temptation," the "mist the heart wears." She says in her poem "New York" ("the savage's romance," "the center of the wholesale fur trade"):

> it is not the atmosphere of ingenuity,
> the otter, the beaver, the puma skins
> without shooting-irons or dogs;
> it is not the plunder,
> but 'accessibility to experience.'

Her syntheses of experience present a jerboa, "The Plumet Basilisk," "The Malay Dragon," "The Tuatera," "The Frigate Pelican," or "The Pangolin" more immediately and significantly than they would appear before us in flesh, feather or scale. This is all the more remarkable in the instances I have chosen, since it is unlikely that Marianne Moore has had a personal encounter with any of them. Yet she can exhibit them, in action in their native surroundings — down to the basilisk "basking on a / horizontal branch / from which sour-grass and orchids sprout" — with more authority than a seasoned member of the Explorers Club.

Direct contact is not obligatory to her observation. (She calls Ireland "the greenest place I've never seen.") It is like the rumored occasion of her being taken to a baseball game by certain Algonquin wits piqued by her infallibility. She began calling strikes and balls, pointing out "So-and-so warming up in the bull pen" and in general displaying a familiarity with the proceedings that would have done credit to the most rabid of fans. "I thought you told us," said one of the party, "that you'd never been to a ball game before in your life." "You're quite right," she said. "But I have read a book on the subject."

What she says of the mind is, then, as far as her own is concerned, a plain statement of fact:

> It has memory's ear
>   that can hear without
> having to hear.

She is free to reconstruct the unfamiliar, to supply, with uncanny accuracies, the living environment of the strange and the faraway, because she has looked so discerningly at what is present. Having watched the activity of a family of mocking-birds until she can reproduce it, in "Bird-Witted," line for line in the movement of her verse, she is able in other poems to extend this gift to what she sees with the mind's eye; to create a Costa Rican setting where

> . . . . Vines suspend
> the weight of something's shadow fixed on silk. . . .

. . . .

. . . . Hollow whistled monkey-notes disrupt
the castanets. Taps from the back of the bow sound odd
on last year's gourd,

or when they touch the
kettledrums — at which, for there's no light,
a scared frog screaming like a bird, leaps out from weeds
in which
it could have hid, with curves of the meteorite,
the curve of whose diving no diver refutes. . . .

Her telescopic observation leaps from fine to superfine; as of "The Pangolin"

. . . . who endures
exhausting solitary
trips through unfamiliar ground at night,
returning before sunrise; stepping
in the moonlight, on the moonlight
peculiarly, that the out-
side edges of his
hands may bear the weight and save the claws
for digging. . . .

Whatever she looks at, whether actually or in the pages of a book, she is able to see alive and can conjure up its distinctive motion. In "The Frigate Pelican" it is the motion of a flock —

. . . . separating, until
not flapping they rise once more,
closing in without looking and move
outward again to the top
of the circle and stop

and blow back, allowing the wind to reverse their direction.

—which is the link between us and this "fleetest foremost fairy among birds." For we have had the experience of just such a cycle of motion in the reciprocating movement of a carrousel.

This physical correspondence is carried out in the circularities, the risings and fallings of the rhythm. We are simultaneously in the position of looking at a merry-go-round and riding it. Just so, watching the motion of the frigate-bird, we find ourselves hypnotically transported out of ourselves. An impossible rapport is established. Confidants of "the unconfiding frigate-bird" who "hides in the height and in the majestic / display of his art," we share his "exclusion." From " a height / so great the feathers look black and the beak does not / show," we too look down and observe

. . . . what went
secretly, as it thought, out of sight
among dense jungle plants. Sent
ahead of the rest, there goes the true
knight in his jointed coat that
covers all but his bat

ears; a-trot, with stiff pig gait — our tame armadillo, loosed by
his master and as pleased as a dog. Beside the
spattered blood — that orchid which the native fears —
the fer-de-lance lies sleeping; centaur-
like, this harmful couple's amity
is apropos. A jaguar
and crocodile are fighting. Sharp-shinned
hawks and peacock-freckled small
cats, like the literal

merry-go-round, come wandering within the circular view
of the high bird for whom from the air they are ants
keeping house all their lives in the crack of a
crag with no view from the top. . . .

Among the sights that come to us from our high-spiraling vantage-point is a scene where

unlikely animals learning to
dance, crouch on two steeds that rear
behind a leopard with a frantic
face, tamed by an Artemis
who wears a dress like his,

and hampering haymaker's hat. . . .

So complete is our rapport that we find we are regarding with surprise the most exotic creature of all: ourselves. The correspondences have amplified the contrasts: "Make hay; keep / the shop; I have one sheep; were a less / limber animal's mottoes."

The poem's magically intricate rhythms begin to run down, like the works of the calliope geared to "the literal merry-go-round" from which "we watch the moon rise on the Susquehanna."

> The tune's illiterate footsteps fail;
> the steam hacks are not to be admired.

Our ride is coming to an end. But not the frigate-bird's, whose carnival never closes:

> The reticent lugubrious ragged immense minuet
> descending to leeward, ascending to windward
> again without flapping, in what seems to be
> a way of resting, are now nearer,
> but as seemingly bodiless yet
> as they were. Theirs are sombre
> quills for so wide and lightboned a bird
> as the frigate pelican
> of the Caribbean.

It is the precision of her imagination that earns Marianne Moore such varieties of freedom. Her refinements of thought and of style are always in the direction of greater, rather than less, inclusiveness.

"It is the honourable characteristic of Poetry," said Wordsworth in the Advertisement to the first edition of *Lyrical Ballads,* "that its materials are to be found in every subject which can interest the human mind." And Marianne Moore is able to use material hitherto considered inappropriate to poetry. The ordinary details of living are revealed in a new way. She says in "Poetry":

> . . . . the bat
> holding on upside down or in quest of something to
>
> eat, elephants pushing, a wild horse taking a roll, a
> tireless wolf under

> a tree, the immovable critic twitching his skin like
> a horse that feels a flea, the base-
> ball fan, the statistician —
> nor is it valid
> to discriminate against 'business documents and
>
> school-books'; all these phenomena are important. . . .

This is by way of reply to Tolstoy's bewilderment as noted in his *Diary:*

> . . . Where the boundary between prose and poetry lies, I shall never be able to understand. The question is raised in manuals of style, yet the answer to it lies beyond me. Poetry is verse; prose is not verse. Or else poetry is everything with the exception of business documents and school books.

Her answer is that poetry is in the use that is made of experience. It is not the experience itself; nor does it consist in a grading of experiences: "this is a fit subject; that is not." All are available, whether eccentric, like an upside-down bat, or common to all, like a bat foraging; deliberate or impulsive; of animal or human origin; special to the point of esoteric, or general to the point of abstract; "nor is it valid to discriminate against" the purely mundane and the didactic.

While this conception goes far beyond conventional ideas of poetry, it is not in the narrow sense revolutionary. It does not turn against the traditionally "emotional" themes, but brings them too into perspective:

> Hands that can grasp, eyes
> that can dilate, hair that can rise
> if it must, these things are important not because a
>
> high-sounding interpretation can be put upon them but
> because they are
> useful. . . .

They are useful until "they become so derivative as to become unintelligible."

Putting these statements together, we are in possession of a definition of poetry that satisfies the bigotries of neither "conservatism" nor "modernism." It is definition by example rather than by limitation. Marianne Moore is too knowing to involve herself very seriously in confirming or denying the alternatives proposed by Tolstoy. By implication she subscribes to the formal distinction of poetry as "verse," distinguished from "prose" by technical considerations of form. These formal considerations can be hair-splitting and tedious, as she has acknowledged at the outset:

> I, too, dislike it: there are things that are important
> beyond all this fiddle.

While admitting their relative unimportance, she is quick to point out what they are there for:

> Reading it, however, with a perfect contempt for it,
> one discovers in
> it after all, a place for the genuine.

The genuine is the main concern, whether we find it in verse or prose. It is the "poetic" in that sense that goes beyond the formalities. For the genuine is the original; it has the stamp of its maker upon it; its maker will determine its form. To define this form, before it is created, is to kill it; for it is to shut ourselves off by restrictive preconceptions from the variety of its possibilities. As for innovation:

> . . . . One must make
> a distinction
> however: when dragged into prominence by half poets,
> the result is not poetry,
> nor till the poets among us can be
> 'literalists of
> the imagination' — above
> insolence and triviality and can present
>
> for inspection, imaginary gardens with real toads in
> them, shall we have
> it. . . .

Poetry is defined by poets. Its definition changes somewhat with each; we cannot predict either its content or its form. All we can say is that, when most complete, it is found to be imagination articulated by fact; as Coleridge characterized it, "lending the charm of imagination to the real" and "lending the force of reality to the imaginary."

Politely, Tolstoy has been put in his place. The question he raised was academic. What does it matter where we find poetry, in what form, so long as we find it?

> . . . In the meantime, if you demand on the one hand,
> the raw material of poetry in
>   all its rawness and
>   that which is on the other hand
>   genuine, then you are interested in poetry.

III

The Metric

THE LIVING DEFINITION in "Poetry" is its form. This is definition in action rather than by pronouncement. Its form exemplifies what it says.

Written at a time when "free verse" was in the air, provoking debate over where prose leaves off and poetry begins, its style bears a superficial resemblance. Nothing could be further from the reality. This is verse of unparalleled strictness.

It is free, that is to say, only in the real sense that it is chosen, Marianne Moore's own form, not a hand-me-down of conventional prosody. It results in the freedom that permits her to use ideas as images, images as ideas, and prose rhythms in lines more regulated than alexandrines.

Between these freedoms, conveying each to each, lies the method of her verse. Its degree of regulation varies from poem to poem. At one pole stands "The Jerboa" — twenty-seven stanzas with every syllable accounted for. At the opposite are those poems like "Sea Unicorns and Land Unicorns," "When I Buy Pictures," "A Grave" and about twelve others written in a style approaching free verse. Although these evade exact analysis, they are characterized by tautness of expression, compression of thought; the residues of discipline. In between are any number of variants, poems in which a basic all-over pattern is interrupted.

"Bird-Witted" illustrates the uniform application of her method. The first two stanzas set the pattern:

> With innocent wide penguin eyes, three
>   large fledgling mocking-birds below
> the pussy-willow tree,
>   stand in a row,
> wings touching, feebly solemn,
> till they see
>   their no longer larger
>   mother bringing
> something which will partially
> feed one of them.
>
> Toward the high-keyed intermittent squeak
>   of broken carriage-springs, made by
> the three similar, meek-
>   coated bird's-eye
> freckled forms she comes; and when
> from the beak
>   of one, the still living
>   beetle has dropped
> out, she picks it up and puts
> it in again.

We see first, as always, the miraculous parallels between the lines of verse and the actions they describe. By its very sparsity and placement, "stand in a row" is a complete linear depiction of the three waiting young birds. This visual writing has the economy of detail of the most accomplished drawing. The breaks in the lines follow the breaks in the drama:

> something which will partially
> feed one of them.

The awkwardness of creatures supposedly relying on "instinct" is reproduced in the wonderfully stumbling gait and clumsy recovery of:

> . . . . and when
> from the beak
> of one, the still living
> beetle has dropped
> out, she picks it up and puts
> it in again.

It is as if, as one often wishes, a witnessed action could be repeated by a wave of the hand, motif and motion are so beautifully blended. When we come to analyze it, we find that this scene, occurring so naturally, is plotted in its execution down to the last syllable.

The first line (rhyming with the third and sixth) contains nine syllables. The second line (rhyming with the fourth) has eight; the third, six; the fourth, four; the fifth (rhyming with the tenth), seven; and the other lines follow: 3, 6, 4, 7 and 4. This syllable and rhyme pattern is duplicated in the second stanza, line for line; in the third, fourth, fifth and concluding sixth. The majority of Marianne Moore's poems employ similar patterns, which vary from poem to poem in the number of lines, their syllabic count and the number and placement of rhymes.

It is more difficult to match syllables than to plot the scheme of a sonnet. But in either case it is not the structure that determines the quality of the poem. A conventional structure does not decree a conventional poem, any more than an original one can insure originality. The quality resides in the use to which the structure is put and its appropriateness to what is being conveyed.

Marianne Moore's metric, however – which would seem to derive from the child's magic of taking so many steps in a square – does have a special virtue. It escapes the prosodic confusions of much of English poetry, which stems from diverse sources. Some of the inherited verse-forms, despite the differences in the two tongues, are adaptations of Latin originals. Longfellow's failure to get the effect of Vergil's "Arma virumque cano Troiae qui primus ab oris" in his "This is the forest primeval, the murmuring pines and the hemlocks" has often been cited to illustrate the fact that Latin depends more on the weight of syllables, English on their accent. What is sonorous and majestic in the one becomes tinkling and insipid in the other.

Marianne Moore's verse-form depends very little if at all on the use of prosodic feet. The syllable-count has no relation to stress or accent, heaviness or lightness of the syllables, or the amount of time they occupy. Phrasing is independent of structure; which gives a play between them, the phrases sometimes ending with the line ("stand in a row"), sometimes beginning at the end ("three / large fledgling mocking-birds") or ending at the beginning ("beetle has dropped / out") and sometimes roving from line to line or for several succeeding lines ("Toward the high-keyed intermittent squeak / of broken carriage-springs, made by / the three similar, meek- / coated bird's-eye / freckled forms she comes").

When read aloud the lines are not always perceptible as such; which is true of more conventional poems unless they are read singsong. But the underlying structure, its interplay with the rhythm, and the varied frequencies of rhyme, all contribute to a tension that unmistakably differentiates the form from prose.

It is in the coincidence of this structure with the content of the poetry that her technical virtuosity by itself amounts to genius. The resolution of opposites, of necessity and freedom, which is her constant theme (Hercules "hindered to succeed," the sea that "in its surrendering / finds its continuing") is nowhere so conclusively demonstrated as in the premeditated spontaneity of this form, at once as fixed as a mosaic and as free as running water.

By its means she has achieved a significant expansion of the limits of poetry. Wordsworth, in reaction to the "poetic diction" of his day, imported the language of prose into his poems; but without seriously altering their structure. The prose rhythms had to adapt themselves. Since few will, the results were often monotonous.

Marianne Moore can import the *rhythms* of prose – any rhythm she chooses – and by subjecting them to the tensions of her verse transform them into poetry. In the alchemy of her style ingredients thought inimical to each other can be brought together: beauty ("A brass-green bird with grass- / green throat smooth as a nut") with wit ("One may be a blameless / bachelor, and it is but a / step to Congreve"); perception ("An aspect may deceive; as the / elephant's columbine-tubed trunk / held waveringly out — / an at will heavy thing — is / delicate") with research (" 'The legendary white- / eared black bulbul that sings / only in pure Sanskrit' "); precision ("in the stiff-leafed tree's blue- / pink dregs-of-wine pyramids / of mathematic / circularity") with feeling ("And what of / our clasped hands that swear, 'By Peace / Plenty; as / by Wisdom Peace.' Alas!"). These quotations are all from "Smooth Gnarled Crape Myrtle."

Typical of her poetry is its inweaving of quotation. In "The Student" she quotes from a lecture, *The Arabian Nights,* three college mottoes, Albert Einstein, Goldsmith, Emerson, Edmund Burke and Henry McBride. Her practice is quite different from T. S. Eliot's. Eliot brings together phrases out of the poetry of the past, applying them to the contemporary scene. While he achieves an ironic effect, his style might almost be said to be formed by its appropriations. The pull is more strongly in the direction of the past.

Marianne Moore's sources are for the most part prose. Not only do her ingenuities transmute them into poetry. A magic of selection and arrangement subjugates them to her own idiom. It is as if, during the course of her varied career, she had assumed a multiplicity of sobriquets — Xenophon, Voltaire, Montaigne, the Reverend E. H. Kellogg, the Comtesse de Noailles, Sir Francis Bacon, Denis O'Sullivan, *The Vest Pocket Manual Of Printing,* Boccaccio, Donn Byrne, Captain John Smith, Carlyle and the travel page of the *New York Sun* — and were engaged in bringing her works up to date.

Free-verse experiments may have paved the way for her use of prose rhythms. But she escapes the two great disadvantages of free verse: its tendency on the one hand to become amorphous, and on the other a restriction arising out of its "freedom," which can be preserved only by excluding much of the language and many of the rhythms of traditional poetry.

Marianne Moore can make use of everything. Her verse-form embodies a principle of limitation that does not limit her, really, in any way. Instead it brings to rhyme, figure of speech, even regular metre, whenever she chooses to employ them, a new freshness.

Using the rhymed couplet sparingly, she intensifies its effect when we come upon it in such passages as:

> Its leaps should be set
> to the flageolet

or:

> the plumet portrays
> mythology's wish
> to be interchangeably man and fish . . .

She passes at will in and out of singing rhythms, setting them off by contrast with their surroundings; or leading up to them so subtly that they return to us in echoes:

> Arranged by two's as peaches are,
> at intervals that all may live—
> eight and a single one, on twigs that
> grew the year before—they look like
> a derivative;
> although not uncommonly
> the opposite is seen—
> nine peaches on a nectarine.

T. S. Eliot has remarked her expert use of light rhyme—

> an
> injured fan

—which gives a half-lilt; and of internal rhyme, an example of which is to be found in the seventh line of "Camellia Sabina," rhyming with the first and eighth lines:

> and the Bordeaux *plum*
>
> . . . .
>
> briar-black *bloom* on black-thorn pigeon's-blood
> is, like Certosa, sealed with foil. Appropriate cus*tom*.

This subdued rhyming, repeated in the seven succeeding stanzas, is very different from the expected "shock." The various *or, ar, ire, er, air, ure* and *ear* sounds through the poem contribute further modulations of which we need not be wholly conscious unless we have analyzed them, but which play upon the inner ear.

"Spenser's Ireland," she says:

> has not altered; —
> the kindest place I've never been,
> the greenest place I've never seen.
> Every name is a tune.

An Irish jig twirls in the middle of each stanza — "of the fly for mid-July" — and in other turns like:

> the guillemot
> so neat and the hen
> of the heath and the
> linnet spinet-sweet . . .

Preparation and placement have given certain of these phrases, although they occur only once, the effect of refrain. The turning rhythms are themselves a turn of the very thought and a twist of the very emotion that is resolved in the magnificently concluding stanza:

> they are to me
> like enchanted Earl Gerald who
> changed himself into a stag, to
> a great green-eyed cat of
> the mountain. Discommodity makes
> them invis ible; they've dis-
> appeared. The Irish say your trouble is their
> trouble and your
> joy their joy? I wish
> I could believe it;
> I am troubled, I'm dissat-
> isfied, I'm Irish.

Plain rhyme, half-rhyme, hidden rhyme and non-rhyme contribute to these effects, and to the wheeling rhythms of "A Carriage From Sweden":

> They say there is a sweeter air
> where it was made, than we have here;
> a Hamlet's castle atmosphere.
> At all events there is in Brooklyn
> something that makes me feel at home.

Submerged rhymes in the first and fifth lines ("there – air" and "some – home") mediate between the couplet of the second and third lines and the unrhymed fourth, ending in this stanza in the wittily ungarnished "Brooklyn." These variations give further impetus to the spoke-like alternations of spinning and stopping rhythm.

Making new uses of these old devices, her style brings the past up to the present. In the same way, her "literalist" imagination makes use of the fabulous. "Sea Unicorns and Land Unicorns" relates mythical to literal experience – not without humor – as a symbol for the imagination; for all poetry:

> So wary as to disappear for centuries and reappear,
> yet never to be caught,
> the unicorn has been preserved
> by an unmatched device
> wrought like the work of expert blacksmiths,
> with which nothing can compare –
> this animal of that one horn
> throwing itself upon which head foremost from a cliff,
> it walks away unharmed;
> proficient in this feat which, like Herodotus,
> I have not seen except in pictures.
> Thus this strange animal with its miraculous elusiveness,
> has come to be unique,
> 'impossible to take alive',
> tamed only by a lady inoffensive like itself –
> as curiously wild and gentle;
> 'as straight and slender as the crest,
> or antlet of the one-beam'd beast'.

Appropriately to its subject, this is written in her freest style. There are all gradations in her poems. In many of the syllabically patterned ones she breaks her own rules. In this category are "Camellia Sabina," "The Frigate Pelican," "Nine Nectarines and Other Porcelain," "Pedantic Literalist," "Critics and Connoisseurs," "The Monkeys," "Black Earth," "Peter," "Picking and Choosing" and about twenty-five others; including five in *Observations* which were omitted from the *Selected Poems*.

The variations are sometimes as slight as one syllable in a poem. Others modify, omit or transpose one or more lines. In "The Plumet Basilisk" a complete break in the original pattern is followed, after several stanzas, by its resumption.

In all but the slightest of these variations a deliberate intent is apparent. The overriding of her metric system in the last stanza of "In the Days of Prismatic Color" seems to be allied to its thought; a self-comment:

> . . . . we have the classic
> multitude of feet. To what purpose! Truth is no Apollo
> Belvedere, no formal thing. The wave may go over it if it
> likes.
> Know that it will be there when it says,
> 'I shall be there when the wave has gone by.'

There are several instances of what appear to be self-comments. The oblique reference to her own style, in "To a Steam Roller," adds to its savor:

> The illustration
> is nothing to you without the application.
> . . . . . . You crush all the particles down
> into close conformity, and then walk back and forth
> on them.

The opening lines of "The Pangolin" are also so pertinent to her millimetrically-thought-out verse-form as to seem self-humorously directed:

Another armored animal — scale
  lapping scale with spruce-cone regu-
  larity until they
form the uninterrupted central
  tail-row. This near artichoke
    with head and legs and grit-equipped giz-
  zard, the night miniature artist-
    engineer, is Leonardo's
      indubitable son.

The name of a friend is incorporated in the inverted acrostic of "The Wood-Weasel." And Marianne Moore would seem to be smilingly involved in the convolutions of "To a Snail":

If 'compression is the first grace of style',
you have it. Contractility is a virtue
as modesty is a virtue.
It is not the acquisition of any one thing
that is able to adorn,
or the incidental quality that occurs
as a concomitant of something well said,
that we value in style,
but the principle that is hid:
in the absence of feet, 'a method of conclusions';
'a knowledge of principles',
in the curious phenomenon of your occipital horn.

In her poetry the absence of prosodic feet is "a method of conclusions." And "the principle that is hid" is partially revealed by the free form of this poem. Her principle does not consist in the replacing of one set of conventions by another, equally rigid. She is committed to the truth that rules — even self-made ones — are for use. They are to be broken when they do not accomplish their intention. For they are an expression of that mind of which she says: "it's conscientious inconsistency."

Her imagination, although it is articulated by fact, is not bound by it. To return to her own image, we may think we have been following a kiwi with its eyes on the ground. But we come to realize that we have been transported by "rain-shawls."

IV

The Enchantment

TECHNICALLY and thematically, in detail and in the round, the art of this poetry is a self-portrait. This is the most beautiful and complete correspondence of all. Interior illumination has been made to shine out, a symbol of integrity, a symptom of wholeness.

This wholeness is not one that has been lost but one toward which we are progressing. Its look is toward the future. It is the continuous process of mind becoming imagination; a process not abstracted from the rest of the person, but in an active sense its total product.

> . . . It's fire in the dove-neck's
>
> iridescence; in the
> inconsistencies
> of Scarlatti.
> Unconfusion submits
> its confusion to proof; it's
> not a Herod's oath that cannot change.

The changes in Marianne Moore's poetry have been in a continuous line of development. The course of this line can be traced from some of the early poems, like "Reticence and Volubility," in *Observations;* through the elaboration of more dramatic reticence and interior climax; to the fully projected emotion which finds expression in *What Are Years*:

> What is our innocence,
> what is our guilt? All are
> naked, none is safe. And whence
> is courage: the unanswered question,
> the resolute doubt, —
> dumbly calling, deafly listening — that
> in misfortune, even death,
> encourages others
> and in its defeat, stirs
>
> the soul to be strong? He
> sees deep and is glad, who
> accedes to mortality
> and in his imprisonment, rises
> upon himself as
> the sea in a chasm, struggling to be
> free and unable to be,
> in its surrendering
> finds its continuing.
>
> So he who strongly feels,
> behaves. The very bird,
> grown taller as he sings, steels
> his form straight up. Though he is captive,
> his mighty singing
> says, satisfaction is a lowly
> thing, how pure a thing is joy.
> This is mortality,
> this is eternity.

In its exultant resolution "What Are Years" achieves the very mastery of experience which is its theme. The coincidence of thought and form is complete; every word is fully charged with its import. Its emotion "steels its form straight up" so that the poem is itself an enchasmed sea, a bird becoming his bars, the bars becoming his music. Image, thought, structure, language and emotion are brought to bear on each other. Each confirms and augments each, like converging searchlights.

One can think in comparison only of the greatest religious poetry; of Hopkins' "The fine delight that fathers thought" and of his other late sonnets, in which a tragic self-questioning is translated into triumph by the very controlled passion of its expression.

The poems that follow, in *What Are Years* and in *Nevertheless,* continue to exhibit this power of outright emotion; as in "The Pangolin":

> Sun and moon and day and night and man and beast
> each with a splen-
> dor which man
> in all his vileness cannot
> set aside; each with an excellence!

The poem concludes on a note of affirmation:

> "Again the sun!
> anew each
> day; and new and new and new,
> that comes into and steadies my soul."

"In Distrust of Merits" I consider the finest poem of the war. The word "fighting" is the refrain:

> There're fighting, fighting, fighting the blind
> man who thinks he sees,—
>
> . . . .
>
> . . . . They're
> fighting in deserts and caves, one by
> one, in battalions and squadrons;

they're fighting that I
may yet recover from the disease, My
Self; some have it lightly, some will die. . . .

. . . .

. . . . We
vow, we make this promise
to the fighting — it's a promise — "We'll
never hate black, white, red, yellow, Jew,
Gentile, Untouchable." We are
not competent to
make our vows. With set jaw they are fighting,
fighting, fighting, —

. . . .

. . . . Some

in snow, some on crags, some in quicksands,
little by little, much by much, they
are fighting fighting fighting that where
there was death there may
be life. . . .

The unremitting pace, the emotional intensity, is at once controlled and accelerated by contrast with the "patience patience patience" which is "the soldier's defense / and hardest armor for / the fight." The refrain leads directly to the moral:

Hate-hardened heart, O heart of iron,
iron is iron till it is rust.
There never was a war that was
not inward; I must
fight till I have conquered in myself what
causes war, but I would not believe it.
I inwardly did nothing.
O Iscariotlike crime!
Beauty is everlasting
and dust is for a time.

Here is technical virtuosity and a genius for detail, with grandeur of conception and nobility of expression. The poet who can arrest the most fleeting of nuances — feelings so elusive we have forgotten we've forgotten them — is equal to the profound emotion of terror overmastered by beauty.

Poetry of this order transcends its immediate occasion. The consecrated fervor of "In Distrust of Merits" locates the true battleground, from which there is no military exemption: "There never was a war that was not inward."

If, outwardly, wars lead only to greater wars ("As contagion / of sickness makes sickness"); if their means invariably dictate their ends ("The enemy could not / have made a greater breach in our / defenses"); if the world is still "an orphan's home" with "pleas of the dying for / help that won't come," it is because the human emotion expressed here is too real to be impersonated by the massive impersonality of nations.

Henry James, in an exhortation to the critic quoted by Alfred Kazin in his book *On Native Grounds,* could have been prefiguring Marianne Moore's many-windowed mind:

> . . . To lend himself, to project himself and steep himself, to feel and feel till he understands, and to understand so well that he can say, and to have perception at the pitch of passion and expression as embracing as the air, to be infinitely curious and incorrigibly patient, and yet plastic and inflammable and determined, patient, stooping to conquer and serving to direct . . .

I have attempted to describe the machinery of her magic; a little of it. "To explain grace requires a curious hand."

It is we who are enchanted.

Part Five

CUMMINGS TIMES ONE

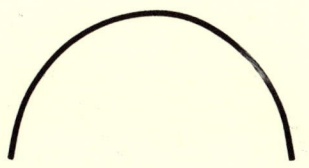

I

To Be, As a Transitive Verb

THE POEMS of E. E. Cummings celebrate individuals. From *Tulips and Chimneys* (1923) on, this has been his continuously expanding theme. To this central conception everything in his work is addressed: his experimental techniques; his resurrecting of language from the dead box of grammar; his reanimation of the cliché and the colloquial; his concern with the look of a poem, how it lies on the page, as well as with the shape it makes in the ear; his audible punctuation, double-duty negatives and all the devices he employs, such as between-statement (an aside from an aside) and parenthetically dispersed words, for achieving immediacy and simultaneity.

This accent on individuals accounts too for his satire, which because of its pungency and point has received perhaps a disproportionate amount of attention. He talks frequently out of the corner of his mouth, in his own brand of the vernacular based, in attitude and idiom, on the American wiseguy.

. . . lift the
poor cuss
tenderly this side up handle

with care
fragile
and send him home

to his old mother in
a new nice pine box

(collect

(from 152, in *Collected Poems*)

This brilliantly destructive, Swiftian satire is the obverse of his passionate regard for individuals, whether people, animals or things. His hatred is primarily of anything that threatens or denies their individuality. His hatreds, therefore, like his loves, are legion. But his love is equally articulate. He is not, as true cynics are, tongue-tied in the presence of emotion.

I had started to say, originally, that Cummings' poetry is a series of definitions of the individual. But "definition" is too static a term for the process of presentation in his poems, and "the individual" too colorless an abstraction for what they present.

Perhaps the closest he has ever come to defining his central conception, in a more or less conventional manner, is in *The Enormous Room* (1922), a more-than-factual account of his internment during the first world war. The high point of the book is his encounter at La Ferté Macé, that French preview of a concentration camp, with certain personages who possess the incorrigible virtue, in brutal surroundings, of remaining themselves. He refers to them, in John Bunyan's language, as Delectable Mountains. One of the Delectable Mountains is described in Chapter IX:

> He did not come and he did not go. He drifted.
>
> His angular anatomy expended and collected itself with an effortless spontaneity which is the prerogative of perhaps fairies, or at any rate of those things in which we no longer believe. But he was more. There

are certain things in which one is unable to believe for the simple reason that he never ceases to feel them. Things of this sort — things that are always inside of us and in fact are us and which consequently will not be pushed off or away where we can begin thinking about them — are no longer things; they and the us which they are, equals A Verb; an IS. The Zulu, then, I must perforce call an IS.

Here Cummings has stated the theme that is to be involved, implied or developed in all of his future writing. Significantly the theme is paralleled by a beginning re-evaluation of language. Two instances of a device he later uses consummately are introduced; the first in the phrase, "the prerogative of perhaps fairies."

"Perhaps," as it is placed here, contributes to a gracious quality in the writing. Its placement is to be even more strategic. In "Spring is like a perhaps hand" (from 75, in *Collected Poems*) the word is put to a double use, stylistically reproducing the shifting emergence of spring. "Perhaps" now has the force of an adjective describing the hand as it moves delicately, tentatively

arranging and changing placing
carefully there a strange
thing and a known thing here) . . .

. . . .

moving a perhaps
fraction of flower here placing
an inch of air there) and

without breaking anything.

"Perhaps" also retains its force as an adverb qualifying the whole statement, making it more realized by its very accurate suggestion of the elusiveness of our thought touching spring. In this it is of a piece with Cummings' use of parenthesis as interjection. We are made to stop, almost unconsciously, to ask ourselves, "Is it really like a hand? yes of course it is."

Cummings has enlarged the vocabulary, intensively rather than extensively, by amplifying its uses, as with "perhaps." This follows his general practice of turning parts of speech back into words.

"Now" in "as these emerging now / hills invent the air" (from 237, in *Collected Poems*) has all the magical immediacy that is traditionally looked for in poetry; an instantaneous effect similar to that found in the fifth line of this stanza from Keats' "Ode to the Nightingale":

> Away! away! for I will fly to thee,
> Not charioted by Bacchus and his pards,
> But on the viewless wings of Poesy,
> Though the dull brain perplexes and retards.
> Already with thee! tender is the night. . . .

The second anticipatory instance in the passage quoted from *The Enormous Room* is the use of "IS." More than one function is now performed by the hitherto verb. Grammatically it has been turned into a noun. Essentially it remains and becomes even more of a verb. It has lost the stigma of inactivity usually associated with existence.

Purists may frown on it; but the device, like many of Cummings', is an extension of common speech. "IS" has been given the force implied in the colloquial expression, "He *is* somebody."

The quality of being, to Cummings, is an active principle. This runs counter to the modern preoccupation with the drama of *doing*. It has become the technical fashion, best exemplified in Hemingway, to present character in and through "action." But to Cummings "he does something" need not imply any marked or interesting degree of existence. He makes the contrast plain in his song to "anyone" (29, in *50 Poems*) in the line

> they sowed their isn't they reaped their same

Here the underlying conception of an IS reappears in negative form. As a matter of record, although it is basic to his philosophy, its verbal occurrence in the poems is infrequent. He is not so much concerned with constructing a watertight, logically consistent system with which to examine experience, as he is with providing symbols for the totality of an experience.

I say "an experience" rather than "experience." Although his poetry looks toward the universal it does so by means of intense particularity. It is a reaction of the whole person to a whole experience.

II

The Metaphor - Poem

BETWEEN CUMMINGS' first definition of an IS, in *The Enormous Room,* and his magnificent reaffirmation in *lxl* (1944), come fifteen books, of which eleven are volumes of poetry. His earlier poems, with certain omissions, are brought together in the *Collected Poems* of 1938. Together with *50 Poems* (1940) and *lxl,* this forms one of the most impressive collections of poetry to be brought out in our time.

Until recently, however, discussion of his work has tended to center about this or that phase of it; its format, for example, or certain innovations of style such as the breaking up of phrases and words. In his *Essay on Rime* Karl Shapiro writes:

> This poet is most concerned with the component
> Integers of the word, the curve of "e,"
> Rhythm of "m," astonishment of "o"
> And their arranged derangement.

Others have been more impressed by the unabashed subjectmatter of some of the poems. And I remember reviews of fifteen or more years ago which announced that the "modernist" Cummings was returning to traditional forms like the sonnet and ballade, although he had been employing such all along.

On the whole, opinion has tended to parallel the variety of the poetry itself. One reason for this may be that, prior to the *Collected Poems,* his books so quickly became collectors' items. Judgments based upon poems or groups of poems encountered in anthologies were at the mercy of the taste of the anthologist. There is also the fact that his poems, despite their variety, possess such distinctive characteristics that they create an illusion of "knowing one, knowing all."

Whatever the cause, rather legendary misconceptions have grown up around his work. For instance, Henry McBride, reviewing an exhibition of Cummings' paintings at the American British Art Center, in 1944, had this astonishing remark to make. Their delicacy, he said, would "come as a surprise to readers of Cummings' poetry."

Now it might be a surprise to readers of his poetry to learn that he has been as prolific a painter as he is a poet. Some of his work in charcoal, ink, oil, pastel and watercolor was reproduced in 1931, in the volume *CIOPW,* which was, however, a limited edition, quickly out of print. But to have overlooked the delicacy (in whatever sense one wishes to mean the word) to be found in his poetry, from *Tulips and Chimneys* on, can only have been due to an exclusive attention paid to his originalities of form and some of his racier poems.

The *Collected Poems* opens with these lines:

> (thee will i praise between those rivers whose
> white voices pass upon forgetting (fail
> me not) whose courseless waters are a gloat
> of silver . . .

This is the first of a recurrent series of love poems, some of which rival, in purity and delicacy of expression, the finest examples of Provençal literature. It is no longer, one hopes, a shock to find the lines beginning in lower case. By this means the capital letter, when it does occur later in the poem, is given more than cursory interest, serving both as emphasis and as typographical embellishment.

The introductory parenthesis, also a characteristic feature, might be regarded as equivalent to the interpretation mark in music, setting the mood for the poem. Here it suggests an indication for the voice: "To be read smoothly, not as beginning but as continuation." Its meaning, like that of words, varies from poem to poem. In another context —

look at this)
a 75 done
this . . .
(from 152, in *Collected Poems*)

— it seems to imply a back-of-the-hand gesture: "This is between you and me."

Apart from these two innovations, this first poem surprises not by its departures from, but by its adherences to, traditional form, language and feeling. It is written in the grand manner and a modified version of the Spenserian stanza. An occasional word or phrase is precursive of more idiomatic speech:

(be with me in the sacred witchery
of almostness . . .

If the several poems that follow leap with the agility of acrobats through Cavalier and Chinese hoops, Poundian epithets, the *Song of Solomon,* a sonnet, a ballad, a nursery rhyme, finally landing on their own spry pins —

O sweet spontaneous
earth how often have
the
doting
        fingers of
prurient philosophers pinched
and
poked

thee
(from 21, in *Collected Poems*)

– they never forget, for all the literary respects they pay, their devotion to a lady, the spring or a landscape. Nor does Cummings, through all his subsequent experimenting with stripped forms and packed meanings, ever lose the ability to summon at will a sustained tone, which grows deeper as it becomes more personal. Nearly every anthology includes

> Always before your voice my soul
> half-beautiful and wholly droll
> is as some smooth and awkward foal,
> whereof young moons begin
> the newness of his skin . . .
>
> (from 15, in *Collected Poems*)

Beautiful as it is it seems, compared with later poems, rather youthfully generalized. Its graces are added, line by line; not quite so integral to the poem as in this sonnet (187):

> after all white horses are in bed
>
> will you walking beside me, my very lady,
> if scarcely the somewhat city
> wiggles in considerable twilight
>
> touch (now) with a suddenly unsaid
>
> gesture lightly my eyes?
> And send life out of me and the night
> absolutely into me. . . . a wise
> and puerile moving of your arm will
> do suddenly that
>
> will do
> more than heroes beautifully in shrill
> armour colliding on huge blue horses,
> and the poets looked at them, and made verses,
>
> through the sharp light cryingly as the knights flew.

Here the feeling is more particularized. It has lost anonymity of setting and exists as to time and place. The allusive chivalric element, which in earlier poems appears in their nostalgic recapture of courtly style, is now more directly related to immediate emotion and present observation. The center of imagination has shifted.

We have already been introduced, in another sonnet (91), to the drayhorses who live next door. They

. . . sleep upstairs
And you can see their ears. Ears win-

k, funny stable. In the morning they go out in pairs:
amazingly, one pair is white
(but you know that) they look at each other. Nudge.

(if they love each other, who cares?)
They pull the morning out of the night.

The horses are linked to the myth of Phoebus' chariot; but the allusion is not intrusive. The sun is not named; the myth is inferred only from the peculiar fact that their stable is upstairs, and "they pull the morning out of the night."

The horse continues to be a symbol for Cummings. An almost obsolete animal, threatened with extinction, he represents the precariousness of beauty in the modern world.

what a proud dreamhorse pulling (smoothloomingly) through
(stepp) this (ing) crazily seething of this
raving city screamingly street wonderful

flowers . . .

. . . .

— to have tasted Beautiful to have known
Only to have smelled Happens — skip dance kids hop point at
red blue yellow violet white orange green-
ness

o what a proud dreamhorse moving (whose feet
almost walk air). now who stops. Smiles.he
stamps

(from 281, in *Collected Poems*)

"IS" reappears in this sonnet, equated with "Love" and "Spring." (In others it equals "Yes" and "Life.") The horse, "whose feet almost walk air," suggests Pegasus. But much more than a symbol he is a horse, (stepp) (ing) into the street of the poem, visibly smiling and audibly stamping. The progression from literary to alive is complete.

Cummings is continually surpassing himself. Certain images form and re-form in his mind, reappearing both more original in themselves and more integrally related to their poems. Development in detail is paralleled by development in structure. Compare, for instance, certain poems in which love and rain are associated. One of the earliest of these associations occurs in Poem 18, of the *Collected Poems*:

the moon is hiding in
her hair.

. . . .

Recite
upon her
flesh
the rain's

pearls singly-whispering.

This is beautiful for its effects, particularly in the last line. But they are more noticeable as "effects" than the more daring imagery to come. The grandiloquent command, too, is typical of young poetry. The lyric impulse often ceases with the cessation of this wish-fulfillment frame of mind, after it has collided with too many evidences of "stern reality." So the lyric is sometimes thought of as incompatible with "maturity." But every now and then a poet succeeds in making his wishes come true.

Pursuing his wishes, Cummings arrives, in Poem 93, at a somewhat more modest conclusion:

i have found what you are like
the rain . . .

This corresponds with his increased powers of observation. The rain is now not so much an image in the mind; it has come out in the open:

(Who feathers frightened fields
with the superior dust-of-sleep. . . .

In Poem 179 his attention has turned more to the person; the comparison is qualified:

you are like the snow only
purer fleeter, like the rain
only sweeter frailler you

But the image is still in his mind. In Poem 225 the sonority of his first poem, with a music now his own, is joined by the increasing precision of his perceptions and a continuing belief in the impossible. The climax of the poem is this image, which has been revolving like a prism until now it catches all the light:

somewhere i have never travelled,gladly beyond
any experience,your eyes have their silence:
in your most frail gestures are things which enclose me,
or which i cannot touch because they are too near

your slightest look easily will unclose me
though i have closed myself as fingers,
you open always petal by petal myself as Spring opens
(touching skilfully,mysteriously) her first rose

or if your wish be to close me,i and
my life will shut very beautifully,suddenly,
as when the heart of this flower imagines
the snow carefully everywhere descending;

nothing which we are to perceive in this world equals
the power of your intense fragility:whose texture
compels me with the colour of its countries,
rendering death and forever with each breathing

(i do not know what it is about you that closes
and opens;only something in me understands
the voice of your eyes is deeper than all roses)
nobody,not even the rain,has such small hands

Like the horse, rain is a recurrent symbol. In Poem 83 it

occurs deeply, beautifully

and i (being at a window
in this midnight)
                    for no reason feel
deeply completely conscious of the rain or rather
Somebody who uses roofs and streets skilfully to make a
possible and beautiful sound . . .

In Poem 231 it

speaks (among leaves Easily
through voices womenlike telling

of death love earth dark)

. . . . . .

    (when
Rain comes;
predicating forever,assuming
the laughter of afterwards—
i spirally understand

What

touching means
or What does a hand
with your hair
in my imagination

To say that rain represents freshness or spontaneity or renewal is to make the symbol less clear. This is not just a case of substitution, like "Grim Reaper" for "death." Rain is incorporated in the symbol. There is rain in the poems. It can be heard drippingly through the leaves, in the heavy syllables of "death love earth dark." Its "spiral understanding" arises from itself. Its feeling of inner coolness is carried with it, not as idea but as sensation, wherever it appears.

here's to opening and upward,to leaf and to sap
and to your (in my arms flowering so new)
self whose eyes smell of the sound of rain
(From 269, in *Collected Poems*)

In Poem 237, in connection with rain, occurs one of Cummings' proportional equations:

be unto love as rain is unto colour;create
me gradually (or as these emerging now
hills invent the air)

This is an algebra of the heart. X:love::rain:colour. In this equation we are the unknown. Multiplied by the relationships observed in nature, we discover ourselves. Or it might be said — remembering Cummings' definition of an IS — we only exist then. All terms in nature are unknowns, becoming visible in the brief eternity of an observed relationship. Poetry is a record of such observations.

Cummings' poetry, both rhythmically and in idea, increasingly comes to depend on calculated equilibriums. The equations become subtler with each book. Compare

be of love (a little)
More careful
Than of everything
(from 287, in *Collected Poems*)

and

who far less lonely than a fire is cool
(from 293, in *Collected Poems*)

with

love is more thicker than forget
more thinner than recall

(from 42, in *50 Poems*)

and all of the foregoing with the following, taken from *lxl*:

love's to giving as to keeping's give;
as yes is to if,love is to yes

(from XXXIV)

(and buds know better
than books
don't grow)

(from LIV)

2

A very intimate relationship between poet and subjectmatter is characteristic of Cummings. The directness of a lovesong is carried over into a wide variety of poems less obviously personal in theme. The first instance of what I have in mind appears early in *Collected Poems* (24):

hist   whist
little ghostthings
tip-toe
twinkle-toe

little twitchy
witches and tingling
goblins
hob-a-nob   hob-a-nob

little hoppy happy
toad in tweeds
tweeds
little itchy mousies

with scuttling
eyes   rustle and run   and
hidehidehide
whisk

whisk   look out for the old woman
with the wart on her nose
what she'll do to yer
nobody knows

for she knows the devil   ooch
 the devil   ouch
the devil
ach   the great

green
dancing
devil
devil

devil
devil

wheeEEE

This is not just a poem *about* ghostthings, witches, goblins, toads and mice. Its form is itself a metaphor, becoming what it describes; recreating childhood. It might be called onomatometaphor, the sounds are so perfectly reproduced. But the shape and feel are also part of the metaphor; the mouse that runs through, tail and all; the small tickle of tweed.

I can think of few prior examples of the metaphor-poem. The nearest comparison that comes to mind is with Hopkins' "The Leaden Echo and the Golden Echo," in which the bells speak. But even there subject is not quite so thoroughly poem.

This corresponds to changes in approach that may be observed in much of modern art. Formerly a cat, for example, might be regarded as the subject, or part of the subject, of a picture; as in Goya's portrait of the little boy with his bird, his toys and his cats. In one of Paul

Klee's paintings a cat becomes the canvas; rather than looking at the cat we are led pictorially into its mind, where we see a little bird. We have an experience of being a cat. This experience might be called the subject of the picture.

These closer relationships with subjectmatter are allied to more primitive ways of experiencing the world. A picture such as Klee's, a poem such as Cummings', are the recapture for their arts of a kind of imitative magic, such as may be seen in African sculpture, Oceanic art and the drawings of children.

There are many other poems in which Cummings, placing himself in this one-to-one relation with his material, achieves comparable feats of emotional transference; a form of poetic decalcomania. To pick out a few, there is

> In Just-
> spring   when the world is mud-
> luscious the little
> lame balloonman
>
> whistles   far   and wee
>
> (from 30, in *Collected Poems*)

There is

> gee i like to think of dead it means nearer because deeper
> firmer since darker than little round water at one end of
> the well . . .
>
> (from 79, in *Collected Poems*)

There is the "little silent Christmas tree" (104), two mice poems (166 and 274), the sonnet to Joe Gould (261), the "proud dream-horse" quoted above, and

> this little bride & groom are
> standing) in a kind
> of crown he dressed
> in black candy she

veiled with candy white
carrying a bouquet of
pretend flowers this
candy crown with this candy

little bride & little
groom in it kind of stands on
a thin ring which stands on a much
less thin very much more

big & kinder of ring & which
kinder of stands on a
much more than very much
biggest & thickest & kindest

of ring & all one two three rings
are cake & everything is protected by
cellophane against anything (because
nothing really exists

(301, in *Collected Poems*)

This is a little world to itself. The poem is of a size with the cake; constructed, like it, in tiers of progressive excitement; and all frosting. What is realized is the cake's essential quality, that which makes it what it is.

This quality, in these poems, is not so much related to the philosopher's "idea" as it is to the "significant form" of the painter. It is not a static abstract entity or essence, but an active principle arrived at not by the method of canvasing the possibilities, cataloguing, eliminating and ordering; but by Cummings' gift of direct emotional interpenetration. Through all the brilliant organization of his material he is able to preserve the spontaneity of internal mimicry; the reflex of his poetry.

Similarly the pantomime art of Jimmy Savo crystallizes in motion the images of a song, translating into gestures the minor tragedies and small triumphs of a little man confronted by a big unwieldy world. He projects the continual oscillation in such a character between "a laugh and a tear." Cummings' poem to him (302, in *Collected Poems*) is a word-picture both of this character and of the enveloping gift of its creator:

so little he is
so.
     Little
ness be

(ing)
comes ex
-pert-
Ly expand:grO

w
  i
?n
  g

Is poet iS
(childlost
so;ul
) foundclown a

-live a
,bird
          !O
& j &

ji
&
jim, jimm
;jimmy

s:
  A
V
o(
  .
   :
    ;
     ,

The interrelationships are so deftly numerous that only a few can be pointed out. "So" begins and concludes the poem. The latter "so" encloses "AV" (a root-form for "bird"), thus confirming in Savo's name the birdlike quality expressed in the poem. Savo's "pert" expertness consists in expanding littleness, but not by blowing up its dimensions. He grOws in a series of circular elations, as the miracle ("L . . . O") of a "wi?ng" causes a bird to grow through space. They grow by what their motion encloses. Savo is a "childlost"; yet like a poet recovers original impulses of living: the child, lost to most of us, is found in poet and clown. "AV" may also allude to another of Savo's expansions, when he suddenly releases a torrent of song in "River Stay Away from My Door." The trailing punctuation at the end recalls the floating particles of paper Savo can incredibly cause to flutter off from his fingers, with infinite lassitude. And of course Savo began as a juggler; a precisionist at balance.

There are many other examples: "sitting in a tree" (47, in *50 Poems*), "old mr ly" (XXVII, in *lxl*), "rain or hail" (XXVIII, in *lxl*) and a poem (XLV, in *lxl*) to a flower-wagon man – "than sunlight older" – who all but disappears into the jonquils he is offering but manages to convey his classic origin:

"my home ionian isles

The first poem in *50 Poems* is one of many instances of Cummings' landscape-portraits:

!blac
k
agains
t

(whi)

te sky
?t
rees whic
h fr

om droppe

d
,
le
af

a:;go

e
s wh
IrlI
n

.g

The wind in the poem has blown some of the words upside down and ravelled others; but as in nature nothing is lost. If we look at it steadily it reassembles itself, more complete in that it includes its own disruption; again an example of balancing opposites.

The transmission of the subject's action into the structure of the poem is also beautifully carried out in Poem 276, of the *Collected Poems:*

r-p-o-p-h-e-s-s-a-g-r
who
a)s w(e loo)k
upnowgath
PPEGORHRASS
eringint(o-
aThe):l
eA
!p:
S a
(r
rIvInG .gRrEaPsPhOs)
to
rea(be)rran(com)gi(e)ngly
,grasshopper;

The subject of the poem is a grasshopper. The action of the poem is the grasshopper "gathering up now to leap." "As we look" we don't see him in the grass; his identity is withheld. But we get hints from the stridulating sounds he makes. These sounds — some soft, some loud, some intermittent — are rearrangements of his name; just as he rearranges himself to rub forewing and hind leg together. Then he "leaps!" clear so that we see him, "arriving to become, rearrangingly, grasshopper."

The motive of such a poem is the same delight in the natural world, the same love toward its inhabitants, that has always inspired poetry; today or in Greece, where Aristophanes reproduced the sound of frogs in the syllables: "Brek-kek-kek-kex, Ko-ax, Ko-ax." In the urgency of this feeling, poets have looked for more and more immediate ways of declaring themselves. Here the wish is to have the grasshopper appear before us with all the surprise and pleasure of a live one.

Internal mimicry, an osmosis of emotion, is the constant factor running through and accounting for the amazing variety of Cummings' poems. It accounts for "Spring is like a perhaps hand" and for

the moon looked into my window
it touched me with its small hands
and with curling infantile
fingers it understood my eyes cheeks mouth
((from 178, in *Collected Poems*)

It accounts too for something as different in tone as

buncha hardboil guys frum duh A.C. fulla
hooch kiddin eachudder bout duh clap an
talkin big how dey could kill
sixereight cops . . .
(from 202, in *Collected Poems*)

Having no sentimental recoil from sentiment, Cummings is also able to make delicate use of the "indelicate." Through all the lustinesses and ribaldries — which are apt to be what first strike the attention of new readers — runs his gift for allowing the person or the scene to present itself. This is true of the various poems to

"kitty". sixteen, 5′ 1″, white, prostitute
(from 34, in *Collected Poems*)

, to Betty, Marj, Lil and the rest; the sonnets (37 and 65) about Dick Mid's Place; the Five Americans (122) and a number of other poems Villonesque or Rabelaisian in flavor though employing the American idiom:

. . . gimme uh swell fite

like up ter yknow Rektuz, Toysday nite;
where uh guy gets gayn troze uh lobstersalad
(from 122, in *Collected Poems*)

He can incorporate, when he wishes, Anglo-Saxon four-letterisms, as in a poem from *ViVa,* not included in the *Collected Poems:*

oil tel duh woil doi sez
dooyuh unnurs tanmih eesez pullih nizmus tash,oi
dough un giv uh shid oi sez. Tom
oi doughwuntuh doot, buttoiguttuh
braikyooz,datswut eesez tuhmih. (Nowoi askyuh
woodundat maik yurarstoin
green? Oilsaisough.) — Hool
spairruh luckih? Thangskeed. Mairsee.
Muh jax awl gawn. Fur Croi saik
ainnoughbudih gutnutntuhplai?
— HAI
youzwidduh poimnuntwaiv un duhyookuhsumpnruddur
givusuhtoonunduhphugnting

All the expressions are in key; that is, they are in character. The shocks are placed just right. When they are, they shock you into sensibility. When they are not, they shock you into insensibility.

The shocks in his poems are so nearly always placed right that it may be of some value to examine two instances in which, it seems to me, they are not. In "the way to hump a cow" (14, in *50 Poems*) neither Cummings nor the poem seems to be speaking in character.

The idiom therefore seems forced and to my way of thinking unpleasantly intrusive. This is not a matter of decorum. It is a far more subtle one of balance. Poem and subject are not integrated. I get the same overweighted feeling from Poem 215, in the *Collected Poems,* which ends:

o live with me in the fewness of
these colours;
alone who slightly
always are beyond the reach of death

and the English.

The surprising thing about such instances is their rarity, considering the latitude Cummings allows himself. And that latitude is more important than its lapses.

In his more strictly satirical poems Cummings ridicules the stereotyped by means of its own platitudes:

come, gaze with me upon this dome
of many coloured glass, and see
his mother's pride, his father's joy,
unto whom duty whispers low

"thou must!" and who replies "I can!"
—yon clean upstanding well dressed boy
that with his peers full oft hath quaffed
the wine of life and found it sweet—

a tear within his stern blue eye,
upon his firm white lips a smile,
one thought alone: to do or die
for God for country and for Yale

(from 149, in *Collected Poems*)

His barbed platitudes fly straight for the hidden motivation, or lack of it, in public utterance:

"next to of course god america i
love you land of the pilgrims' and so forth oh
say can you see by the dawn's early my
country 'tis of centuries come and go
and are no more what of it we should worry
in every language even deafanddumb
thy sons acclaim your glorious name by gorry
by jingo by gee by gosh by gum
why talk of beauty what could be more beautiful than these heroic happy dead
who rushed like lions to the roaring slaughter
they did not stop to think they died instead
then shall the voice of liberty be mute?"

He spoke. And drank rapidly a glass of water

(147, in *Collected Poems*)

The point of his satire, its implied contrast, is always a distinction between "public" and "human." His poems, themselves extensions of personal speech, are addressed to the man. For all the devastation of his wit, he reaches the heights of expression in the more inclusive beauty of such songs as "anyone lived in a pretty how town" (29, in *50 Poems*) and the unsurpassed "my father moved through dooms of love" (34, in *50 Poems*).

III

Algebra of the Heart

In *lxl* Cummings has drawn the strands of his poetry more closely together than ever before. He has reformulated, now in poetic terms, the definition of an individual first stated in *The Enormous Room,* setting it against the perspective of our times.

> there's nothing as something as one
>
> one hasn't a why or because or although
> (and buds know better
> than books
> don't grow)
> one's anything old being everything new
>
> . . . .
>
> (with a spin
> leap
> alive we're alive)
> we're wonderful one times one
>
> (from LIV)

To be "one," an IS, a Yes, is for Cummings a form of aristocracy. The individual is "quality." This aristocracy is more potent than that implied in ruling, making money, depriving others of same, possessing social position, family or any other fortuitous advantage. The individual may have all or none of these; they are not what make him individual.

There is no question of "one" being superior to "another." Neither is there any question of equality if that is taken to mean sameness. One is as valuable as another, but not because they are alike. The disease of sameness with which man is afflicted would reduce us to the status of products. Between Ford cars no metaphor is possible.

Only the individual can live because only the individual can love. Mass emotions go in negative directions.

> Huge this collective pseudobeast
> (sans either pain or joy)
> does nothing except preexist
> its hoi in its polloi
>
> (from IV)

In his literal-minded attempts to equalize, man destroys not only poetry but himself. Becoming the abstractions he worships he is crushed between his own ideologies.

> pity this busy monster,manunkind,
>
> not. Progress is a comfortable disease:
> your victim (death and life safely beyond)
>
> plays with the bigness of his littleness
> — electrons deify one razorblade
> into a mountainrange;lenses extend
>
> unwish through curving wherewhen till unwish
> returns on its unself.
>   A world of made
> is not a world of born — pity poor flesh
>
> and trees,poor stars and stones,but never this
> fine specimen of hypermagical

ultraomnipotence. We doctors know

a hopeless case if — listen:there's a hell
of a good universe next door;let's go

(XIV)

There are degrees of aliveness. Some mice, maples, mountains, are more alive than some men. The quality of non-being, as I have earlier suggested, is just as present to Cummings' awareness as the quality of Yes-Life-Love-Spring-IS, and he inveighs against it with all the fervor of an old-line hell-fire-and-damnation preacher. But he is more specific:

a salesman is an it that stinks Excuse

Me whether it's president of the you were say
or a jennelman name misder finger isn't
important whether it's millions of other punks
or just a handful absolutely doesn't
matter and whether it's in lonjewray

or shrouds is immaterial it stinks

(from IX)

This poem anticipates Erich Fromm's diagnosis, in *Man For Himself* (Rinehart, 1947) of "the marketing personality," a peculiarly modern phenomenon. In the market of today, Dr. Fromm shows, the emphasis is on exchange value rather than on use value. People "package" themselves along with their commodities, altering their traits to conform with changing fashions. In time their "personalities," like their values, become abstract.

Fromm contrasts this and other restrictions of the self with "the productive personality." The mature man has realized his potentialities; he "feels himself one with his powers," which "are not masked and alienated from him." This parallels in a striking manner Cummings' early definition of an IS, and his subsequent portrayal of individuals. The pungency of his satire is matched by the passion of his affirmations. He is in every sense a revivalist:

what if a much of a which of a wind
gives the truth to summer's lie;
bloodies with dizzying leaves the sun
and yanks immortal stars awry?
Blow king to beggar and queen to seem
(blow friend to fiend:blow space to time)
—when skies are hanged and oceans drowned,
the single secret will still be man

(From XX)

The Arch-Fiend in his universe may be summed up in the word abstraction, meaning any idea to which a man subscribes as if it were more living than himself—

(leaving a perfectly distinct unhe;
a ticking phantom by prodigious time's
mere brain contrived: a spook of stop and go)

(from XVIII)

—and from which he expects (if only everyone else would equally subscribe) automatic benefits.

(really unreal world, will you perhaps do
the breathing for me while i am away?)

(from XVIII)

An abstraction is a convenience in thinking; a labor-saving device like machinery. Misused, both come to be symbols of man's laziness. The sins of mankind need no Sky Police; caught in his own machinery, his own abstractions, man is goaded on as by fifty devils. Chief among them is an abstraction whose colossal *un*carnation is The State.

dead every enormous piece
of nonsense which itself must call
a state submicroscopic is—
compared with pitying terrible
some alive individual

(from XXI)

Implicit faith in The State, as a divine agency to which all of our personal wishes can safely be entrusted, reached its apogee in Hitler's Germany. In *Eimi* (1933), written during a visit to Russia, Cummings recorded his impressions of a people who were also, he felt, submerging their identities in an abstraction. But the disease is not confined to this or that country.

Basically it is the belief that an abstraction, such as "mostpeople" (to which Cummings refers in the Introduction to the *Collected Poems*), has an independent existence. A "majority" cannot have an opinion. You and I can. When you and I, as we often do, take over a majority opinion we cease to have any of our own. Superficially democratic, we are really subscribing to a totalitarian conception; to an abstraction which will surely destroy us.

War is one of the catastrophic workings of this principle. Wars could not exist if they depended upon our personal wishes. But since these have been entrusted to States we are involved, whether we wish or not, in the very tangible collisions of these abstractions.

Cummings, who referred to the first world war in the most scathing of terms (39, 144, 147, 149, 150, 151, 152, 204, of *Collected Poems*), did not suffer a temporary lapse at the advent of the second. War continues to be what "general / (yes / mam) / sherman" (from XIII) called it.

armies (than hate itself and no
meanness unsmaller) armies can
immensely meet for centuries
and(except nothing)nothing's won

(from XL)

Perhaps one myth upon which wars are based has never been so savagely exposed as in Poem VII:

ygUDuh

ydoan
yunnuhstan

ydoan o
yunnuhstan dem
yguduh ged

yunnuhstan dem doidee
yguduh ged riduh
ydoan o nudn
LISN bud LISN

dem
gud
am

lidl yelluh bas
tuds weer goin

duhSIVILEYEzum

"War," he had said in the catalogue to his 1944 exhibition of paintings, "is the science of inefficiency. Peace is the inefficiency of science." Science, by which Cummings means the superstitious belief that "to measure is to know," is another mythical abstraction, which like The State threatens to usurp us. Perhaps it is ungracious to labor the point now, when the scientists of the atom project are so desperately trying to disentangle themselves and the world from the logical results of their achievement.

Cummings measures with a different ruler:

one's not half two. It's two are halves of one:
which halves reintegrating,shall occur
no death and any quantity;but than
all numerable mosts the actual more

minds ignorant of stern miraculous
this every truth — beware of heartless them
(given the scalpel,they dissect a kiss;
or,sold the reason,they undream a dream)

(from XVI)

To escape the prospect that the scientists' painstaking and dramatically verified measurements have opened up, many are fleeing into the arms of another abstraction, The Church. But, says Cummings,

> it's over a (see just
> over this) wall
> the apples are (yes
> they're gravensteins) all
> as red as to lose
> and as round as to find.
>
> . . . .
>
> But over a (see just
> over this) wall
> the red and the round
> (they're gravensteins) fall
> with kind of a blind
> big sound on the ground

(from III)

To get back from partial truths, which abstractions are, to life, which poetry indicates and to which everything – even an abstraction – is contributory, is Cummings' message. To the alive, especially the alive who are in love (and who else are alive?) "nothing except the impossible shall occur" because

> Life's life and strikes my your our blossoming sphere

(from XLII)

The spectral conflicts of our age, its catastrophic shadow-boxings between equivocal protagonists, have led Cummings to assert more forcibly than ever the elementary struggle underlying all life and all his poetry; that between No and Yes, Un and IS, denial and affirmation.

darling!because my blood can sing
and dance (and does with each your least
your any most very amazing now
or here) let pitiless fear play host
to every isn't that's under the spring

. . . .

doubting can turn men's see to stare
their faith to how their joy to why
their stride and breathing to limp and prove

. . . .

but if a look should april me
. . . Hills jump with brooks:
trees tumble out of twigs and sticks;

(from XL)

IV

The Whole Idea

In *Santa Claus* (1946) Cummings brings the two halves of his whole idea together. Cast in the form of a Morality, like the *Everyman* play of fifteenth-century England, it employs conventional symbols — Santa Claus, Death, a Mob, a Child, a Woman — to make an allegorical blueprint illuminating the connection between what his satire has ridiculed and what his lyrics have celebrated. It is consequently neither so satirical nor so lyric as his other work. Its poetry lies in the clarity of its action. With mathematical precision his symbols revolve through the negative and positive poles of human motivation.

Twice before Cummings has deliberately used stock figures to project in dramatic form his feelings about the world. Neither the ballet *Tom* (1935) nor the play *Him* (1927) is in verse. Both are poetic in conception and treatment. *Tom* is based on Harriet Beecher Stowe's *Uncle Tom's Cabin.* The novel is treated as a part of folklore; which is what it has become. Cummings' words provide the structure and mood-indications for a poem in motion, for which the choreography is yet to be supplied. The story is translated into a sequence of exalted, dreamlike episodes conveying the inner integrity and nobility of the slave Tom. He is another symbol, or example, of the individual.

Him was one of the outstanding successes of the Provincetown Players, in their adventurous days. Designed kaleidoscopically, it oscillates between a series of interior and exterior scenes illustrating the predicament of the artist — the individual — in the modern world. The exterior scenes are developed in front of flats, in the manner of vaudeville skits and circus sideshows. Characterizing the modern world is the recurrent scene of the Three Fates, the Misses Weird, who sit with their backs to the audience, knitting and exchanging nonsensical gossip and advertising slogans. The interior scenes develop the inner life of the artist, symbolized by the attempts of the lover, Him, to understand the beloved, Me. These five scenes are played in a room, three walls of which are visible and the fourth — that between the players and the audience — invisible. The room revolves from scene to scene so that the imaginary fourth wall is successively a mirror, a window, a door, a blank wall, and no wall at all (in the fifth scene the players become aware of the audience). The five revolutions are five metaphors of the relation of art to life. The play is a reflection of life; a view of life; a passage to it; life itself, private and self-contained; and finally — since it *is* life — common to all. Him is Me (Mih) reversed.

The chief stock figure in *Him* is the play itself, whose mechanics reveals us to ourselves. In *Santa Claus* it is the capacious symbol celebrated once a year: the spirit of giving. From Cummings' poems we know that giving equates with Yes, with IS, with Spring, with Life, with Love. In the Morality, Santa Claus is youth in disguise.

Santa Claus is at an impasse because no one wants what he has to offer: understanding. What they want is knowledge; half of understanding. To break a whole experience in two leads neither to life nor to death, but to an intermediate realm; the realm of abstractions.

> Imagine if you can, a world so blurred
> that its inhabitants are one another
> — an idiotic monster of negation:

so timid, it would rather starve itself
eternally than run the risk of choking;
so greedy, nothing satisfies its hunger
but always huger quantities of nothing—
a world so lazy that it cannot dream;
so blind, it worships its own ugliness:
a world so false, so trivial, so unso,
phantoms are solid by comparison.

Santa Claus meets Death, the spirit of taking. Death is in similar plight; there is nothing for him to take. Where there is no living, there can be no dying. Death's mask is therefore a crude imitation of himself.

Death and Santa Claus exchange masks. In a world of abstractions, death mixes with life. Our best impulses turn into our worst. Being half himself, Santa Claus cuts giving in half: he sells. What he sells is not understanding but knowledge.

The world is now not a world but a side-show. Santa Claus, passing himself off as a Scientist, does a brisk trade. The knowledge he sells takes the form of shares in a non-existent "wheelmine," a device by which the world will run itself. The Mob wants the taking end of Christmas: something for nothing. Its credulity is that a system can be invented by which work will work itself, life will live itself, and everything will be super for "superladies and supergentlemen."

. . . Science
is no mere individual. Individuals
are, after all, nothing but human beings;
and human beings are corruptible.

Science, capitalized, and the Salesman — Cummings' favorite villains — are abstractions; half-ideas which we suppose to be whole ones. Here he shows that they are Siamese twins: the notion that all you need is the "know-how" in order to get something for nothing, or to sell nothing for something. This is the pathetic fallacy of realists.

Cummings as a poet knows that wishes come true, even non-wishes. This particular non-wish comes true with a vengeance. Santa Claus as the Scientist is mystified when people perish in the wheelmines.

The reciprocal operations of belief have come into play. We are not so far removed from the so-called primitive who, when he accidentally violated a taboo, dropped dead. Putting our faith in non-existent values, we lose our identity. The wheelmines become real; their nothingness invades humanity. Santa Claus can redeem himself only by renouncing his pretensions to knowledge, returning to a faith in the whole experience of life, and rediscovering love.

Cummings' Morality plays on two stages at once: the world arena and the private theatre of the heart. His characters consequently are to be interpreted on two levels. They symbolize our personal impulses as well as the conflicts of groups and nations. The inner and the outer worlds mirror each other.

A distrust of "progress" Cummings has always had, and expressed when its expression was unpopular. This is what gives point to his satire, directed against a faith in the manipulations of Science, industry or government. This half of his whole idea is now in the public domain. It has become fashionable for advertisers to ridicule advertising, for politicians to expose politics, for soldiers to debunk the army.

But savagely as Cummings attacked the easy optimisms of the Twenties, it was never with the desperate cynicism now prevalent. There has always been a logical, emotional and necessary connection between his satire and his lyrics; between what he has denied and what he has affirmed: "one's not half two. It's two are halves of one."

Part Six

VARIATIONS ON WALLACE STEVENS

I

Fictive Music

H*armonium,* first published in 1923, introduced a poet with a vocation for taking delight. In the root sense Wallace Stevens is a dilettant. He takes delight seriously. His poems, again in the root sense, are precious, being concerned with price, with prizing and praising. A great appreciator, he makes his own values with which to appraise experience. His poems are the scales on which he interprets gross and gossamer.

Some of his adjustments are so delicate indeed that they are considered precious in the slighting sense. This is a commentary on the age rather than on Stevens. In the open war between duty and delight, one consecrated to the latter is thought to shirk the former. Refinements of poetry are suspect; while those of science, the paring of Plutonium, are respected whether we understand them or not.

It is not inappropriate to apply double-edged epithets to Wallace Stevens. He makes constant use of such ironies. In "Le Monocle de Mon Oncle" poets are called "the fops of fancy." A poet is concerned with niceties of language and precisions of image; the cut of his thought. Fop is related too to the verb fob, to fool or cheat. Poets, like novelists, openly deceive. The fictive character of poetry Stevens has stressed from "Earthy Anecdote," the first poem in *Harmonium,* to "It Must Give Pleasure," the concluding section of his long poem "Notes Toward a Supreme Fiction" in *Transport to Summer* (1947). Stevens uses his fictions, as the scientist uses hypotheses, to explore phases of reality. The physicist is a dilettant of time, space and energy. Stevens explores relations and correspondences between inner and outer reality. His poems make a series of exquisite accordances.

Harmonium perfectly conveys the scale, range of intensities and formality of Wallace Stevens' early poems. A household instrument, rather outmoded, the harmonium was associated with the parlor, the "best" part of the house; often kept shut except on Sundays and special occasions. Stevens, a lawyer, was writing in his spare time, the "best" part of the day.

More modestly volumed, the harmonium can simulate the grandiose tones of an organ and yet remain intimate, appropriate to family hymns. Many of Stevens' poems are hymns to life. Never Miltonic, their cultivated crescendos employ the harmonium's several stops for imitating woodwinds, brasses and stringed instruments. Stevens has taken such pleasure in plucking and strumming effects that he called his third book *The Man with the Blue Guitar* (1937). Most appropriately, the harmonium is an instrument that depends on breath; on alternate respirations.

Alternation is what strikes us first about the first poem in *Harmonium,* his free verse "Earthy Anecdote":

> Every time the bucks went clattering
> Over Oklahoma
> A firecat bristled in the way.

The bucks, swerving to avoid the danger, re-encounter it, re-swerve, and are finally resolved with it; apparently by being eaten. The path of their swervings makes the pattern of the poem. A continuous alternation between "bucks" and "firecat," "clattering" and "bristled," "right" and "left," supplies an equivalent of rhyme, in effect a series of identical rhymes. These opposed elements are connected by partial rhymes: "clattering" and "firecat," "right" and "left." The partial rhymes follow the action of the poem and are resolved in "slept":

> Later the firecat closed his bright eyes
> And slept.

This principle of alternation leading to final resolution is typical of many of Stevens' poems, although seldom worked out as obviously.

Several of the poems that follow introduce themes and methods that will recur. "Invective Against Swans," in his favorite metre, iambic pentameter, is arranged by irregularly rhymed couplets:

> The soul, O ganders, flies beyond the parks
> And far beyond the discords of the wind.
>
> A bronze rain from the sun descending marks
> The death of summer, which that time endures
>
> Like one who scrawls a listless testament
> Of golden quirks and Paphian caricatures . . .

His complaint against the birds is that their "chilly chariots" remind him of approaching winter. Summer, her soul departing as the leaves' "bronze rain" descends, inscribes her last will "Of golden quirks and Paphian caricatures": the swirling leaves and revealed attitudes of trees. Her amorous grandeurs, like those of the Paphian Aphrodite, are now ribald hieroglyphs. The figure keeps returning on itself, as convoluted as the shapes of swans.

A practice of Stevens' poems is to make their points by puns of appearance. What are called figures of speech are apt to be literally, in his case, visual figures. He does not present fully rounded descriptions, but salient details by which we may summon up the whole. We take part in the poems by a selective rehearsal of our own experience.

One of Stevens' signatures is his use of *k* sounds. Here they suggest the plucking of the wind and the scratching of a pen. It is as if the testament, and the poem, were being written by the swans' quills. The wintry swans will be inherited by winter; summer is

> Bequeathing your white feathers to the moon
> And giving your bland motions to the air.

The pall-bearers are gathering:

> Behold, already on the long parades
> The crows anoint the statues with their dirt.

Three symbols from this poem recur throughout Stevens' poetry. The park, like the parlor, is a "best" part of town. Many of this Sunday poet's poems seem to have been composed or to have had their origin there. The park statues, usually inferior as works of art, memorialize the past: an event or a hero. These memories of the great and the noble are continually being obliterated by the ordinary activities of life, the crows who "anoint the statues with their dirt."

In "The Paltry Nude Starts on a Spring Voyage" Botticelli's ornate "Birth of Venus" has inspired him to paint the contrasting nudes of spring and summer. Spring is "paltry"; her habitat more likely to be the harbor than the sea:

> But not on a shell, she starts,
> Archaic, for the sea.
> But on the first-found weed
> She scuds the glitters,
> Noiselessly, like one more wave.

Miracles of scale, both in imagery and in resonance, set this "meagre play" of the spring goddess, "In the scurry and water-shine," against that "goldener nude" of summer, who

> Will go, like the centre of sea-green pomp,
> In an intenser calm,
> Scullion of fate,
> Across the spick torrent, ceaselessly,
> Upon her irretrievable way.

These richer harmonies have been prepared for by the "discontent" of the spring nude, who

. . . would have purple stuff upon her arms,
Tired of the salty harbors,
Eager for the brine and bellowing
Of the high interiors of the sea.

The surface qualities of the poem, its alternations between plucking and thrumming sounds, reproduce its theme.

"The Plot Against the Giant" launches another recurrent theme. Three girls plot how to thwart "this yokel" – the humdrum giant – when he comes "Whetting his hacker." The first will diffuse "the civilest odors / Out of geraniums and unsmelled flowers." The second will arch before him "cloths besprinkled with colors / As small as fish-eggs." The giant's subjugation is by now so certain that the third can afford to pity him: "Oh, la . . . le pauvre!" This is the first use of Stevens' interjectional immediacy, which in later poems often has the effect of musical obbligato: the guitar brought into the guitar-poem, the bird-cry accompanying the image of the bird. Here the device anticipates and illustrates the stratagem of the third girl:

I shall whisper
Heavenly labials in a world of gutturals.
It will undo him.

The poem is not without its relevance to the position of the arts in an indifferent, if not hostile, culture. Stevens has never made a frontal attack, nor engaged in direct satire. Instead he puts his feelings into anecdotes, little fictions whose ironies double back on themselves; as here, in the fragility of the confidence expressed by the Three Graces.

2

One of the finest early poems is "The Snow Man":

One must have a mind of winter
To regard the frost and the boughs
Of the pine-trees crusted with snow;

And have been cold a long time
To behold the junipers shagged with ice,
The spruces rough in the distant glitter

Of the January sun; and not to think
Of any misery in the sound of the wind,
In the sound of a few leaves,

Which is the sound of the land
Full of the same wind
That is blowing in the same bare place

For the listener, who listens in the snow,
And, nothing himself, beholds
Nothing that is not there and the nothing that is.

The essential quality of cold is conveyed by the correspondence of inner and outer weather. The scene is cold, and the listener is cold. This effect is heightened by the omission of any definite place or person. The bareness of "the same bare place" is like the blank stare of a snowman's anthracite eyes.

The effect is further emphasized by the subtly interlinking sounds that take the place of rhyme. They work all through the poem in a manner too intricate for full analysis, their result being to reduce all sounds to the same value, reproducing the effect of an all-covering snow punctuated by glints of ice. Typical of this is the interrelationship of the end-words. Following the path of those that most nearly echo each other we have, starting from the first line: "winter," "glitter," "think," "wind," "land," "wind," "is"; from the second line: "boughs," "ice," "place," "is"; from the third: "snow" (itself a tone away from "boughs"), "snow," "beholds," "is." Any path we choose leads us to "is"; even "leaves," the least related sound, as the leaves themselves are least related to winter. If we extend the analysis to include the beautifully scattered *s* sounds whistling through the poem, and a few of the interior progressions (*"mind," "winter," "pine-*trees," *"time," "jun*ipers," "spr*u*ces," *"Janu*ary *sun"* – "winter," "glitter," "listener" – *"frost," "boughs,"* "pine-*trees," "crus*ted," "juni*pers,"* "mi*ser*y" – "bare," "there") we begin to realize the deliberate extent of the imitative magic worked upon us. Cold has penetrated the poem. The poem is not simply descriptive; it is becoming before our eyes what it is telling us about. Coldness has become an object; the object is the poem.

Such an intensification of immediacy is typical of modern poetry; not that it is exhibited in all modern poems, or that it is their exclusive property. In T. S. Eliot's "Triumphal March," a parade is reproduced in the beat of the verse:

> Stone, bronze, stone, steel, stone, oakleaves, horses' heels
> Over the paving.

This suggests a children's chant, such as might accompany the bouncing of a ball, or other rhythmic game. In Marianne Moore's "A Carriage from Sweden," the spinning and stopping rhythms and the fluctuations of rhyme translate into sound the visible motion of wheels. The form of many of Cummings' poems are determined by the action of wind on a landscape, the falling and trickling away of rain, a grasshopper's leap, the tiered shape of a wedding-cake surmounted by bride and groom and encased in cellophane "because / nothing really exists."

Wallace Stevens' "listener" — who may be anybody; himself, the reader — may remind us of Walter de la Mare's "The Listeners." De la Mare's poem too, while it is in an earlier tradition of the romantic ballad — with its own deft modifications of that tradition — achieves its eery effect as much by what is omitted as by his impeccable selection of what to include. We are told nothing of the identity of the Traveler "Knocking on the moonlit door." Why did he come? Who was it he expected to meet? The scene is presented as if we were there; as if we were the ghosts making no answer to his knock.

The heightening of immediacy by exclusion is present in Robert Frost's poems, which for all their homely particularity and apparent forthrightness, choose to be reticent on certain crucial points. Where was "I" going in "The Road Not Taken"?

> Two roads diverged in a yellow wood,
> And sorry I could not travel both
> And be one traveler, long I stood . . .

"I" has put just enough of himself into the poem to indicate character:

> Two roads diverged in a wood, and I—
> I took the one less traveled by,
> And that has made all the difference.

By implication a whole life is summed up in the last line. And yet the line is perfectly ambiguous as to the accomplishment of that life. Was it a great success or a complete failure? We are not told. What we are made to share is an awareness of consequences, flowing from apparently casual decision.

In Stevens' "The Snow Man" we are made to share an interpenetrating cold. Yet coldness is itself only part of the subject of the poem; an illustration of an underlying principle. The method of communication is part of the communication. As he says in *The Man with the Blue Guitar:* "Poetry is the subject of the poem." Stevens' poetry is principally concerned with a two-way relationship between the beholder and the thing beheld. This relationship is both active and passive at once; an alternating current. Neither "winter" nor "a mind of winter" is subject or object. Each is both.

II

Harlequin's Progress

"Le Monocle de Mon Oncle," the first long poem in *Harmonium,* is a series of inspections. The monocle suggests a single view; the moon; poetry. Is my uncle the man in the moon? the poet in his poetry? The poet is looking for his monocle; for the kind of poetry that will be appropriate to his time. To find it, he looks through it; but what he looks through is not yet a poetry of his own. It is, like the monocle, antiquated; a fastidious way of viewing life that has been bequeathed to him, not in a direct line of descent, but from a foreign uncle. Stevens' influences are primarily French and Chinese. He looks through them for a technique of his own.

The development of his early poems is circular and decorative; a linking of overtones. He strikes a note and lets its reverberations spread. There is often a blurring of effects, as the tones of a harmonium blur and blend. Echoes of traditional rhetoric may lead us to expect logical development. To arouse such an expectation may be part of his irony. These nostalgic echoes have led some critics to prefer his earlier to his later, more mature style.

If we think of the echoes as examining themselves, as a style inspecting themes to create a style, the method of "Le Monocle de Mon Oncle" becomes clear. It is a series of such inspections. The spotlight falls successively on faith and disillusionment; on the inspiration of youth and the sadness of age; on the passing of beauty and the continually renewed freshness of experience; on innocence and sophistication. No final judgment is made; alternating impressions are recorded. The first stanza states the theme and illustrates the method:

> "Mother of heaven, regina of the clouds,
> O sceptre of the sun, crown of the moon,
> There is not nothing, no, no, never nothing,
> Like the clashed edges of two words that kill."
> And so I mocked her in magnificent measure.
> Or was it that I mocked myself alone?
> I wish that I might be a thinking stone.
> The sea of spuming thought foists up again
> The radiant bubble that she was. And then
> A deep up-pouring from some saltier well
> Within me, bursts its watery syllable.

Which is real? A faith that exceeds experience, or a bitter, mocking skepticism? The poet vouches for neither. In mocking the first, he may be mocking himself. To resolve the conflict he would have to return to earth, become a stone. His monocle presents him with both: two ways of viewing the world: through the "radiant bubble" of faith, or through the "watery syllable" of a tear.

His bifocal monocle, ranging over experience, picks out near things and far; the "firefly's quick, electric stroke," the crickets that came "Out of their mother grass, like little kin," and

> The mules that angels ride come slowly down
> The blazing passes, from beyond the sun.
> Descensions of their tinkling bells arrive.

Beauty and ugliness come to it at once:

Last night, we sat beside a pool of pink,
Clippered with lilies scudding the bright chromes,
Keen to the point of starlight, while a frog
Boomed from his very belly odious chords.

The poem ends with the observation: "That fluttering things have so distinct a shade." If age, wisdom, love, death – the major themes – are involved in mystery, even the most elusive things cast their shadow and can be dealt with. It is his precisions of the elusive – the distinctions he draws between shades, tones and nuances – that chiefly distinguish his early poems. Their variety of mood and virtuosity of technique are suggested by his own apostrophe in "Le Monocle":

I quiz all sounds, all thoughts, all everything
For the music and manner of the palladins
To make oblation fit. Where shall I find
Bravura adequate to this great hymn?

A study adequate to the bravura would have to take it up poem by poem; line by line. Since each poem suggests far more than it says, the result would be a compendious encyclopedia of bravura. We shall only touch a few highlights and illustrate a few principles. As examples of the sounds quizzed, there are his musical interjections; the guitar first brought into the poem in "The Ordinary Women":

The lacquered loges huddled there
Mumbled zay-zay and a-zay, a-zay.

Moonlight is transposed into a noiseless sound; it "Fubbed the girandoles." There are many boisterous irruptions like the "Tum-ti-tum, / Ti-tum-tum-tum!" of "Ploughing on Sunday"; as well as the more subtle evocation of an echo in the mind, in "Of Heaven Considered as a Tomb":

Make hue among the dark comedians,
Halloo them in the topmost distances
For answer from their icy Élysée.

The two types are related in "A High-Toned Old Christian Woman" ("Poetry is the supreme fiction, madame"):

> Such tink and tank and tunk-a-tunk-tunk,
> May, merely may, madame, whip from themselves
> A jovial hullabaloo among the spheres.

In "Depression Before Spring" the poet bewails the absence of his "queen." Midway the poem becomes a cock deserted by his hen:

> Ho! Ho!
>
> But ki-ki-ri-ki
> Brings no rou-cou,
> No rou-cou-cou.

His "intricate assonantals" and "beautiful rigmarole of sounds" include word-fooleries: "Le Monocle de Mon Oncle"; "The Anatomy of Monotony"; "The Jack-Rabbit" who "carolled in caracoles"; the rigid parent in "Two at Norfolk" for whom "the softest word went gurrituck in his skull"; in "Owl's Clover" the "word in the mind that sticks at artichoke / And remains inarticulate." "Cortège for Rosenbloom" proceeds:

> To a chirr of gongs
> And a chitter of cries
> And the heavy thrum

It is not simply to surprise the reader that he cries "Pardie!" or introduces "thunder's rattapallax" and "Ohoyaho, / Ohoo," "The heavy bells are tolling rowdy-dow," "The skreak and skritter of evening gone," "Dew-dapper clapper-traps" or "A dithery gold falls everywhere." Every level, no matter how playful, has a serious intention. As he says in "Notes Toward a Supreme Fiction": "Life's nonsense pierces us with strange relation."

Stevens' intention is often not so much to go beyond surface resemblances as it is to bring out their significance by rendering them with precision. An explicit statement of this theme is made in his "Anecdote of Men by the Thousand":

The soul, he said, is composed
Of the external world.

There are men of the East, he said,
Who are the East.

. . . .

The mandoline is the instrument
Of a place.

Are there mandolines of western mountains?
Are there mandolines of northern moonlight?

In "Floral Decorations for Bananas" he epitomizes the art of interior decoration:

These insolent, linear peels
And sullen, hurricane shapes
Won't do with your eglantine.

The bananas are inappropriate to the expected "women of primrose and purl," for whom

You should have had plums tonight,
In an eighteenth-century dish,
And pettifogging buds,

. . . .

But bananas hacked and hunched . . .
The table was set by an ogre,

. . . .

Pile the bananas on planks.
The women will be all shanks
And bangles and slatted eyes.

Personality and surroundings affect each other. The theme, "clothes make the man," is wittily expanded in the sixth of "Six Significant Landscapes":

Rationalists, wearing square hats
Think, in square rooms,
Looking at the floor,
Looking at the ceiling.
They confine themselves
To right-angled triangles.
If they tried rhomboids,
Cones, waving lines, ellipses —
As, for example, the ellipse of the half moon —
Rationalists would wear sombreros.

"Tea at the Palaz of Hoon" is one of the many direct commentaries he has made on his art. Here he provides a reason for his use of the bizarre. Placing himself in an exotic setting, he concludes:

I was the world in which I walked, and what I saw
Or heard or felt came not but from myself;
And there I found myself more truly and more strange.

In "Theory" he illustrates the explicit statement: "I am what is around me." And in "Tattoo" the interaction of light and eyes is thought of as an indelible design traced over the surface of things by light and by sight. Which is tattooer and which tattooed?

2

His long poem "The Comedian as the Letter C" might have been called "Harlequin's Progress." It is the logbook of a philosophical voyage; a traveling among bright distinctions. Crispin, the French equivalent of the Italian clown Arlecchino, is Stevens' mask; the antecedent of Stevens as Academician. He is referred to in his traditional rôle of valet and barber. Nature's lackey, he dresses up and trims the world to suit himself. These trimmings and dressings are the names and images he puts upon the world. He is a "lutanist of fleas"; a patchwork figure: "The ribboned stick, the bellowing breeches, cloak / Of China, cap of Spain." Whatever he writes is descriptive of himself:

This auditor of insects! He that saw
The stride of vanishing autumn in a park
By way of decorous melancholy; he
That wrote his couplet yearly to the spring,
As dissertation of profound delight . . .

On his "simple jaunt" – "Bordeaux to Yucatan, Havana next, / And then to Carolina" – he is confronted by the sea, an experience exceeding his metaphors. How can he picture himself in its terms?

What word split up in clickering syllables
And storming under multitudinous tones
Was name for this short-shanks in all that brunt?
Crispin was washed away by magnitude.

The aesthetic experience is so comprehensive as to be religious. "The valet in the tempest was annulled." He is reduced to humility, seeing himself "A skinny sailor peering in the sea-glass." One of Stevens' delicious ironies is here to present Crispin's inadequacies in terms of tremendous word-panoramas of the sea:

. . . A wordy, watery age
That whispered to the sun's compassion, made
A convocation, nightly, of the sea-stars,
And on the clopping foot-ways of the moon
Lay grovelling. Triton incomplicate with that
Which made him Triton, nothing left of him,
Except in faint, memorial gesturings . . .

In the face of this reality, Triton, the conventional poetic symbol, is inadequate. Crispin has lost the romantic illusion that man is the measure of his universe, "the intelligence of his soil," as the poem had begun. He must regard himself rather as the letter *C*; a mere initial or intimation of a cosmic comedian revolving its own metaphors, of which Crispin may be one. *C* suggests also the new moon, and a crooked smile.

Crispin, overwhelmed but "a man made vivid by the sea," looks for something to replace the romantic illusion. "Into a savage color he went on." He plunges into the tropics, "an earth, / So thick with sides and jagged lops of green . . . [it] was like a jostling festival"

Of seeds grown fat, too juicily opulent,
Expanding in the gold's maternal warmth.

Exploring his own sources in this exotic and original country, the "affectionate emigrant" — in the pure sense "affected" by all — "Found a new reality in parrot-squawks." He encounters a thunderstorm:

Gesticulating lightning, mystical,
Made pallid flitter. . . .

Taking refuge in a cathedral "with the rest," he reflects that the elemental powers exceed man's forms of worship. A fresh "Andean breath" frees his mind and leaves him "more than free, elate, intent, profound / And studious of a self possessing him."

Now he turns his sharpened observations on the imagination: "The book of moonlight is not written yet." The alternating sequence of his travels sends him north again, toward an imaginary north of "legendary moonlight": "The spring came there in clinking pannicles / Of half-dissolving frost . . ." There he might find "the relentless contact he desired":

Perhaps the Arctic moonlight really gave
The liaison, the blissful liaison
Between himself and his environment,
Which was, and is, chief motive, first delight,
For him, and not for him alone. . . .

But the imagination seems now "Illusive, faint, more mist than moon, perverse," to one who postulates as his theme

The vulgar, as his theme and hymn and flight,
A passionately niggling nightingale.

. . . .

Thus he conceived his voyaging to be
An up and down between two elements,
A fluctuating between sun and moon . . .

He arrives at the Carolina he has imagined:

And as he came he saw that it was spring,
A time abhorrent to the nihilist
Or searcher for the fecund minimum.

. . . .

. . . Tilting up his nose,
He inhaled the rancid rosin, burly smells
Of dampened lumber, emanations blown
From warehouse doors, the gustiness of ropes,
Decay of sacks, and all the arrant stinks
That helped him round his rude aesthetic out.

Embracing "the essential prose" –

To which all poems were incident, unless
That prose should wear a poem's guise at last

– he becomes a "realist" and formulates the proposition: "his soil is man's intelligence." His prime purpose is now

. . . to drive away
The shadow of his fellows from the skies,
And from their stale intelligence released,
To make a new intelligence prevail.

To that end, Crispin determines to establish a colony, which will propagate, institutionalize and perpetuate his aesthetic and religious discoveries: "Commingled souvenirs and prophecies" – such as, "The natives of the rain are rainy men." This colony will be dedicated to the celebration of life through appropriate ceremonies.

The man in Georgia waking among pines
Should be pine-spokesman. . . .

His regionalism extends to "smart detail":

The melon should have apposite ritual,
Performed in verd apparel, and the peach,

When its black branches came to bud, belle day,
Should have an incantation. . . .

But his revolutionary phase is short-lived. He realizes that his wish to replace the old order is a repetition of its pathetic fallacy:

These bland excursions into time to come,
Related in romance to backward flights,
However prodigal, however proud,
Contained in their afflatus the reproach
That first drove Crispin to his wandering.
He could not be content with counterfeit . . .

His "idea of a colony" shrinks. Instead of "Loquacious columns by the ructive sea," he builds a cabin and turns "to salad-beds again." Instead of wanting to change reality, he accepts an idea of reality that includes within it the idea of its own change:

The plum survives its poems. It may hang
In the sunshine placidly, colored by ground
Obliquities of those who pass beneath,
Harlequined and mazily dewed and mauved
In bloom. Yet it survives in its own form,
Beyond these changes, good, fat, guzzly fruit.
So Crispin hasped on the surviving form,
For him, of shall or ought to be in is.

In love he finds an inclusive metaphor, at once personal and universal. It is an expanding metaphor, leading naturally to other and unpredictable metaphors: four daughters, four ways of life. He has become a "fatalist."

The world, a turnip once so readily plucked,
Sacked up and carried overseas, daubed out
Of its ancient purple, pruned to the fertile main,
And sown again by the stiffest realist,
Came reproduced in purple, family font,
The same insoluble lump. . . .

A "mythology of self," the poem has incidentally charted a progression in the idea of metaphor. Metaphor is first conceived of as an equal-sign conveying a static relationship, a one-to-one correspondence between reality and the imagination. This is a passive, traditionally romantic conception. An experience exceeding the poet's metaphors severs the relationship. Reality is "true"; the imagination, "false." He attempts to discover "pure" reality in the jungle of his origins. The relationship between reality and imagination is becoming active. The direction of this action alternates. First it is reality, isolated through observation, that is acting on his imagination; an empirical phase. The poet must employ metaphor, if only as a descriptive device. Observing this unavoidable intrusion of imagination, he passes through an idealistic phase. Perhaps "pure" imagination — the "Arctic moonlight" of his dreams – is alone "true." But the imagination, so isolated, now acts upon and sharpens his perceptions of the actual world; a realistic phase. His new-found realism is in conflict with traditional forms of worship. Intent on founding a religion based on right relationships, he entertains briefly a revolutionary phase. But this attempt would involve him in the very traditional fallacy he is combatting; the belief that "truth" can be imposed, or finally established. Truth simply exists; it need not be imposed. Change is part of it; it cannot be established. (So Stevens entitles one of his short poems, "The Only Emperor is the Emperor of Ice Cream.") He retires into the simple existence of his personal life; an individualistic phase. Now finally he observes, in his own life, the constant and unpredictable interaction of reality and imagination. The metaphor is active and passive at once; a relationship between reality and the imagination that acts in both directions. This fatalistic poetry is a fiction paralleling life.

3

These unfoldings of attitude may have a bearing on changes in Stevens' celebrated poem "Sunday Morning." Originally published in *Poetry* as a five-stanza hymn to life, it was increased in *Harmonium* to eight stanzas and rearranged. Paradoxically, the alterations clarify the poem by making it more indefinite. In the first version the line of emotion is from traditionally religious feeling ("The holy hush of ancient sacrifice") to a questioning of religious symbols, a delight in natural beauty, despair at its evanescence, the search for "some imperishable bliss," the acceptance of death as "the mother of beauty" and a culminating worship of the mystery of life:

> Supple and turbulent, a ring of men
> Shall chant in orgy on a summer morn
> Their boisterous devotion to the sun,
> Not as a god, but as a god might be,
> Naked among them, like a savage source.
>
> . . . .
>
> And whence they came and whither they shall go,
> The dew upon their feet shall manifest.

This apparently corresponds to Stevens' "revolutionary phase"; a celebration of the earth and the visible universe as being, in themselves, more mysterious and holy than any supernatural idea. In the later version, a new second stanza intensifies the questioning of the Christian myth:

> Why should she give her bounty to the dead?
> What is divinity if it can come
> Only in silent shadows and in dreams?

Human emotions are to be "cherished like the thought of heaven," for they "are the measures destined for her soul." In Stanza III a theme is introduced that will recur in later poems: the enrichment of life through myth. Ideas of the supernatural enhance our idea of the earth the more we recognize them as "fiction" and their "paradise" as an abstract symbol: "Jove in the clouds had his inhuman birth." Where did these symbols come from, if not from ourselves? They give hope to our aspirations.

Insisting on the literal truth of such symbols, and a human incarnation of the supernatural, we are driven to questioning them literally, as in Stanza VI:

> Is there no change of death in paradise?
> Does ripe fruit never fall? Or do the boughs
> Hang always heavy in that perfect sky,
> Unchanging, yet so like our perishing earth,
> With rivers like our own that seek for seas
> They never find, the same receding shores
> That never touch with inarticulate pang?

Death is truly "the mother of beauty, mystical." The sense of its imminence is what gives value to the transient. When we think to penetrate its mystery, we merely provide ourselves with ideas of perfection. The poem now ends less conclusively:

> At evening, casual flocks of pigeons make
> Ambiguous undulations as they sink,
> Downward to darkness, on extended wings.

Anthologists have usually preferred the earlier version. Conrad Aiken, in *A Comprehensive Anthology of American Poetry* and *Twentieth-Century American Poetry* (Modern Library, 1944 editions), alternates between them. One change does not seem for the better; from the lines, "She causes boys to bring sweet-smelling pears / And plums in ponderous piles," to "She causes boys to pile new plums and pears / On disregarded plate."

A mystical glorification of transient, though recurrent, beauty, is central to both versions:

> There is not any haunt of prophecy,
> Nor any old chimera of the grave,
> Neither the golden underground, nor isle
> Melodious, where spirits gat them home,
> Nor visionary south, nor cloudy palm
> Remote on heaven's hill, that has endured
> As April's green endures . . .

This anticipates the explicit formulation in the concluding section of "Peter Quince at the Clavier":

Beauty is momentary in the mind—
The fitful tracing of a portal;
But in the flesh it is immortal.

In these lines, and in the ensuing development of his poetry, Stevens resolves an uneasy antithesis between philosopher and poet. The philosopher is often thought of as being concerned primarily with ideas; to that extent anti-emotional. The poet is regarded as being concerned primarily with emotion; to that extent anti-intellectual. The implication is that each rules out the other. But for Stevens poetry is a realm where "mind" and "emotions" are resolved in the imagination. As he prays, in his hymn "To the One of Fictive Music":

Unreal, give back to us what once you gave:
The imagination that we spurned and crave.

III

A Chair of Poetry

In *Ideas of Order* Stevens' ideas of correspondence are growing more active. He has not painlessly renounced the romantic correspondence, the one-to-one relationship. His nostalgia for its feeling of delightful passivity, its sense of instant rapport, provides the tension of "Sailing After Lunch," where it is contrasted with the "heavy historical sail" of present reality:

> It is only the way one feels, to say
> Where my spirit is I am,
> To say the light wind worries the sail,
> To say the water is swift today,
>
> To expunge all people and be a pupil
> Of the gorgeous wheel and so to give
> That slight transcendence to the dirty sail,
> By light, the way one feels, sharp white,
> And then rush brightly through the summer air.

"There are these sudden mobs of men," he says in "Sad Strains of a Gay Waltz." Yet the nostalgic element, strongly expressed, is not Stevens' permanent attitude. In "The Idea of Order at Key West" he reverses its direction. The "blessed rage for order" is always the condition of the poet; not something he has lost, but something he is continually seeking:

The maker's rage to order words of the sea,
Words of the fragrant portals, dimly-starred,
And of ourselves and of our origins,
In ghostlier demarcations, keener sounds.

By observing the present truly and intensely enough, the poet may hope, symbolically, to resolve its conflicts. "Mozart, 1935" begins:

Poet, be seated at the piano.
Play the present, its hoo-hoo-hoo,
Its shoo-shoo-shoo, its ric-a-nic,
Its envious cachinnation.

His relation to this present, where "they carry down the stairs / A body in rags," is intimate. He is not the politician's collective "you," but the artist's singular "thou":

Be thou the voice,
Not you. Be thou, be thou
The voice of angry fear,
The voice of this besieging pain.

Be thou that wintry sound
As of the great wind howling,
By which sorrow is released,
Dismissed, dissolved
In a starry placating.

The significant transition in *Ideas of Order* is Stevens' change of mask from harlequin to academician. This corresponds to changes in the impetus and texture of his poetry, but not its fictive quality. "Jot these milky matters down," he says in "Academic Discourse at Havana." "They nourish Jupiters." Philosophy is his favorite form of fiction. Defining it, in a paper in *The Sewanee Review* (Autumn, 1944) as "the official view of being," he goes on to define poetry as "the unofficial view." If Plato would have excluded poets, Stevens will magnanimously include Plato.

To indulge his taste for ideas he has created his own Academy of Fine Ideas. Before this body, garbed as its chief philosopher, he makes periodic appearances to expound, elaborate and elucidate his theory of resemblances. For his philosophy, like his harlequinade, is based on the nature of metaphor, as this continues to grow in his mind.

The transition is signaled by the opening poem in *Ideas of Order,* "Farewell to Florida." This is a leavetaking of the tropic luxuriance of his earlier style – what he had called in *Harmonium,* "O Florida, Venereal Soil" – for a more northerly latitude of ideas. But if he is to be less preoccupied with bravura for its own sake, it will continue an integral part of his design. He quizzes not only all sounds but all sights. His choice and treatment of the harlequin as hero was related to a painting tradition that includes Watteau and Picasso. His "pool of pink, / Clippered with lilies scudding the bright chromes" suggests a Monet. Various of his landscape poems – "Of the Surface of Things," "Six Significant Landscapes," "Thirteen Ways of Looking at a Blackbird," "Variations on a Summer Day" – are influenced by Oriental painting, as well as by its poetry. "Study of Two Pears" in *Parts of a World* (1942) was quite possibly inspired by a still-life of Cézanne:

> The yellow glistens.
> It glistens with various yellows,
> Citrons, oranges and greens
> Flowering over the skin.

And a partial list of his titles suggests a joint exhibition of Klee, Chirico and Miró: "The Man Whose Pharynx was Bad," "The Place of the Solitaires," "The Curtains in the House of the Metaphysician," "Two Figures in Dense Violet Night," "Nomad Exquisite," "The

Surprises of the Superhuman," "The Revolutionists Stop for Orangeade," "Lunar Paraphrase," "Ghosts as Cocoons," "Dance of the Macabre Mice," "A Fish-Scale Sunrise," "Gallant Château," "The Mechanical Optimist," "Mystic Garden & Middling Beast," "Romanesque Affabulation," "A Rabbit as King of the Ghosts," "A Weak Mind in the Mountains," "The Sense of the Sleight-of-Hand Man," "So-And-So Reclining on Her Couch," "Somnambulisma," "Crude Foyer," "Description of a Platonic Person," "Man Carrying Thing," "A Completely New Set of Objects," "Men Made Out of Words," "Chaos in Motion and Not in Motion," "Mountains Covered with Cats," "Attempt to Discover Life," "A Lot of People Bathing in a Stream." Klee's description, in his *Pedagogical Sketchbook,* of "a line taking a walk" is congenial to the course of a Stevens' poem. Similarly congenial are Klee's discussion of lines and planes, his studies of structure and dimension, his dissections of direction and assignments of balance, and especially his distinctions between atmospheric and cosmic energies.

2

Energetic distinctions animate *The Man With the Blue Guitar,* a title that suggests the paintings of Juan Gris, or of Picasso's Cubist period. The poem is a series of musings on the relation of the poet to his art ("The man bent over his guitar, / A shearsman of sorts"); and of art ("things as they seem") to life ("things as they are"). The poet as observer is part of what he observes. So Stevens asks, in front of a picture of Picasso's, if "this 'hoard / Of destructions' " is

> . . . a picture of ourselves,
>
> Now, an image of our society?
> Do I sit, deformed, a naked egg,
>
> Catching at Good-bye, harvest moon,
> Without seeing the harvest or the moon?

Stevens' correspondences are now more subtly evaluated. They have never been exactly point-by-point. When the poet says they are, Stevens now says, he is setting up a fiction. The relations posed by such fictions are like, but not identical with, the relations of life. " 'Things are they are / Are changed upon the blue guitar.' " Yet he is asked to fulfill his traditional rôle of prophet:

And they said then, "But play, you must,
A tune beyond us, yet ourselves,

A tune upon the blue guitar
Of things exactly as they are."

However much the poet may try to do this, he always fails:

I cannot bring a world quite round,
Although I patch it as I can.

I sing a hero's head, large eye
And bearded bronze, but not a man,

Although I patch him as I can
And reach through him almost to man.

Nevertheless, it remains his chief desire:

Ah, but to play man number one,
To drive the dagger in his heart,

To lay his brain upon the board
And pick the acrid colors out,

To nail his thought across the door,
Its wings spread wide to rain and snow,

To strike his living hi and ho,
To tick it, tock it, turn it true,

To bang it from a savage blue,
Jangling the metal of the strings . . .

His wish is to be God: to summon and sum up life with all the immediacy of the sounds of the strings, *in* the sounds of the strings. Intermittently, he feels, he succeeds:

. . . as the blue guitar

After long strumming on certain nights
Gives the touch of the senses, not of the hand,

But the very senses as they touch
The wind-gloss. . . .

So that he san say, "Tom-tom, c'est moi." He can consider, though he questions, rendering "A million people on one string." He can foresee a rôle for poetry exceeding Matthew Arnold's prophecy:

Do not speak to us of the greatness of poetry,
Of the torches wisping in the underground,

Of the structure of vaults upon a point of light.
There are no shadows in our sun,

Day is desire and night is sleep.
There are no shadows anywhere.

The earth, for us, is flat and bare.
There are no shadows. Poetry

Exceeding music must take the place
Of empty heaven and its hymns,

Ourselves in poetry must take their place,
Even in the chattering of your guitar.

In this prophetic mood the poet, the player of the blue guitar, is

. . . merely a shadow hunched

Above the arrowy, still strings,
The maker of a thing yet to be made;

The color like a thought that grows
Out of a mood, the tragic robe

Of the actor, half his gesture, half
His speech, the dress of his meaning, silk

Sodden with his melancholy words,
The weather of his stage, himself.

The poem proceeds through a series of alternations between "is" and "seems" until, like Tom Sawyer's aunt counting the silver, we give up the distinction entirely. Our ideas of reality are fictions; but the fictions are part of reality. The alternations are part of reality. If "Slowly the ivy on the stones / Becomes the stones," it is equally true that "brick / Is a weed."

Poetry is the subject of the poem,
From this the poem issues and

To this returns. Between the two,
Between issue and return, there is

An absence in reality,
Things as they are. Or so we say.

But are these separate? Is it
An absence for the poem, which acquires

Its true appearances there, sun's green,
Cloud's red, earth feeling, sky that thinks.

From these it takes. Perhaps it gives,
In the universal intercourse.

No matter how aloof, poetry is a part of life. A study of its relations is a method of insight. We may think of it as a special case; but all forms of existence are special cases. Poetry, Stevens seems to be saying over and over again, is the special case that brings together the other special cases and reveals their astonishing unity. It parallels life without ever quite meeting it. Yet it comes closest to this meeting the more it succeeds in paralleling. This aesthetic paradox, for Stevens, supplies the place of religious belief. It is belief stripped of dogma. The poet's impulse is the impulse of the prophet; a prophet who knows he is inventing fictions:

> He held the world upon his nose
> And this-a-way he gave a fling.
>
> His robes and symbols, ai-yi-yi—
> And that-a-way he twirled the thing.
>
> Sombre as fir-trees, liquid cats
> Moved in the grass without a sound.
>
> They did not know the grass went round.
> The cats had cats and the grass turned gray
>
> And the world had worlds, ai, this-a-way:
> The grass turned green and the grass turned gray.
>
> And the nose is eternal, that-a-way.
> Things as they were, things as they are,
>
> Things as they will be by and by . . .
> A fat thumb beats it out ai-yi-yi.

Having invented the fictions, he can continually dispense with them. They are his examinations of himself and the world through the medium of poetry, through the very machinery of his own poems. By their means he progresses toward ever more inclusive and direct apprehensions:

> Throw away the lights, the definitions,
> And say of what you see in the dark
>
> That it is this or that it is that,
> But do not use the rotted names.

How should you walk in that space and know
Nothing of the madness of space,

Nothing of its jocular procreations?
Throw the lights away. Nothing must stand

Between you and the shapes you take
When the crust of shape has been destroyed.

You as you are? You are yourself.
The blue guitar surprises you.

3

Having made his peace with the blue guitar, having resolved reality and the imagination as parts of each other, and having discovered time – not "Time in its final block" but "time / To come, a wrangling of two dreams" – Stevens returns, in "Owl's Clover," to the reconsideration of an earlier theme:

Another evening in another park
A group of marble horses rose on wings
In the midst of a circle of trees, from which the leaves
Raced with the horses in bright hurricanes.

The title suggests the wisdom of the imagination, which forages at night by the reflected light of the moon. The statue, the finished work of art, is viewed successively; first by the foresight of the sculptor. He had foreseen the natural setting into which his work would fit, and how they would enhance each other:

. . . autumn,
The sky above the plaza widening
Before the horses, clouds of bronze imposed
On clouds of gold, and green engulfing bronze,
The marble leaping in the storms of light.

Next the statue is viewed by what the sculptor had not foreseen: the old woman: "the bitter mind / In a flapping cloak." This rational mind, a black crow of reality, whose fantasy is that there is no imagination, is impoverished by the moonlight. "So destitute that nothing but herself / Remained," she impoverishes what she beholds: "The mass of stone collapsed to marble hulk."

Then the statue is viewed by the revolutionist:

> The thing is dead . . . . . Everything is dead
> Except the future. . . .
>
> . . . .
>
> These are not even Russian animals.
>
> . . . .
>
> The stones
> That will replace it shall be carved, *"The Mass*
> *Appoints These Marbles Of Itself To Be*
> *Itself."* No more than that, no subterfuge,
> No memorable muffing, bare and blunt.

The statue, revolving, into the real, into the future ("An abysmal migration into a possible blue"), is next whirled to Africa, "The Greenest Continent"; a jungle reality, whose only god is fate, against which the angels of Europe recurrently contend.

> But could the statue stand in Africa?
> The marble was imagined in the cold.

The finished work of art is appropriate to its culture, its own time and place, the memories and desires that surround it. It cannot encompass all of reality. Yet reality, the god of Africa, "Fatal Ananke is the common god."

> He, only, caused the statue to be made
> And he shall fix the place where it will stand.
> Be glory to this unmerciful pontifex,
> Lord without any deviation, lord
> And origin and resplendent end of law,
> Sultan of African sultans, starless crown.

The statue is now considered in the light of its own civilization.

> The workers do not rise, as Venus rose,
> Out of a violet sea. They rise a bit
> On summer Sundays in the park, a duck
> To a million . . .

They have lost the freedom and boldness of the pioneers, "For whom men were to be ends in themselves":

> . . . for these, day comes,
> A penny sun in a tinsel sky, unrhymed,
> And the spirit writhes to be wakened, writhes
> To see, once more, this hacked-up world of tools.

Of what are they thinking? Are they all thinking the same thought? Has "equality" prevailed?

> Then Basilewsky in the band-stand played
> "Concerto for Airplane and Pianoforte,"
> The newest Soviet reclame. Profound
> Abortion, fit for the enchanting of basilisks.
> They chanced to think: suppose the future fails.

If it does, "What man of folk-lore shall rebuild the world?" For it is "As the man the state, not as the state the man." Who will be the orator that

> Confounds all opposites and spins a sphere
> Created, like a bubble, of bright sheens,
> With a tendency to bulge as it floats away.
> Basilewsky's bulged before it floated, turned
> Caramel and would not, could not float. And yet
> In an age of concentric mobs would any sphere
> Escape all deformation . . . ?

Although the work of art, the statue, is misapprehended by the multitude, it is there to be seen; real because of its integrity:

The statue is white and high, white brillianter
Than the color white and high beyond any height
That rises in the air. The sprawlers on the grass
See more than marble in their eyes . . .

. . . .

The statue is the sculptor not the stone.
In this he carved himself, he carved his age,
He carved the feathery walkers standing by . . .

And the people too, for all their unreality, are real and have a meaning.

The civil fiction, the calico idea,
The Johnsonian composition, abstract man,
All are evasions like a repeated phrase,
Which, by its repetition, comes to bear
A meaning without a meaning.

The people of the mass are revealed, "For a moment, once each century or two."

. . . But then so great,
So epical a twist, c a t a s t r o p h e
For Isaac Watts: the diverting of the dream
Of heaven from heaven to the future, as a god,
Takes time and tinkering, melodious
And practical. . . .

The poem ends with an apostrophe to intuition,

. . . a subman under all
The rest, to whom in the end the rest return,
The man below the man below the man,
Steeped in night's opium, evading day.

This man "Imagines and it is true, as if he thought / By imagining." He sees the "sprawling portent" that moves "high up in heaven." He knows the future because he knows the past, and "The future must bear within it every past."

The portent may itself be memory;
And memory may itself be time to come
And must be, when the portent, changed, takes on
A mask up-gathered brilliantly from the dirt . . .

The portent moves over the statue "in a crow's perspective of trees," altering, magnifying and diminishing it until, when "night / And the portent end in night":

The statue stands
In hum-drum space, farewell, farewell, by day
The green, white, blue of the ballad-eye, by night
The mirror of other nights combined in one.

. . . .

Night and the imagination being one.

I have given skeletal indications of a poem composed not in a straight line of development, but like the statue it describes, in a whirl of movement. The passages quoted are some of the central points of this movement. Such a method of presentation must slight many of the contributing forces, such as the savage parody of Mussolini's Ethiopian adventure:

Forth from their tabernacles once again
The angels come, armed, gloriously to slay
The black and ruin his sepulchral throne.
Hé quoi! Angels go pricking elephants?
Wings spread and whirling over jaguar-men?
Angels tiptoe upon the snowy cones
Of palmy peaks, sighting machine-guns? These,
Seraphim of Europe? . . .

. . . .

. . . This must
Be merely a masquerade or else a rare
Tractatus, of military things, with plates,

. . . .

In Leonardo's way, to magnify
Concentric bosh. . . .

IV

Theories of Resemblance

P*arts of a World* (1942) and *Transport to Summer* continue the development of Stevens' theories of resemblance. To trace this development step by step would require the persevering pedantry and etherial imagination of an angelic Ph.D. thesis. For its progress is not only a logical unfolding of ideas. It is a progression by imaginative leaps. These insights form the individual poems. Periodically they are gathered together and consolidated with previous insights in a series of extended discourses, of which the most prominent in *Parts of a World* are "Extracts from Addresses to the Academy of Fine Ideas" and "Examination of the Hero in a Time of War"; and in *Transport to Summer,* "Esthétique du Mal," "The Pure Good of Theory," "Credences of Summer" and the surmounting "Notes Toward a Supreme Fiction." These supply the very angelic theses of which I have been speaking. It will be impossible to touch on more than a few highlights; what follows might well be called, "Notes Toward a Supreme Study of Wallace Stevens."

Stevens' genius in dealing with ideas is his ability to reproduce their *sensations*. This is an extension by reversal of his ability, through uncanny mimicry, to make ideas of sensations:

> Then, while the music makes you, make, yourselves,
> Long autumn sheens and pittering sounds like sounds
> On pattering leaves . . .

These lines from "Owl's Clover" illustrate how he can state movement, almost as if it were an object. In "Parochial Theme," the first poem in *Parts of a World,* he speaks of the voices in the wind that

> Have shapes that are not yet fully themselves,
>
> Are sounds blown by a blower into shapes,
> The blower squeezed to the thinnest *mi* of falsetto.

Being able to render action, even imaginary action, so definitively, he has extended this gift to catch the action of ideas; the very inflection and rhythm of thought as it passes through the mind. In "Prelude to Objects," which incidentally illuminates the fictitious character of his own Academy, he plays upon the terms of philosophic disquisition; the repeated, and by placement overemphasized, "ifs" and condescending "granteds":

> If he will be heaven after death,
> If, while he lives, he hears himself
> Sounded in music, if the sun,
> Stormer, is the color of a self
> As certainly as night is the color
> Of a self, if, without sentiment,
> He is what he hears and sees and if,
> Without pathos, he feels what he hears
> And sees, being nothing otherwise,
> Having nothing otherwise, he has not
> To go to the Louvre to behold himself.

"Granted" all these things — that "each picture is a glass" and "the walls are mirrors multiplied" —

. . . It comes to this:
That the guerilla I should be booked
And bound. . . .
. . . Academies
As of a tragic science should arise.

In these academies the poet should conceive "the diviner health / Disclosed in common forms." For "Poet," he says: "We are conceived in your conceits." The command is one that Stevens himself is carrying out. His poetry is just such an academy of the self.

He continues his examination of resemblances in "The Glass of Water":

That the glass would melt in heat,
That the water would freeze in cold,
Shows that this object is merely a state,
One of many, between two poles. So,
In the metaphysical, there are these poles.

Here in the centre stands the glass. Light
Is the lion that comes down to drink. There
And in that state, the glass is a pool.
Ruddy are his eyes and ruddy are his claws
When light comes down to wet his frothy jaws

And in the water winding weeds move round.
And there and in another state — the refractions,
The *metaphysica,* the plastic parts of poems
Crash in the mind — But, fat Jocundus, worrying
About what stands here in the centre, not the glass,

But in the centre of our lives, this time, this day,
Is a state, this spring among the politicians
Playing cards. In a village of the indigenes,
One would have still to discover. Among the dogs
and dung,
One would continue to contend with one's ideas.

The poet is one of the states he is describing. Resemblances are contained within resemblances, like a nest of boxes. The nature of the poet is the nature of man. Poetry, a fiction, is true in that it is our native method of grasping reality.

He carries this further in "Add This to Rhetoric":

> It is posed and it is posed.
> But in nature it merely grows.
> Stones pose in the falling night;
> And beggars dropping to sleep,
> They pose themselves and their rags.
> Shucks . . . lavender moonlight falls.

The moonlight has ruined the beggars' calculated effect. So the poet's calculations, in his poems, are constantly modified by incursions; details that will not yield to his intentions. These intrusions are to be thought of as assertions of exterior reality. Stevens seems to be building his poems up, before our eyes, out of just such surprises; his calculations might be called the setting of a trap for them. Sometimes the trap catches only a fragment. At other times the trap is itself entrapped:

> Tomorrow when the sun,
> For all its images,
> Comes up as the sun, bull fire,
> Your images will have left
> No shadow of themselves.

This is an irony of ironies. Stevens uses the conclusive image, "bull fire," to prove his contention that all images are inconclusive. They are inadequate to a final seizure of reality. But they are inescapable; not just necessary to thought; they *are* the action of thought. We cannot approach "raw nature" because at every point our own images, our own fictions, intervene. To say "raw nature" or to say "sun" is to employ such a fiction. But the more deliberate our fictions, the more we are driven to an apprehension, almost a sensation, of unseizable reality.

Reality thought of in this way, as it might be by a Zen-Buddhist, becomes an apprehension behind all apprehensions, a figment of figments; something sensed as unchangeable behind all change.

Now reversing himself, looking for an image of stability — a stability that endures through all change and yet is created *by* change — Stevens arrives at the image of the dump. He revolves this image in one of his finest poems, "The Man on the Dump":

Day creeps down. The moon is creeping up.
The sun is a corbeil of flowers the moon Blanche
Places there, a bouquet. Ho-ho . . . The dump is full
Of images. Days pass like papers from a press.
The bouquets come here in the papers. So the sun,
And so the moon, both come, and the janitor's poems
Of every day, the wrapper on the can of pears,
The cat in the paper-bag, the corset, the box
From Esthonia: the tiger chest, for tea.

The freshness of night has been fresh a long time.
The freshness of morning, the blowing of day, one says
That it puffs as Cornelius Nepos reads, it puffs
More than, less than or it puffs like this or that.
The green smacks in the eye, the dew in the green
Smacks like fresh water in a can, like the sea
On a cocoanut — how many men have copied dew
For buttons, how many women have covered themselves
With dew, dew dresses, stones and chains of dew, heads
Of the floweriest flowers dewed with the dewiest dew.
One grows to hate these things except on the dump.

Now, in the time of spring (azaleas, trilliums,
Myrtle, viburnums, daffodils, blue phlox),
Between that disgust and this, between the things
That are on the dump (azaleas and so on)
And those that will be (azaleas and so on),
One feels the purifying change. One rejects
The trash.

That's the moment when the moon creeps up
To the bubbling of bassoons. That's the time
One looks at the elephant-colorings of tires.

Everything is shed; and the moon comes up as the moon
(All its images are in the dump) and you see
As a man (not like an image of a man),
You see the moon rise in the empty sky.

One sits and beats an old tin can, lard pail.
One beats and beats for that which one believes.
That's what one wants to get near. Could it after all
Be merely oneself, as superior as the ear
To a crow's voice? Did the nightingale torture the ear,
Pack the heart and scratch the mind? And does the ear
Solace itself in peevish birds? Is it peace,
Is it a philosopher's honeymoon, one finds
On the dump? Is it to sit among mattresses of the dead,
Bottles, pots, shoes and grass and murmur *aptest eve*:
Is it to hear the blatter of grackles and say
Invisible priest; is it to eject, to pull
The day to pieces and cry *stanza my stone?*
Where was it one first heard of the truth? The the.

Having discarded the appearances, the images, as trash, he has arrived at an ultimate idea of reality: the *the*; the thinnest *mi* of idea. Even this is an image, this trashcan; an ultimate fiction. Consequently his next move, in "On the Road Home," is to pitch this out too, in order to return to appearances; the substance of reality:

It was when I said,
"There is no such thing as the truth,"
That the grapes seemed fatter.
The fox ran out of his hole.

2

The reciprocating action of reason and observation plays through his poems. He denies the one in order to isolate the sensation of the other. As "The Latest Freed Man" he is "Tired of the old descriptions of the world."

> "I suppose there is
> A doctrine to this landscape. Yet, having just
> Escaped from the truth, the morning is color and mist,
> Which is enough . . ."

His new description of the world is: "To be without a description of to be." "It was everything bulging and blazing and big in itself." And in "A Rabbit as King of the Ghosts" he captures the basking sensation of this self, a rabbit at evening forgetting its danger: "the cat slopping its milk all day."

> And to feel that the light is a rabbit-light,
> In which everything is meant for you
>
> . . . .
>
> A self that touches all edges,
>
> You become a self that fills the four corners of night.
> The red cat hides away in the fur-light
> And there you are humped high, humped up,
>
> You are humped higher and higher, black as stone—
> You sit with your head like a carving in space
> And the little green cat is a bug in the grass.

Although his thinking leads him continually toward it, he continually evades the fallacy of finality. His poems, in their play and resolution of opposites, would appear to support an Hegelian dialectic. But that too is a fiction. He says, in "Connoisseur of Chaos":

> I
>
> A. A violent order is disorder; and
> B. A great disorder is an order. These
> Two things are one. (Pages of illustrations.)

II

If all the green of spring was blue, and it is;
If the flowers of South Africa were bright
On the tables of Connecticut, and they are;
If Englishmen lived without tea in Ceylon, and they do;
And if it all went on in an orderly way,
And it does; a law of inherent opposites,
Of essential unity, is as pleasant as port,
As pleasant as the brush-strokes of a bough,
An upper, particular bough in, say, Marchand.

III

After all the pretty contrast of life and death
Proves that these opposite things partake of one,
At least that was the theory, when bishops' books
Resolved the world. We cannot go back to that.
The squirming facts exceed the squamous mind,
If one may say so. And yet relation appears,
A small relation expanding like the shade
Of a cloud on sand, a shape on the side of a hill.

IV

A. Well, an old order is a violent one.
This proves nothing. Just one more truth, one more
Element in the immense disorder of truths.
B. It is April as I write. The wind
Is blowing after days of constant rain.
All this, of course, will come to summer soon.
But suppose the disorder of truths should ever come
To an order, most Plantagenet, most fixed. . .
A great disorder is an order. Now, A
And B are not like statuary, posed
For a vista in the Louvre. They are things chalked
On the sidewalk so that the pensive man may see.

V.

The pensive man. . . He sees that eagle float
For which the intricate Alps are a single nest.

The pensive man, the mind that divides chaos into A and B and attempts to resolve them, is himself part of the relation he observes. He cannot observe all around it, for the very observation creates a new horizon; a new ring around himself, like the growth of a tree. These rings become wider and wider. They do not expand to infinity, which would be *mere* idea; but they get stronger apprehensions of it; of "that eagle . . . For which the intricate Alps is a single nest."

The imagination as a continuous activity tends to go in alternating directions. From a fictional heaven it looks back to earth, in section IV of "The Blue Buildings in the Summer Air":

Look down now, Cotton Mather, from the blank.
Was heaven where you thought? It must be there.
It must be where you think it is, in the light
On bed-clothes, in an apple on a plate.
It is the honey-comb of the seeing man.
It is the leaf the bird brings back to the boat.

In "Life on a Battleship" Stevens' expanding and contracting metaphysics defines and exalts the individual. He takes as theme the totalitarian concept of imposed unity. The "rape of the bourgeoisie" has been accomplished; the war between classes has ended. What is the next step in this classless society? As the captain of the conquering gunboat, *The Masculine,* explains, it will be "the war between individuals."

"... In time,
When earth has become a paradise, it will be
A paradise full of assassins. Suppose I seize
The ship, make it my own and, bit by bit,
Seize yards and docks, machinery and men,
As others have, and then, unlike the others,
Instead of building ships, in numbers, build

A single ship, a cloud on the sea, the largest
Possible machine, a divinity of steel,
Of which I am captain. . . ."

This ship, symbol of the triumph of "solidarity" and the "final conflict," would be "the centre of the world." The world's ruler would be the captain. And

" . . . the sorrow of the world, except
As man is natural, would be at an end."

The captain draws up "rules of the world," the first being: "The grand simplifications reduce / Themselves to one." The ship, the totalitarian idea, having prevailed, is a law unto itself. Might is right. *The Masculine* is

. . . life compressed
Into its own illustration, a divinity
Like any other, rex by right of the crown,
The jewels in his beard, the mystic wand . . .

Such a justification, says Stevens, does not go far enough. A true simplification exists everywhere, not needing to impose itself. The divinity of self-asserted divinities — kings, laws, *The Masculine* — is pretended.

. . . But if
It is the absolute why must it be
This immemorial grandiose, why not
A cockle-shell, a trivial emblem great
With its final force, a thing invincible
In more than phrase? There's the true masculine,
The spirit's ring and seal, the naked heart.

The captain's second rule is that "The part / Is the equal of the whole." It is interesting to observe that the rules the captain draws up correspond in principle to what Stevens believes. What he is showing is their false application. The captain takes his second rule to mean that he alone is the equal of the whole; the dictator's justification.

But by trying to prove it, he disproves it. For it is simply true, not just for him, but for every other part; every other "I."

"This is a thing to twang a philosopher's sleep . . .

. . . .

On *The Masculine* one asserts and fires the guns.
But one lives to think of this growing, this pushing life,
The vine, at the roots, this vine of Key West, splurging,
Covered one morning with blue, one morning with white,
Coming from the East, forcing itself to the West,
The jungle of tropical part and tropical whole."

The two rules are resolved in a third: "The whole cannot exist without / The parts." To destroy any part is, then, to destroy the whole: "The gunman of the commune / Kills the commune."

Captain, high captain, how is it, now,
With our affair, our destiny, our hash?
Your guns are not rhapsodic strophes, red
And true. . . .

Stevens has defined the function of myth in the act of creating it. It is necessary to imagine a heaven, a divine authority, in order to return the conception to ourselves; to learn that we cannot arrive at the "ultimate simplification." What we can learn and be ruled by is our own good – which is not only part of the "ultimate simplification" but creates it. "Our fate is our own."

One of the clearest statements of the poet's intentions occurs in number XIV of "Variations on a Summer Day":

Words add to the senses. The words for the dazzle
Of mica, the dithering of grass,
The Arachne integument of dead trees,
Are the eye grown larger, more intense.

This has to do with the devices of immediacy that punctuate Stevens' poems; the onomatopoeia of "Chome! clicks the clock"; his translations of sight-patterns into sound-patterns: "The shiddow-shaddow of light revolving"; his equations between sensations and ideas: "The moon follows the sun like a French / Translation of a Russian poet." It relates such immediacies of detail to a larger, more inclusive immediacy.

"Of Modern Poetry" defines and exhibits this. The poem is itself the act of writing the poem; the act of apprehension along with what is being apprehended:

> The poem of the mind in the act of finding
> What will suffice. It has not always had
> To find: the scene was set; it repeated what
> Was in the script.
>   Then the theatre was changed
> To something else. Its past was a souvenir.
>
> It has to be living, to learn the speech of the place.
> It has to face the men of the time and to meet
> The women of the time. It has to think about war
> And it has to find what will suffice. It has
> To construct a new stage. It has to be on that stage
> And, like an insatiable actor, slowly and
> With meditation, speak words that in the ear,
> In the delicatest ear of the mind, repeat,
> Exactly, that which it wants to hear, at the sound
> Of which, an invisible audience listens,
> Not to the play, but to itself, expressed
> In an emotion as of two people, as of two
> Emotions becoming one. The actor is
> A metaphysician in the dark, twanging
> An instrument, twanging a wiry string that gives
> Sounds passing through sudden rightnesses, wholly
> Containing the mind, below which it cannot descend,
> Beyond which it has no will to rise.
>   It must
> Be the finding of a satisfaction, and may
> Be of a man skating, a woman dancing, a woman
> Combing. The poem of the act of the mind.

In "Arrival at the Waldorf" the hotel and Guatemala are symbols for the opposite poles of poetry: reality and imagination. Which is the real and which the imaginary? One makes trips between them. Arrived back at the Waldorf, "You touch the hotel the way you touch moonlight . . . After that alien, point-blank, green and actual Guatemala."

"Landscape with Boat" satirizes Stevens' own proclivity for pushing thought to the verge of abstraction:

> He brushed away the thunder, then the clouds,
> Then the collossal illusion of heaven. Yet still
> The sky was blue. He wanted imperceptible air.

Parodying the logical development and conjectural mannerisms of philosophy, he searches the *locus* of truth:

> . . . If
> It was nowhere else, it was there and because
> It was nowhere else, its place had to be supposed,
> Itself had to be supposed, a thing supposed
> In a place supposed . . .
>
> . . . .
>
> He never supposed
> That he might be truth, himself, or part of it,
> That the things that he rejected might be part
> And the irregular turquoise, part, the perceptible blue
> Grown denser, part, the eye so touched, so played
> Upon by clouds, the ear so magnified
> By thunder, parts, and all these things together,
> Parts, and more things, parts. . . .
>
> . . . .
>
> Had he been better able to suppose:
> He might sit on a sofa on a balcony
> Above the Mediterranean, emerald
> Becoming emeralds. He might watch the palms
> Flap green ears in the heat. He might observe

A yellow wine and follow a steamer's track
And say, "The thing I hum appears to be
The rhythm of this celestial pantomime."

So in "Extracts from Addresses to the Academy of Fine Ideas" he comes to the thesis, supported by brilliant illustrations, "The false and true are one." This begins a series of examinations: into the idea of evil ("The good is evil's last invention"); of a religion of all men ("The lean cats of the arches of the churches, / That's the old world. In the new, all men are priests"); the distinction between reality and abstraction ("That difference between the and an") which is like the difference between spring and winter, water and ice; of the clash of ideas in "the mass of meaning" and of the one idea that prevails ("the assassin that remains and sings / In the high imagination, triumphantly"); of the quality of belief ("Ecstatic identities / Between one's self and the weather"); and of the "stanzas of final peace" that in a time of war "lie in the heart's residuum":

If earth dissolves
Its evil after death, it dissolves it while
We live. . . .

. . . .

Behold the men in helmets borne on steel,
Discolored, how they are going to defeat.

"Examination of the Hero in a Time of War" revolves, in unrhymed sonnets, our ideas and emotions concerning the hero. He is eccentric; yet he shares what is common to all, the common fortune

. . . induced by nothing,
Unwished for, chance, the merest riding
Of the wind, rain in a dry September,
The improvisations of the cuckoos
In a clock-shop. . . .

We have to believe in him. Therefore "devise" him. "Make him of mud." There have been classic heroes.

And there are many bourgeois heroes.
There are more heroes than marbles of them.
The marbles are pinchings of an idea,
Yet there is that idea behind the marbles,
The idea of things for public gardens,
Of men suited to public ferns. . . .

The hero, then, is not a person. And if not, "the emblem / Of him . . . seems / To stand taller than a person stands." But he is not an image:

The hero is a feeling, a man seen
As if the eye was an emotion,
As if in seeing we saw our feeling
In the object seen and saved that mystic
Against the sight, the penetrating,
Pure eye. Instead of allegory,
We have and are the man, capable
Of his brave quickenings, the human
Accelerations that seem inhuman.

Stevens' hero recalls the "portent" that sprawled "high up in heaven." Like the future, he is "a cloud no larger than a man's hand." Both are in our hands when our ideas of them, like our ideas of the divine, return to where they originated: in ourselves. The rôle of the poet is to clarify this recognition.

V

The Grandest Metaphor

INCREASINGLY DOMINANT, Stevens' theme of the human origin of ideas of divinity is carried further, in *Transport to Summer,* by "Chocorua to Its Neighbor," a meditation on the distinctions between forms (mountains) and aggregates (cities and armies):

> To say more than human things with human voice,
> That cannot be; to say human things with more
> Than human voice, that, also, cannot be;
> To speak humanly from the height or from the depth
> Of human things, that is acutest speech.

Man's lot is a continual lifting of his bootstraps by means of what Eliot has called "the high dream." Where Eliot seems to emphasize the cleavage between the dream and the bootstrap, Stevens isolates and criticizes each in order to show their necessary connection. He says in "Crude Foyer":

Thought is false happiness: the idea
That merely by thinking one can,
Or may, penetrate, not may,
But can, that one is sure to be able—

That there lies at the end of thought
A foyer of the spirit in a landscape
Of the mind, in which we sit
And wear humanity's bleak crown . . .

This, again, defines by example. The desire for finality is a universal wish. It is shared by the reader, who reads "the critique of paradise" and says "it is the work / Of a comedian, this critique." It is shared by the poet, or he should not have the awareness of its

False happiness, since we know that we use
Only the eye as faculty, that the mind
Is the eye, and that this landscape of the mind

Is a landscape only of the eye . . .

Another "poem of the act of the mind," its ripples of criticism widen to criticize itself, the very act of the mind that composed it. The shifting qualifications of thought form the rhythms of the poem: "by thinking one can, / Or may, penetrate, not may, / But can, that one is sure to be able—."

That such awarenesses of awareness, constantly returning on themselves, do not end in the despair of utter futility, is evidence of the delight Stevens takes in living; in its continuous alternation of movement and balance. Each of his insights is the prelude, the "crude foyer," to another. Having pushed too far into the realm of abstraction, his ideas, stripped of everything but themselves, perceive their own non-existence except as re-entrances into life.

We are ignorant men incapable
Of the least, minor, vital metaphor, content,
At last, there, when it turns out to be here.

His delight is the delight in being human; of pushing consciousness to the point of being conscious of what it cannot be conscious of. In "Esthétique Du Mal" he extracts a delight from evil, pain and suffering; not because they are evil, but because their experience is part of the experience of full consciousness. As he says near the beginning:

> Except for us, Vesuvius might consume
> In solid fire the utmost earth and know
> No pain (ignoring the cocks that crow us up
> To die). This is a part of the sublime
> From which we shrink. And yet, except for us,
> The total past felt nothing when destroyed.

One of the limitations of consciousness is to conceive of everything in its own terms. So god, the unknown, becomes the man-god. Heaven and hell, conjectural realms, realize themselves in a heaven-hell on earth:

> His firm stanzas hang like hives in hell
> Or what hell was, since now both heaven and hell
> Are one, and here, O terra infidel.
>
> The fault lies with an over-human god,
> Who by sympathy has made himself a man . . .

"False engagements of the mind" cause the "fault" that "Falls out on everything." To be is, inescapably, to be human; although that includes wanting to be more than human. The phrases "Be near me, come closer, touch my hand,"

> . . . phrases
> Compounded of dear relation, spoken twice,
> Once by the lips, once by the services
> Of central sense, these minutiae mean more
> Than clouds, benevolences, distant heads.

Yet we retain "damasked memories" of "the golden forms, / Before we were wholly human and knew ourselves." We are, then, eminently ourselves; yet our selves, of their very nature, share in all creation. We share the imperfections of the sun:

> The sun, in clownish yellow, but not a clown,
> Brings the day to perfection and then fails. He dwells
> In a consummate prime, yet still desires
> A further consummation. For the lunar month
> He makes the tenderest research, intent
> On a transmutation which, when seen, appears
> To be askew. And space is filled with his
> Rejected years. . . .

In consciousness each of us shares in everyone else. We share the soldier's death:

> How red the rose that is the soldier's wound,
> The wounds of many soldiers, the wounds of all
> The soldiers that have fallen, red in blood,
> The soldier of time grown deathless in great size.
>
> . . . .
>
> A woman smoothes her forehead with her hand
> And the soldier of time lies calm beneath that stroke.

In contrast with the concrete symbols of the past, our modern notions of evil are abstract:

> The death of Satan was a tragedy
> For the imagination. A capital
> Negation destroyed him in his tenement
> And, with him, many blue phenomena.

He was killed off, not by a "Julian thunder-cloud," but by a simple act of negation: "He was denied." The phantoms of our thought, departing, have left a blank in our thinking:

> . . . How cold the vacancy
> When the phantoms are gone and the shaken realist
> First sees reality. . . .

But vacuums, even of the imagination, are to be filled:

> The tragedy, however, may have begun,
> Again in the imagination's new beginning,
> In the yes of the realist spoken because he must
> Say yes, spoken because under every no
> Lay a passion for yes that had never been broken.

We require "Another chant, an incantation, as in / Another and later genesis." This will be found, not by a return to the discarded symbols, the "nostalgias," but in the pursuit of "The softest woman, / Because she is as she was, reality . . . " It is "the last nostalgia" to believe that reality can ever be explained and finally understood. "Life is a bitter aspic." Suffering, pain and evil are integral parts of it; inseparable even from the coldest utilitarianism: "At dawn / The paratroopers fall and as they fall / They mow the lawn." Revolution – that "affair of logical lunatics," imposing their single idea – cannot banish evil. Life is, after all, the activity of living:

> The greatest poverty is not to live
> In a physical world, to feel that one's desire
> Is too difficult to tell from despair. Perhaps,
> After death, the non-physical people, in paradise,
> Itself non-physical, may, by chance, observe
> The green corn gleaming and experience
> The minor of what we feel. . . .
>
> . . . .
>
> This is the thesis scrivened in delight,
> The reverberating psalm, the right chorale.
>
> . . . .
>
> And out of what one sees and hears and out
> Of what one feels, who could have thought to make
> So many selves, so many sensuous worlds,
> As if the air, the mid-day air, was swarming
> With the metaphysical changes that occur,
> Merely in living as and where we live.

Our hope cannot lie in the bed of the past, wanting the return of its ghosts, he says in "The Bed of Old John Zeller":

> This structure of ideas, these ghostly sequences
> Of the mind, result only in disaster. . . .

We add to the disaster if we simply substitute another structure, with "other ghostly sequences."

> This is the habit of wishing, as if one's grandfather lay
> In one's heart and wished as he had always wished, unable
>
> To sleep in that bed for its disorder, talking of ghostly
> Sequences that would be sleep and ting-tang tossing . . .

The very bed, the jangling of its springs, entered into their ghostly cogitations. From this we learn, what is "more difficult":

> . . . to accept the structure
> Of things as the structure of ideas. It was the structure
> Of things at least that was thought of in the old peak of night.

"Less and Less Human, O Savage Spirit" must be our conception of divinity, if we must have one:

> If there must be a god in the house, must be,
> Saying things in the rooms and on the stair,
>
> Let him move as the sunlight moves on the floor,
> Or moonlight, silently . . .
>
> . . . .
>
> It is the human that is the alien,
> The human that has no cousin in the moon.
>
> It is the human that demands his speech
> From beasts or from the incommunicable mass.

If there must be a god in the house, let him be one
That will not hear us when we speak: a coolness,

A vermilioned nothingness, any stick of the mass
Of which we are too distantly a part.

To pass from skepticism to deliberate fiction, created myth, he says in "The Pure Good of Theory," is to realize the essence of faith:

To say the solar chariot is junk

Is not a variation but an end.
Yet to speak of the whole world as metaphor
Is still to stick to the contents of the mind

And the desire to believe in a metaphor.
It is to stick to the nicer knowledge of
Belief, that what it believes in is not true.

The prayer of "Flyer's Fall" is one of the forms of this worship:

This man escaped the dirty fates,
Knowing that he did nobly, as he died.

Darkness, nothingness of human after-death,
Receive and keep him in the deepnesses of space—

Profundum, physical thunder, dimension in which
We believe without belief, beyond belief.

"Description Without Place" interweaves ideas and sounds, *seems* and *is*. Seemings become being. The actual world is flowing out of the ideas of Nietzsche and Lenin. But the activity does not end there:

Things are as they seemed to Calvin or to Anne
Of England, to Pablo Neruda in Ceylon,

To Nietzsche in Basel, to Lenin by a lake.
But the integrations of the past are like

A *Museo Olimpico,* so much
So little, our affair, which is the affair

Of the possible: seemings that are to be,
Seemings that it is possible may be.

These are the "potential seemings, arrogant / To be, as on the youngest poet's page." "Description is revelation. . . . Thus the theory of description matters most."

It is the theory of the word for those

For whom the word is the making of the world,
The buzzing world and lisping firmament.

"Two Tales of Liadoff" is an allegory of the actual and the ideal. Civilization is a rocket into which the townspeople crowd, touch the fuse and take off. The rocket crosses the path of a dead musician.

Do you remember how the rocket went on
And on, at night, exploding finally
In an ovation of resplendent forms—

Ovation on ovation of large blue men
In pantaloons of fire and of women hatched,
Like molten citizens of the vacuum?

Do you remember the children there like wicks,
That constantly sparkled their small gold? The town
Had crowded into the rocket and touched the fuse.

That night, Liadoff, a long time after his death,
At a piano in a cloud sat practicing,
On a black piano practiced epi-tones.

Do you remember what the townsmen said,
As they fell down, as they heard Liadoff's cloud
And its tragical, its haunted arpeggios?

And is it true that what they said, as they fell,
Was repeated by Liadoff in a narration
Of incredible colors ex, ex and ex and out?

The interaction is conveyed by the design of the poem. Everything is turning into everything else. The visual effects of the rocket, its repeated bursts and fallings-away, are reproduced in the syllables of the reiterated word "ovation." The people are the rocket from which they are scattered – its "resplendent forms" – and the "large blue" sky against which they appear.

The rocket of civilization, exploding, follows the arc of the musician's inspiration. An ambiguity in time conveys an ambiguity in the relationship of art to life. Do we repeat, in mass disaster, the tragic inspiration of the artist? Or was his inspiration – as William Blake said it was – truly prophetic? Is the spirit of the musician seated *now* in the cloud, repeating the speech of the falling townsmen? Either way, their explosive mysteries have become identical: "ex, ex and ex and out."

This first half of the poem has isolated the moment at which the actual world becomes epic. It is on the *return* from disaster that the townspeople begin to speak. They are conscious *after* the fact.

In the second half, Stevens isolates the moment at which the epic foretells the actual. Liadoff's inspiration, his personal rocket, has projected him into an ether where no communicable speech is possible. His "epi-tones" signalize a change in direction; a return from that abstract realm toward the reality of human feelings.

The feeling of Liadoff was changed. It is
The instant of the change that was the poem,
When the cloud pressed suddenly the whole return

From thought, like a violent pulse in the cloud itself,
As if Liadoff no longer remained a ghost
And, being straw, turned green, lived backward, shared

The fantastic fortune of fantastic blood,
Until his body smothered him, until
His being felt the need of soaring, the need

Of air . . . But then that cloud, that piano placed
Just where it was, oh beau caboose . . . It was part
Of the instant to perceive, after the shock,

That the rocket was only an inferior cloud.
There was no difference between the town
And him. Both wanted the same thing. Both sought

His epi-tones, the colors of the ear,
The sounds that soon become a voluble speech —
Voluble but archaic and hard to hear.

"His epi-tones, the colors of the ear," reinforces and resolves the relationship between townspeople and musician, by reversing "an ovation of resplendent forms." This prose interpretation can hope only to point to a few of the interior relationships. At each return to the poem we discover new meanings, until we approach that condition of total rapport in which they seem to flow into us through the senses. As he says in "Man Carrying Thing":

The poem must resist the intelligence
Almost successfully. Illustration:

A brune figure in winter evening resists
Identity. . . .

If some poems explode like rockets, others quietly merge. Their desire is to encompass life by losing themselves in it — almost. This is quite opposite from wanting to depict it literally. The attitude, and the images chosen, are Chinese.

But the impulse toward a literal depiction is never far absent. There is constant tension between imagined fact and imagined imagination. "Credences of Summer" muses on maturity and the poems of maturity:

Postpone the anatomy of summer, as
The physical pine, the metaphysical pine.

Let's see the very thing and nothing else.
Let's see it with the hottest fire of sight.
Burn everything not part of it to ash.

Trace the gold sun about the whitened sky
Without evasion by a single metaphor.
Look at it in its essential barrenness
And say this, this is the centre that I seek.
Fix it in an eternal foliage

And fill the foliage with arrested peace,
Joy of such permanence, right ignorance
Of change still possible. Exile desire
For what is not. This is the barrenness
Of the fertile thing that can attain no more.

2

Stevens' poems are constant preparation for poems to come. So it is as if all he has so far written has been to lead up to his "Notes Toward a Supreme Fiction." Stevens' re-creation of myth is "an end and a beginning"; his myth a preparation for myth.

Here, as before that Academy of Fine Ideas in full assembly, he discourses fluently on the central problems of poetry and belief. The myths that have come down to us do not suffice, since we no longer "believe" them. We either deny or make dogma of them; both pretensions to "knowledge."

For faith to be reanimated, the myth to come must fulfill three conditions, which form the three divisions of the poem. It must be a going beyond what we know: "It Must Be Abstract." It cannot be final or conclusive: "It Must Change." And, like any other work of art: "It Must Give Pleasure."

Inventing an imaginary world, an idol of reality, we enlarge our ideas of reality; a true form of worship.

> . . . The sun
> Must bear no name, gold flourisher, but be
> In the difficulty of what it is to be.

It is our nature to expand by contradiction. If we determine to worship the sun, the true sun, the sun beyond and behind all names for the sun, we are impelled in the next breath to name it: "bull fire"; "gold flourisher." Naming it, we come that much closer to an apprehension of its nameless qualities:

> It is the celestial ennui of apartments
> That sends us back to the first idea, the quick
> Of this invention; and yet so poisonous
>
> Are the ravishments of truth, so fatal to
> The truth itself, the first idea becomes
> The hermit in a poet's metaphors,
>
> Who comes and goes and comes and goes all day.
> May there be an ennui of the first idea?
> What else, prodigious scholar, should there be?

This hermit, this first idea, this fiction

> . . . knows that what it has is what is not
> And throws it away like a thing of another time,
> As morning throws off stale moonlight and shabby sleep.

The poem, says Stevens, "refreshes life so that we share, / For a moment, the first idea." Should this fiction include an idea of deity, "the giant of the weather"?

> It feels good as it is without the giant,
> A thinker of the first idea. Perhaps
> The truth depends on a walk around a lake,
>
> A composing as the body tires, a stop
> To see hepatica, a stop to watch
> The definition growing certain and

A wait within that certainty, a rest
In the swags of pine-trees bordering the lake.
Perhaps there are times of inherent excellence,

As when the cock crows on the left and all
Is well, incalculable balances,
At which a kind of Swiss perfection comes

And a familiar music of the machine
Sets up its Schwärmerei, not balances
That we achieve but balances that happen,

As a man and woman meet and love forthwith.
Perhaps there are moments of awakening,
Extreme, fortuitous, personal, in which

We more than awaken, sit on the edge of sleep,
As on an elevation, and behold
The academies like structures in a mist.

The music of poetry is the prayer and proper speech of this worship:

The romantic intoning, the declaimed clairvoyance
Are parts of apotheosis, appropriate
And of its nature, the idiom thereof.

They differ from reason's click-clack, its applied
Enflashings. . . .

Never has "reason" — the "applied enflashings," for example, of such criticism as I am now writing — been more roundly nor more justly put in its place. This first section concludes with "the major abstraction": "the idea of man," central to man's worship. MacCullough, "the major man," is only part, "Though an heroic part," of this abstraction.

The major abstraction is the commonal,
The inanimate, difficult visage. Who is it?

What rabbi, grown furious with human wish,
What chieftan, walking by himself, crying
Most miserable, most victorious,

Does not see these separate figures one by one,
And yet see only one, in his old coat,
His slouching pantaloons, beyond the town,

Looking for what was, where it used to be?
Cloudless the morning. It is he. The man
In that old coat, those sagging pantaloons,

It is of him, ephebe, to make, to confect
The final elegance, not to console
Nor sanctify, but plainly to propound.

"It Must Change": the myth must be a continuous creation. Its forms cannot be fixed: "The seraph / Is satyr in Saturn, according to his thoughts."

The President ordains the bee to be
Immortal. The President ordains. But does
The body lift its heavy wing, take up,

Again, an inexhaustible being, rise
Over the loftiest antagonist
To drone the green phrases of its juvenal?

What has happened to past ideas of permanence? What of the statue?

The great statue of the General Du Puy
Rested immobile, though neighboring catafalques
Bore off the residents of its noble Place.

The right, uplifted foreleg of the horse
Suggested that, at the final funeral,
The music halted and the horse stood still.

On Sundays, lawyers in their promenades
Approached this strongly-heightened effigy
To study the past, and doctors, having bathed

Themselves with care, sought out the nerveless frame
Of a suspension, a permanence, so rigid
That it made the General a bit absurd,

Changed his true flesh to an inhuman bronze.
There never had been, never could be, such
A man. The lawyers disbelieved, the doctors

Said that as keen, illustrious ornament,
As setting for geraniums, the General,
The very Place Du Puy, in fact, belonged

Among our more vestigial states of mind.
Nothing had happened because nothing had changed.
Yet the General was rubbish in the end.

What is the principle of change?

Two things of opposite natures seem to depend
On one another, as a man depends
On a woman, day on night, the imagined

On the real. This is the origin of change.

. . . .

And North and South are an intrinsic couple
And sun and rain a plural, like two lovers
That walk away as one in the greenest body.

These opposites not only attract, but merge with each other:

The partaker partakes of that which changes him.
The child that touches takes character from the thing,
The body, it touches. The captain and his men

Are one and the sailor and the sea are one.
Follow after, O my companion, my fellow, my self,
Sister and solace, brother and delight.

The apostrophe has gayer implications than Eliot's quotation, in *The Waste Land,* of Baudelaire: "You! hypocrite lecteur! — mon semblable, — mon frère!" Eliot's readers are companions in evil. His nightingale sings " 'jug jug' to dirty ears." Stevens proposes a rounder affinity:

Bethou me, said sparrow, to the crackled blade,
And you, and you, bethou me as you blow,
When in my coppice you behold me be.

Ah, ké! The bloody wren, the felon jay,
Ké-ké, the jug-throated robin pouring out,
Bethou, bethou, bethou me in my glade.

This recalls his command to the poet in "Mozart": "Be thou the voice, / Not you. Be thou, be thou . . . " In its present context "bethou" has become metaphor. Birdsong and what it expresses are one. So for the poet the machinery of his poem becomes the poem; a motion of ideas and images, of idea-images and imaginary ideas. Stevens' poetry plays a game of living statues, whirling and freezing, freezing and whirling. His poems combine the attitudes taken, with the whirl from attitude to attitude; the kaleidoscope, and the kaleidoscope shaken. Rather mockingly he had said, in "The Pleasures of Merely Circulating" (in *Ideas of Order*):

The garden flew round with the angel,
The angel flew round with the clouds,
And the clouds flew round and the clouds flew round
And the clouds flew round with the clouds.

Is there any secret in skulls,
The cattle skulls in the woods?
Do the drummers in black hoods
Rumble anything out of their drums?

Mrs. Anderson's Swedish baby
Might well have been German or Spanish,
Yet that things go round and again go round
Has rather a classical sound.

Now he relates this more seriously to another circularity:

The poem goes from the poet's gibberish to
The gibberish of the vulgate and back again.
Does it move to and fro or is it of both

At once? Is it a luminous flittering
Or the concentration of a cloudy day?

What is it the poet seeks?

It is the gibberish of the vulgate that he seeks.
He tries by a peculiar speech to speak

The peculiar potency of the general
To compound the imagination's Latin with
The lingua franca et jocundissima.

We are reminded of Eliot's "the formal word" and "the common word" which "move in concorde" in the stately measures of *Four Quartets.* Stevens' measures combine stateliness and gaiety, in the humorous implications of his language. The dead language of his imagination is revived by an everyday vulgate.

He is still a frequenter of parks:

A bench was his catalepsy, Theatre
Of Trope. He sat in the park. The water of
The lake was full of artificial things . . .

. . . .

Of these beginnings, gay and green, propose
The suitable amours. Time will write them down.

"It Must Give Pleasure" opens with an ironic distinction between easy and difficult delights:

> To sing jubilas at exact, accustomed times,
> To be crested and wear the mane of a multitude
> And so, as part, to exult with its great throat,
>
> To speak of joy and to sing of it, borne on
> The shoulders of joyous men, to feel the heart
> That is the common, the bravest fundament,
>
> This is a facile exercise. . . .
>
> . . . .
>
> But the difficultest rigor is forthwith,
> On the image of what we see, to catch from that
>
> Irrational moment its unreasoning,
> As when the sun comes rising, when the sea
> Clears deeply, when the moon hangs on the wall
>
> Of heaven-haven. These are not things transformed.
> Yet we are shaken by them as if they were.
> We reason about them with a later reason.

The tribute to Hopkins in "heaven-haven" testifies to Stevens' sense of the religious quality of everyday experience. The great Jesuit poet, for all his "jubilas at exact, accustomed times," celebrated most in his poems the image of what he saw, the unreasoning delight of the "irrational moment."

At such moments customary events of the sun, of the sea, of the moon, come to us with an effect of transformation. But, says Stevens, they are not really transformed. They are only truly perceived then; perceived by the whole man as, in "A Dish of Peaches in Russia" (in *Parts of a World*), he had said: "With my whole body I taste these peaches."

It is the perceptions that heighten and diminish. At heightened moments we receive, with immediacy, a full impact. It is at diminished moments that we supply the notion of transformation. We "reason about them with a later reason."

Recognized as fiction, such reasoning contributes to our further awareness. Taken as "the truth," it imposes its fallacies:

. . . to impose is not
To discover. To discover an order as of
A season, to discover summer and know it,

To discover winter and know it well, to find,
Not to impose, not to have reasoned at all,
Out of nothing to have come on major weather,

It is possible, possible, possible. It must
Be possible. It must be that in time
The real will from its crude compoundings come,

Seeming, at first, a beast disgorged, unlike,
Warmed by a desperate milk. To find the real,
To be stripped of every fiction except one,

The fiction of an absolute — Angel,
Be silent in your luminous cloud and hear
The luminous melody of proper sound.

"What am I to believe?" he asks. Is the Angel real, or do I imagine him. "Is it he or is it I that experience it?" The question is rhetorical, irrelevant, so long as there is

. . . an hour
Filled with expressible bliss, in which I have

No need, am happy, forget need's golden hand,
Am satisfied without solacing majesty,
And if there is an hour there is a day,

There is a month, a year, there is a time
In which majesty is a mirror of the self . . .

Like the repetitions of the birds, "these things at least comprise," he says:

> An occupation, an exercise, a work,
>
> A thing final in itself and, therefore, good:
> One of the vast repetitions final in
> Themselves and, therefore, good, the going round
>
> And round and round, the merely going round,
> Until merely going round is a final good,
> The way wine comes at a table in a wood.
>
> And we enjoy like men, the way a leaf
> Above the table spins its constant spin,
> So that we look at it with pleasure, look
>
> At it spinning its eccentric measure. Perhaps,
> The man-hero is not the exceptional monster,
> But he that of repetition is most master.

His worship is of nature: "Fat girl, terrestrial, my summer, my night." Yet he must think of her as constantly changing; and in her constant changes giving delight:

> You remain the more than natural figure. You
> Become the soft-footed phantom, the irrational
>
> Distortion, however fragrant, however dear.
> That's it: the more than rational distortion,
> The fiction that results from feeling. Yes, that.
>
> They will get it straight one day at the Sorbonne.
> We shall return at twilight from the lecture
> Pleased that the irrational is rational,
>
> Until flicked by feeling, in a gildered street,
> I call you by name, my green, my fluent mundo.
> You will have stopped revolving except in crystal.

We must always seek what we can never finally find. The delight, the joy, is in the constant seeking, renewed by partial findings.

Stevens' poetry fulfills and exceeds Matthew Arnold's critical prophecy. It does not supplant the religious impulse. It *is* that impulse, faithfully directed: directed in the direction of faith. To this occupation it brings all the resources of a technique itself constantly gyring on itself: a study of relations in the relations themselves. Each poem is an adventure in interpretation. No one poem, no one way of thought, is the key to all the others. As soon as one way of thought has congealed into a device, he uses the device to reach beyond itself.

So his poems disclose their meanings, their shades on shades and exquisite gradations, gradually. To fathom the rightness of their balances, it is necessary to participate in the balancing act. All art is participatory.

I have tried to indicate certain constant but developing principles. There is a moment in the repeated reading of each poem at which suddenly "everything becomes plain." Sometimes it disappoints by seeming to mean *less* than we had supposed while it still remained nebulous. Now, returning again, we find new meanings beginning to emerge from its new simplicity. Like a waterplant unfolding, it may take another soundless spreading leap, into a new dimension of meaning; a seriousness underlying and including its own delight, that sings

In the high imagination, triumphantly.

Part Seven

SEVEN POETS

Seven Poets

TOWARD OUR UNDERSTANDING of modern poetry James Stephens' transitional forms have served as a link with the more familiar forms of the past. His novels provide an additional span between prose and verse. T. S. Eliot's criticism too, defining and developing the "historic sense," leads to a fuller appreciation of the time-amalgams of his poetry.

Reading these poets and Marianne Moore, E. E. Cummings and Wallace Stevens, we experience the qualities of immediacy and simultaneity characteristic of much modern poetry. But the poems of each do not consist primarily of features that lend themselves to convenient crystallization. Our arrangements are structural afterthoughts. If the tendency is toward intensification, poets intensify in quite different ways.

The following pages deal with seven other poets. Their sequence is roughly chronological, not to imply an order of excellence or historical importance. The amount of space devoted to each is not calculated to convey a tacit appraisal. They are chosen to suggest, not to exhaust, the variety of modern poetry.

The temptation of criticism is to tidy poetry away in neat compartments. It is like Charlie Chaplin packing his traveling bag. Everything hanging out is efficiently sheared off. In spite of necessary compression I have tried to avoid summing up the work of living poets. That would be a disservice, I feel, not only to them but to the readers's anticipation.

I

Ezra Pound

FROM WHATEVER VANTAGE one chooses to regard the modern period, loosely the last forty years, its poetic activity is dominated by the figure of Ezra Pound. Pound is the great reanimator of our time. His conversations with Yeats at Rapallo are said to have had a direct bearing on the reinvigorated style of Yeats' later poems. T. S. Eliot, in *Poetry: A Magazine of Verse* (September, 1946), acknowledged Pound's "critical genius" in editing *The Waste Land,* "a sprawling, chaotic poem . . . which left his hands, reduced to about half its size, in the form in which it appears in print."

These are incidental examples of his effect on other poets, summarized by James Joyce's tribute in 1933: "Nothing could be more true than to say we all owe a great deal to him. But I, most of all, surely." Innovator and instigator of new forms, critical precisionist, founder of movements which he immediately abandoned for others, one-man academy and physicist of poetry, he brought influences to bear on influences.

An "instructor with professorial functions" at twenty, Pound, like Frost and Eliot, gained his first recognition abroad, where most of his poetry was published. It is now collected in *Personae* (Liveright, 1926, distributed by New Directions), which contains all of his poetry to date with the exception of eighty-four *Cantos* (New Directions, 1948) of a projected one hundred.

Personae displays nearly every traditional current entering the main stream of present-day poetry. Many of his early poems read like fine translations; and his translations have the ring of original poems. The charm and archaic flavor of the earliest is illustrated in "The Tree":

> I stood still and was a tree amid the wood,
> Knowing the truth of things unseen before;
> Of Daphne and the laurel bow
> And that god-feasting couple old
> That grew elm-oak amid the wold.
> 'Twas not until the gods had been
> Kindly entreated, and been brought within
> Unto the hearth of their heart's home
> That they might do this wonder thing;
> Nathless I have been a tree amid the wood
> And many a new thing understood
> That was rank folly to my head before.

His Phoenician commerce begins at once, with his tribute in "Mesmerism" to Robert Browning — "Old Hippety-Hop o' the accents," "Clear sight's elector!" — and with his translations and paraphrases of Villon, Leopardi, Propertius, Apuleius and the Provençal poets. In "Ballatetta" it is as if Pound himself were a Provençal:

> The broken sunlight for a healm she beareth
> Who hath my heart in jurisdiction.

And his rendering of "Sestina: Altaforte" makes Bertrans de Born a contemporary of Pound:

> Damn it all! all this our South stinks peace.

His excursions among the poets are not all as admiring as his "Translations and Adaptations from Heine." There is also "Mr. Housman's Message":

O woe, woe,
People are born and die,
We also shall be dead pretty soon
Therefore let us act as if we were
dead already.

The bird sits on the hawthorn tree
But he dies also, presently.
Some lads get hung, and some get shot.
Woeful is this human lot.
Woe, woe, etcetera. . . .

London is a woeful place,
Shropshire is much pleasanter.
Then let us smile a little space
Upon fond nature's morbid grace.
Oh, Woe, woe, woe, etcetera. . . .

"Portrait d'Une Femme," rather Browningesque in treatment, bears interesting resemblances to Eliot's "Portrait of a Woman," especially in the lines:

And now you pay one. Yes, you richly pay.
You are a person of some interest, one comes to you
And takes strange gain away:
Trophies fished up; some curious suggestion;
Fact that leads nowhere; and a tale or two,
Pregnant with mandrakes, or with something else
That might prove useful and yet never proves,
That never fits a corner or shows use,
Or finds its hour upon the loom of days . . .

Nothing illustrates his versatility more strikingly than the transition from the graces of Provençal rhythm to the strong stress of Anglo-Saxon in "The Seafarer":

May I for my own self song's truth reckon,
Journey's jargon, how I in harsh days
Hardship endured oft.

Almost at once he returns to the tenderest of his love poems, "A Virginal":

No, no! Go from me. I have left her lately.
I will not spoil my sheath with lesser brightness,
For my surrounding air hath a new lightness;
Slight are her arms, yet they have bound me straitly
And left me cloaked as with a gauze of aether;
As with sweet leaves; as with subtle clearness.
Oh, I have picked up magic in her nearness
To sheathe me half in half the things that sheathe her.
No, no! Go from me. I have still the flavour,
Soft as spring wind that's come from birchen bowers.
Green come the shoots, aye April in the branches,
As winter's wound with her sleight hand she staunches,
Hath of the trees a likeness of the savour:
As white their bark, so white this lady's hours.

"Come, let us pity those who are better off than we are," he says in "The Garret" and launches a series of intimate songs railing at the age: "O generation of the thoroughly smug and thoroughly uncomfortable," "Go, little naked and impudent songs," "Come, my songs, let us express our baser passions," and

Come, my songs, let us speak of perfection—
We shall get ourselves rather disliked.

A translation from the Provençal of Bertrans de Born, "Dompna Pois de me No'us Cal," symbolizes Pound's search for perfection. Its theme is that of the "borrowed lady," recurrent in Troubadour poetry; one that Pound has used or alluded to many times. Maent, the perfect lady, having withheld her favors, the poet seeks from each famous beauty her most perfect feature. From Bels Cembelins, he takes "her colour"; of Midons Aelis "Her straight speech free-running"; from the Viscountess of Chalais "Her two hands and her throat," the locks of Lady Anhes, the form of Audiart, the body of Miels-de-ben, the white teeth of the Lady Faidita and the "Tall stature and gaiety" of Bels Mirals. Of these he constructs a phantom to equal the cruel Maent.

A full length study of Pound's poetic phantom would have to account in detail for all its borrowed lineaments. Their interweaving in the Cantos is more readily understood in the light of his longing, expressed in "Provincia Deserta":

> I have walked over these roads;
> I have thought of them living.

The route of his pious pilgrimage led next to *Cathay,* "For the most part from the Chinese of Rihaku, from the notes of the late Ernest Fenollosa, and the decipherings of the Professors Mori and Ariga." Typical of these adaptations is "The River-Merchant's Wife: A Letter":

> While my hair was still cut straight across my forehead
> I played about the front gate, pulling flowers.
> You came by on bamboo stilts, playing horse . . .

"Near Perigord" weaves the theme of the "borrowed lady" with those of politics and economics which are later to play so dominant a rôle in Pound's thinking. Was Bertrans' song a subtle disguise for his political ambitions? Did he seek to make alliances and stir up jealousies by his seemingly purely amorous praises of the distinctive features of these ladies of great castles?

> Is it a love poem? Did he sing of war?
> Is it an intrigue to run subtly out,
> Born of a jongleur's tongue, freely to pass
> Up and about and in and out the land,
> Mark him a craftsman and a strategist?
>
> . . . .
>
> Oh, there is precedent, legal tradition,
> To sing one thing when your song means another . . .

Here Pound leaves it in doubt. It was one or the other, or both. For his interest is not now in issues, but in the recapture of the living doubts and ambiguities. In *Langue d'Oc* he returns to a courtly celebration of love, as in the purity of its introductory song "Alba":

> When the nightingale to his mate
> Sings day-long and night late
> My love and I keep state
> In bower,
> In flower,
> 'Till the watchman on the tower
> Cry:
>   "Up! Thou rascal, Rise,
>   I see the white
>   Light
>   And the night
>   Flies."

But his urgency that the poetic phantom be realized in life contributes a growing tone of bitterness, as in the caustic "Cantico del Sole":

> The thought of what America would be like
> If the Classics had a wide circulation
>   Troubles my sleep,
> The thought of what America,
> The thought of what America,
> The thought of what America would be like
> If the Classics had a wide circulation
>   Troubles my sleep.
> Nunc dimittis, now lettest thou thy servant,
> Now lettest thou thy servant
>   Depart in peace.
> The thought of what America,
> The thought of what America,
> The thought of what America would be like
> If the Classics had a wide circulation . . .
>   Oh well!
>   It troubles my sleep.

One of the first specific mentions of usury, which he has come to regard as the core of evil in the world, occurs in a series of poems written shortly after the first world war, "Hugh Selwyn Mauberley." Pound's savage denunciations of that war include:

> There died a myriad,
> And of the best, among them,
> For an old bitch gone in the teeth,
> For a botched civilization,
>
> Charm, smiling at the good mouth,
> Quick eyes gone under earth's lid,
>
> For two gross of broken statues,
> For a few thousand battered books.

In 1917 appeared his *Homage to Sextus Propertius,* brilliant adaptations rather than translations of the Roman poet. These alone would establish Pound as a great trafficker between civilizations. They include one of the most beautiful lines in the language: "Me happy, night, night full of brightness."

2

It would be premature to attempt a full estimate of the incomplete *Cantos,* of which Yeats spoke with affection and some perplexity in *A Vision* (Macmillan, 1938). They are among the most difficult and most rewarding long poems of our time. As Yeats said of them, "I have often found there brightly printed kings, queens, knaves, but have never discovered why all the suits could not be dealt out in some quite different order. Now at last he explains that it will, when the hundredth canto is finished, display a structure like that of a Bach Fugue. There will be no plot, no chronicle of events, no logic of discourse, but two themes, the Descent into Hades from Homer, a Metamorphosis from Ovid, and, mixed with these, mediaeval or modern historical characters."

Their whole design is gradually becoming plain, although there are many discoveries yet to be made. Pound's apparent intention is to present "ideas in action"; the living ideas of the past to counteract the dead ideas of the modern world, in which usury has triumphed. Pound notes in the margin of one recent interpretation of his central purpose: "vide verso 17." Verses 17 and 18 of the first Canto read:

> The ocean flowing backward, came we then to the place
> Aforesaid by Circe.

If "The ocean flowing backward" represents his conception of civilization at the time he was beginning the Cantos, his battle since has been like that of Yeats' Cuchulain, who "fought with the invulnerable tide."

The first Canto sets the location of Pound's epic. Like Eliot and Joyce, he has gone to Homer's *Odyssey*. His scene is Book XI, "The Book of the Dead," where Odysseus, sent to consult the prophet Teiresias, converses with the spirits of the departed great. Pound uses this as framework for his own conversations with the dead. Among the first of these, in Canto II, are Browning

> And poor old Homer blind, blind, as a bat,
> Ear, ear, for the sea-surge . . .

Pound's own ear for the sea-surge accounts for many passages of surpassing beauty. In the early Cantos water-images recur: the seduction of Tyro by the sea-god, whose "twisted arms . . ."

> Lithe sinews of water, gripping her, cross-hold,
> And the blue-gray glass of the wave tents them,
> Glare azure of water, cold-welter, close cover.

And:

> Grey peak of the wave,
> wave, colour of grape's pulp . . .

In them the forms of the past shift and dissolve. In Canto IV the swallows come flying over, calling "Ityn!" and other variations on the name of Philomela's brother.

> . . . the swallows crying:
> 'Tis. 'Tis. Ytis!

Philomela, having been ravished by Tereus, contrived with her sister Procne, Tereus' wife, to kill and serve up to him his son Itys. For these mutual betrayals all three were transformed into birds. Pound relates this to the Troubadour story of Cabestan, slain by his mistress' husband, who served up Cabestan's heart to her.

> "It is Cabestan's heart in the dish?
> "No other taste shall change this."
> And she went toward the window,
> the slim white stone bar
> Making a double arch;
> Firm even fingers held to the firm pale stone;
> Swung for a moment,
> and the wind out of Rhodez
> Caught in the full of her sleeve.

Actaeon is set upon by dogs for having seen the nakedness of Diana, bathing, with her nymphs about her:

> Nymphs white-gathered about her, and the air, air,
> Shaking, air alight with the goddess,
> fanning their hair in the dark,
> Lifting, lifting and waffing . . .

The golden appearance of the goddess anticipates the introduction of Danaë to whom Zeus appeared in a shower of gold. The theme of gold, symbolizing for Pound perhaps the vanished beauty, the "real value" of the world, of life lived for and of itself, recurs in a series of subtle modulations throughout the early Cantos, and relates to Pound's emerging theme of the destruction of real value through usury.

The gold is brightest in antiquity. Slowly it begins to fade. By Canto XI, where he is recounting political and military manoeuvres in fifteenth-century Italy: "In the gloom, the gold gathers the light against it." In the next Canto comes his first long tirade against the

Director, dealers through holding companies,
Deacons in churches, owning slum properties,
Alias usurers in excelsis,
        the quintessential essence of usurers,
The purveyors of employment, whining over their 20 p. c.
        and the hard times
And the bust-up of Brazilian securities
        (S. A. securities),
And the general uncertainty of all investment
Save investment in new bank buildings,
        productive of bank buildings,
And not likely to ease distribution . . .

While Kung walks "by the dynastic temple / and into the cedar grove," exchanging with his disciples the wisdom of a useful life, Pound pays his respects to the politicians, financiers and "betrayers of language" wallowing in hell; that is, in the present. In Canto XVII the ancient gods briefly reappear:

                "In the gloom the gold
Gathers the light about it."...

By Canto XXI: "Gold fades in the gloom." He is by now involved with the theme of

War, one war after another,
Men start 'em who couldn't put up a good hen-roost.

The heroes and the villains of all history, of the American Revolution, of Italy, of the Chinese dynasties, are contending together in an active version of the *Divine Comedy*. The relative positions assigned the blessed and the damned in Dante are the results of action. Pound gives the action, especially the action of their ideas. It is an expansion of Eliot's technique in *The Waste Land,* to which Pound makes at least two allusions, the first beginning Canto VIII:

> These fragments you have shelved (shored).
> "Slut!" "Bitch!" Truth and Calliope
> Slanging each other sous les lauriers . . .

The second begins Canto XLVI:

> And if you will say that this tale teaches...
> a lesson, or that the Reverend Eliot
> has found a more natural language...you who think you will
> get through hell in a hurry...

Increasingly his desire to isolate the ideas, and the relation of the ideas, that are at the core of action, complicates the scheme of his later Cantos. We are most grateful for the lyric interludes that less frequently punctuate his course, such as the beautiful Canto XXXVI, beginning:

> A lady asks me
> I speak in season
> She seeks reason for an affect, wild often
> That is so proud he hath Love for a name
> Who denys it can hear the truth now
> Wherefore I speak to the present knowers
> Having no hope that low-hearted
> Can bring sight to such reason
> Be there not natural demonstration
> I have no will to try proof-bringing
> Or say where it hath birth
> What is its virtu and power
> Its being and every moving
> Or delight whereby 'tis called "to love"
> Or if man can show it to sight.

And in XLV, after countless instances that by their very number come to seem petulant, his indignation itself swells to lyric proportion:

With *Usura*

> With usura hath no man a house of good stone
> each block cut smooth and well fitting
> that design might cover their face . . .

The middle reaches of the Cantos are heavy going, yet in the midst of his most drily expository sections, as in Canto LXIV where he is dealing with the Stamp Act, we come upon Byles saying: "Our grievances red-dressed." And in LXV:

> Smoke, smell of sea coal, of stagnant and putrid water
> Increase the qualminess but do not occasion it

and his description of the "hurrycane." He terminates Canto LXXX: "sunset grand couturier."

I should not like to add to the confusion already surrounding Pound's position during the last war. In the absence of complete evidence, any conclusions we may draw are based on supposition. One supposition is that he considered fascism a stage in the establishment of a new system of credit, which would do away with usury. If this is true, his tragedy would seem to be an an inordinate faith in the power of ideas as such, and a consequent distortion of human values.

Whether such a supposition is correct or not, this imbalance is what I find to be the central weakness in the design of the Cantos, especially the later ones. They are a great mosaic of ideas; of ideas in the words of the men who had them; a device Pound seems to believe retains their action. Their mutual tensions provide the drama of his epic.

But the poet who once founded a school whose distinguishing tenet was "to present an image" has in the later Cantos gone to the extreme of leaving out almost all visual representation. His wish to isolate the "action" of ideas springs from the same desire for compression and crystallization that has always animated his work. Yet a conference, even such a magnificent colloquy between the centuries as Pound has here assembled, is a very partial presentation of the action of ideas. The Chinese ideogram, which has influenced him profoundly, itself often includes a picture, or residual image.

Whatever place the Cantos will eventually take in the shifting hierarchy of literature, Pound's poetic and critical work will remain of inestimable value to poets. There they will find, as they have found already, so many directions explored, so many paths laid out, so much of their preliminary work done for them, that a Chair of Comparative Prosody alone could be founded on them. Pound, whose vehemences have included so many diatribes against "professors," is himself the greatest "professor" of them all.

11

William Carlos Williams

THE EPITHET that might most quickly characterize William Carlos Williams is happy champion of the vernacular. If Pound, like Eliot, tracked back through all the past in search of language and metre, Williams has consistently avoided traditional form. Thoroughly contemporary in speech and subjectmatter, he has denounced the sonnet as a played-out form. Speaking of rhyme, in the middle of his poem "This Florida: 1924" (from *The Complete Collected Poems of William Carlos Williams: 1906–1938,* New Directions, 1938), he throws light on his intentions:

> e-e i-i o-o u-u a-a
> Shall I write it in iambs
> Cottages in a row
>
> all radioed and showerbathed?
> But I am sick of rime —
> The whole damned town

is riming up one street
and down another, yet there is
the rime of her white teeth

the rime of glasses
at my plate, the ripple rime
the rime her fingers make —

And we thought to escape rime
by imitation of the senseless
unarrangement of wild things —

the stupidest rime of all —

. . . .

The fullest statement of what his poetry is about is given in the opening to Book I of his projected four-part *Paterson* (New Directions, 1946): ": a local pride; spring, summer, fall and the sea; a confession; a basket; a column; a reply to Greek and Latin with the bare hands; a gathering up; a celebration;" and in some lines near its close:

Plaster saints, glass jewels
And those apt paper flowers, bafflingly
complex — have here
their forthright beauty, beside:

Things, things unmentionable
the sink with the waste farina in it and
lumps of rancid meat, milk-bottle-tops: have
here a still tranquility and loveliness
Have here (in his thoughts)
a complement tranquil and chaste.

In the Preface to an earlier *Collected Poems: 1921–1931* (The Objectivist Press, 1934) Wallace Stevens, speaking of Williams' "passion for the anti-poetic," says: "Williams, by nature, is more of a realist than is commonly true in the case of a poet." But he has a romantic, even sentimental side, says Stevens, pointing out "how often the essential poetry is the result of the conjunction of the unreal and the real, the sentimental and the anti-poetic, the constant interaction of two opposites. . . . It will be found that he has made some veritable additions to the corpus of poetry, which certainly is no more sacred to anyone than to him. His special use of the anti-poetic is this. The ambiguity produced by bareness is another. The implied image, as in 'Young Sycamore,' the serpent that leaps up in one's imagination at his prompting, is an addition to imagism, a phase of realism which Williams has always found congenial."

In Williams' hands free verse, which in English is at least as old as the King James Version, has become a truly flexible and contemporary instrument. He may be said to have rescued it from the influence of Walt Whitman, whose pervasive beat, Biblical utterance and large sweeping vision reappear, as echoes of grandeur, in the work of his followers. A great poet is not to be blamed for his imitators. Whitman is not to be blamed because his great natural overabundance has degenerated into a cheerleading approach to poetry, his successors whipping themselves up into the appropriate mood by chanting a catalogue of Indian place names.

Williams has refined and applied the principle of Whitman, not the manner. The most obvious difference is in the comparative shortness of his lines, which correspond more closely to breaths taken in talking. An observer of the everyday surburban scene, with which he has grown familiar as a baby doctor in Rutherford, New Jersey, and a recorder of its speech, Williams uses these typical inspections and inflections to build up his poems. Although he has had his panoramic moods, as in "The Wanderer," he returns most happily to what one encounters walking down a street. One of his early poems in this vein is "Pastoral":

When I was younger
it was plain to me
I must make something of myself.
Older now
I walk back streets
admiring the houses
of the very poor:
roof out of line with sides

the yards cluttered
with old chicken wire, ashes,
furniture gone wrong;
the fence and outhouses
built of barrel-staves'
and parts of boxes, all,
if I am fortunate,
smeared a bluish green
that properly weathered
pleases me best
of all colors.

No one
will believe this
of vast import to the nation.

Merging completely, if vocally, with his background, he is nevertheless aware of the individual's essential isolation. This theme he treats gravely in "El Hombre":

It's a strange courage
you give me ancient star:

Shine alone in the sunrise
toward which you lend no part!

In "Danse Russe" he returns to it with a proper disregard for propriety:

If I when my wife is sleeping
and the baby and Kathleen
are sleeping
and the sun is a flame-white disc
in silken mists
above shining trees, —
if I in my north room
danced naked, grotesquely
before my mirror
waving my shirt round my head
and singing softly to myself:

"I am lonely, lonely.
I was born to be lonely,
I am best so!"
If I admire my arms, my face
my shoulders, flanks, buttocks,
against the yellow drawn shades,—

Who shall say I am not
the happy genius of my household?

Lonely or not, "Lighthearted William" enjoys a rapport with the weather that leads to instantaneous transformation:

Lighthearted William twirled
his November moustaches
and, half dressed, looked
from the bedroom window
upon the spring weather.

Heigh-ya! sighed he gaily
leaning out to see
up and down the street
where a heavy sunlight
lay behind some blue shadows.

Into the room he drew
his head again and laughed
to himself quietly
twirling his green moustaches.

He treats his man-made surroundings as a part of nature. Among the series of quick sketches, in diary form, which make up the poem he calls "The Descent of Winter," there is this entry for "10/30":

To freight cars in the air

all the slow
    clank, clank
    clank, clank
moving above the treetops

the
    wha, wha
of the hoarse whistle

    pah,   pah,   pah
    pah, pah, pah, pah, pah

    piece and piece
    piece and piece
moving still trippingly
through the morningmist

long after the engine
has fought by
                and disappeared
in silence
          to the left

Wallace Stevens characterized in his Preface the unique effect and importance of "Young Sycamore":

I must tell you
this young tree
whose sound and firm trunk
between the wet

pavement and the gutter
(where water
is trickling) rises
bodily

into the air with
one undulant
thrust half its height—
and then

dividing and waning
sending out
young branches on
all sides—

hung with cocoons—
it thins
till nothing is left of it
but two

eccentric knotted
twigs
bending forward
hornlike at the top

Stevens mentions particularly his flower poems. "Primrose," with its storm of images and gustily accelerating rhythms, is one of many fine examples. From their particular observation he is able to achieve the serene grand single image in "Flowers by the Sea":

When over the flowery, sharp pasture's
edge, unseen, the salt ocean

lifts its form—chickory and daisies
tied, released, seem hardly flowers alone

but color and the movement—or the shape
perhaps—of restlessness, whereas

the sea is circled and sways
peacefully upon its plantlike stem

His poems of social protest, such as "Paterson: The Strike" and, in *The Broken Span* (New Directions, 1941), "Impromptu: The Suckers," spring from indignation, and from a warm human sympathy most immediately conveyed in "To a Poor Old Woman"

Munching a plum on
the street a paper bag
of them in her hand

They taste good to her
They taste good
to her. They taste
good to her.

You can see it by
the way she gives herself
to the one half
sucked out in her hand

comforted
a solace of ripe plums
seeming to fill the air
They taste good to her

In their clear detail and industrial subjectmatter, some of his poems have affinities with the watercolors of Charles Sheeler, to one of whose exhibitions Williams wrote an introduction. He has dedicated a poem to Charles Demuth; and the latter's "My Egypt" is suggested in Williams' poem, "Classic Scene":

A power-house
in the shape of
a red brick chair
90 feet high

on the seat of which
sit the figures
of two metal
stacks — aluminum —

commanding an area
of squalid shacks
side by side —
from one of which

buff smoke
streams while under
a grey sky
the other remains

passive today —

One of his finest poems, which in its precision of observed detail may remind us of Marianne Moore, is "The Yachts."

THE YACHTS

contend in a sea which the land partly encloses
shielding them from the too heavy blows
of an ungoverned ocean which when it chooses

tortures the biggest hulls, the best man knows
to pit against its beatings, and sinks them pitilessly.
Mothlike in mists, scintillant in the minute

brilliance of cloudless days, with broad bellying sails
they glide to the wind tossing green water
from their sharp prows while over them the crew crawls

ant like, solicitously grooming them, releasing,
making fast as they turn, lean far over and having
caught the wind again, side by side, head for the mark.

In a well guarded arena of open water surrounded by
lesser and greater craft which, sycophant, lumbering
and flittering follow them, they appear youthful, rare

as the light of a happy eye, live with the grace
of all that in the mind is feckless, free and
naturally to be desired. Now the sea which holds them

is moody, lapping their glossy sides, as if feeling
for some slightest flaw but fails completely.
Today no race. Then the wind comes again. The yachts

move, jockeying for a start, the signal is set and they
are off. Now the waves strike at them but they are too
well made, they slip through, though they take in canvas.

Arms with hands grasping seek to clutch at the prows.
Bodies thrown recklessly in the way are cut aside.
It is a sea of faces about them in agony, in despair

until the horror of the race dawns staggering the mind,
the whole sea become an entanglement of watery bodies
lost to the world bearing what they cannot hold. Broken,

beaten, desolate, reaching from the dead to be taken up
they cry out, failing, failing! their cries rising
in waves still as the skillful yachts pass over.

It is this clarity of focus and Williams' ability to suggest by expressively casual detail that give his novels *White Mule* and *In the Money* their quiet excellence. Now combined in a single volume, *First Act* (New Directions, 1947), they have never had the appreciation they deserve. They are not simply faithful and brilliant reportage of middle-class family life in the early Nineteen Hundreds; although in this respect alone their selection of incident lifts them above better-known examples of the realistic genre, whose effects are usually gained by relentless accumulation. What causes these to transcend the very genre itself is their central poetic conception. The "white mule," the infant who is born and reaches the age of two during the course of the action, is at all times central to this action and dominates it. We come to realize, through strategically placed episodes, that everything in the story of Joe Stecher and his ambitiously driving wife is having its empathic effect on the baby. In the unrolling events the future is being prepared.

Here Williams' linear development, typical of many of his poems which often are close to the technique of prose, completes itself. His poems always have lines of suggestion going off from them. But some of them, separately, leave me unsatisfied. They seem to ask for more detail; for a continuity that comes only by reading them in context with surrounding poems.

His poetry is acquiring new depth and roundness of expression in the geographical biography *Paterson,* establishing the interidentity of person and place. Williams' clusters of impression have now their unifying conception; in his words, "that a man in himself is a city, beginning, seeking, achieving and concluding his life in ways which the various aspects of a city may embody — if imaginatively conceived — any city, all the details of which may be made to voice his most intimate convictions."

The episodic design, shuttling between the topography of the resting giant, the local legends that are his dreams, the people he thinks or who think him, allows for many delightful cross-references:

> Twice a month Paterson receives
> communications from the Pope and Jacques
> Barzun
>
> . . . .
>
> Say it! No ideas but in things. Mr.
> Paterson has gone away
> to rest and write. Inside the bus one sees
> his thoughts sitting and standing. His
> thoughts alight and scatter —

While awaiting the full development of Williams' double exposure, we may question one of his observations: "Certainly I am not a robin nor erudite."

III

Ogden Nash

IN AMERICA the light-verse tradition has seldom been combined with the intentions of serious poetry. The quality of musical-comedy lyrics has occasionally, as with Ira Gershwin and Moss Hart, been high, if seldom matching the cleverness of Noel Coward. We have had the acidulous wit of Dorothy Parker. We have had the fine light and free verse of Don Marquis, with its wonderful "toujours gai" refrain. And we have the original talent of Ogden Nash, who has mastered the art of writing a poetry to accompany the reading of prose.

There is a real play in his work between the intentions of prose and the intentions of poetry. With a patter as distinctive as W. S. Gilbert's, yet remarkably distinct from it, he makes marginal comments on his time and place that are quite as apposite as those of Gilbert for nineteenth-century England.

Placed as he expected to be, and very frequently is, next to columns of magazine prose, Nash developed a form that lures the eye by the clumped arrangement of its lines, halfway between prose and verse. The ear is teased by a scansion that catches the breathless rhythm of silent reading. Delayed-action rhymes have an effect very much like the one described in "How to Tell a Quail from a Partridge":

> You all know the story of the insomniac who got into such a state
> Because the man upstairs dropped one shoe on the floor at eleven o'clock and the unhappy insomniac sat up until breakfast time waiting for him to drop the mate.
> Well, here I lie in the interval between the beginning of day and the end of night,
> Waiting for a Bob White to finish saying Bob White . . .

These rhymes frequently become as preposterous as the fantasy that accompanies them. In "Curl Up and Diet":

> No matter how underfed to you a lady's anatomy seemeth,
> She describes herself as Leviathan or Behemoth;
> To the world she may appear slinky and feline,
> But she inspects herself in the mirror and cries, Oh, I look like a sea lion.

A diet that really worked, he reflects, would be disastrous, because

> . . . I fear me one ten-pound loss would only arouse the craving for another,
> So it wouldn't do any good for ladies to get their ambition and look like somebody's fourteen-year-old brother,
> Because, having accomplished this with ease,
> They would next want to look like somebody's fourteen-year-old brother in the final stages of some obscure disease,
> And the more success you have the more you want to get of it,
> So then their goal would be to look like somebody's fourteen-year-old brother's ghost, or rather not the ghost itself, which is fairly solid, but a silhouette of it,
> So I think it is very nice for ladies to be lithe and lissome,
> But not so much so that you cut yourself if you happen to embrace or kissome.

Among his cleverest are "England Expects — " which begins:

> Let us pause to consider the English,
> Who when they pause to consider themselves they get
> all reticently thrilled and tinglish . . .

"A Clean Conscience Never Relaxes," with its lines:

> Remorse is a violent dyspepsia of the mind,
> But it is very difficult to treat because it cannot even be
> defined,
> Because everything is not gold that glisters and everything
> is not a tear that glistens,
> And one man's remorse is another man's reminiscence . . .

"Columbus," who

> . . . went and tried to borrow some money from
> Ferdinand
> But Ferdinand said America was a bird in the bush and
> he'd rather have a berdinand . . .

and his meditation on the ambiguities of poetry, "Very Like a Whale":

> One thing that literature would be greatly the better
> for
> Would be a more restricted employment by authors
> of simile and metaphor.
> Authors of all races, be they Greeks, Romans, Teutons
> or Celts,
> Can't seem just to say that anything is the thing it is
> but have to go out of their way to say that it is
> like something else.
> What does it mean when we are told
> That the Assyrian came down like a wolf on the fold?
> In the first place, George Gordon Byron had had
> enough experience
> To know that it probably wasn't just one Assyrian, it
> was a lot of Assyrians.

However, as too many arguments are apt to induce apoplexy and thus hinder longevity,
We'll let it pass as one Assyrian for the sake of brevity.
Now then, this particular Assyrian, the one whose cohorts were gleaming in purple and gold,
Just what does the poet mean when he says he came down like a wolf on the fold?
In heaven and earth more than is dreamed of in our philosophy there are a great many things,
But I don't imagine that among them there is a wolf with purple and gold cohorts or purple and gold anythings.
No, no, Lord Byron, before I'll believe that this Assyrian was actually like a wolf I must have some kind of proof;
Did he run on all fours and did he have a hairy tail and a big red mouth and big white teeth and did he say Woof woof woof?
Frankly I think it very unlikely, and all you were entitled to say, at the very most,
Was that the Assyrian cohorts came down like a lot of Assyrian cohorts about to destroy the Hebrew host.
But that wasn't fancy enough for Lord Byron, oh dear me no, he had to invent a lot of figures of speech and then interpolate them,
With the result that whenever you mention Old Testament soldiers to people they say Oh yes, they're the ones that a lot of wolves dressed up in gold and purple ate them.
That's the kind of thing that's being done all the time by poets, from Homer to Tennyson;
They're always comparing ladies to lilies and veal to venison,
And they always say things like that the snow is a white blanket after a winter storm.
Oh it is, is it, all right then, you sleep under a six-inch blanket of snow and I'll sleep under a half-inch blanket of unpoetical blanket material and we'll see which one keeps warm,
And after that maybe you'll begin to comprehend dimly
What I mean by too much metaphor and simile.

IV

W. H. Auden

SINCE THE THIRTIES it has been difficult to find a first book of poems untouched by the influence of W. H. Auden. The most versatile of the between-wars generation of English poets, Auden has taught his style to apply what he knows as an intensely educated man to what he perceives as an acute observer of the contemporary scene. He has a particular flair for the significant detail of city and situation, the public and private dilemmas of our time.

Auden's wit, his technical virtuosity and enormous facility allow him a wide range in modes of expression. In "Law Like Love," which begins in a light vein, Kafka's *The Trial* is crossed with A. A. Milne:

Law, say the gardeners, is the sun,
Law is the one
All gardeners obey
Tomorrow, yesterday, today.

Law is the wisdom of the old
The impotent grandfathers shrilly scold;
The grandchildren put out a treble tongue,
Law is the senses of the young.

Law, says the priest with a priestly look,
Expounding to an unpriestly people,
Law is the words in my priestly book,
Law is my pulpit and my steeple.

Law, says the judge as he looks down his nose,
Speaking clearly and most severely,
Law is as I've told you before,
Law is as you know I suppose,
Law is but let me explain it once more,

Law is The Law. . . .

One of the most brilliant of his lighter verses was published in *The Double Man* (Random House, 1941), written after Auden had come to this country. In *The Collected Poetry of W. H. Auden* (1945), which contains most of the poems I quote, it is called "The Labyrinth" and goes, in part:

"Where am I? Metaphysics says
No question can be asked unless
It has an answer, so I can
Assume this maze has got a plan.

If theologians are correct,
A Plan implies an Architect:
A God-built maze would be, I'm sure,
The Universe in miniature.

Are data from the world of Sense,
In that case, valid evidence?
What in the universe I know
Can give directions how to go?

All Mathematics would suggest
A steady straight line as the best,
But left and right alternately
Is consonant with History.

Aesthetics, though, believes all Art
Intends to gratify the Heart:
Rejecting disciplines like these,
Must I, then, go which way I please?

Such reasoning is only true
If we accept the classic view,
Which we have no right to assert,
According to the Introvert.

His absolute pre-supposition
Is — Man creates his own condition:
This maze was not divinely built,
But is secreted by my guilt.

The centre that I cannot find
Is known to my Unconscious Mind;
I have no reason to despair
Beacuse I am already there. . . ."

It is easier for a rich man to enter the kingdom of heaven than for a clever man to write lyric poetry. Auden's double gift reveals him as a poet who, for relaxation or discipline, writes clever verses to manipulate ideas and techniques. It is true that some quantity of his work seems located in a precarious between-region. There I find his sonnets to Edward Lear, to Montaigne, to Rimbaud and Luther, and the poems to Matthew Arnold, Pascal and Herman Melville. These exhibit an excessively polished neatness, a playing with the ABC's of abstraction, and a jog-trot rhythm. An example is the sonnet "Who's Who":

A shilling life will give you all the facts:
How Father beat him, how he ran away,
What were the struggles of his youth, what acts
Made him the greatest figure of his day . . .

But if at times Auden's characteristically witty and oblique style can seem merely facetious, at others, when the wit fuses with great lyrical power, it becomes a unique instrument for expressing the complexities of the age; what he has called, in "Kairos and Logos," "the smells and furniture of the known world." Then all his manipulations elsewhere are seen to be necessary exercises. For one of his great talents lies in the ability to reclothe abstractions; to particularize the principles — or lack of them — under which modern man lives. He has a way of personalizing them, of so characterizing and setting them in motion that we feel them for what they are: forces working not only at and against us, but in and through us.

> Certainly our city with its byres of poverty down to
> The river's edge, its cathedral, its engines, its dogs;
>   Here is the cosmopolitan cooking
>   And the light alloys and the glass.
>
> Built by the conscience-stricken, the weapon-making,
> By us. . . .

There is his hymn to love which begins:

> O Love, the interest itself in thoughtless Heaven,
> Make simpler daily the beating of man's heart; within,
> There in the ring where name and image meet,
>
> Inspire them with such a longing as will make his thought
> Alive like patterns a murmuration of starlings,
> Rising in joy over wolds, unwittingly weave.

It ends with the magnificent line: "For the virgin roadsteads of our hearts an unwavering keel." There is the poem to "Oxford":

> Nature is so near: the rooks in the college garden
> Like agile babies still speak the language of feelings;
> By the tower the river still runs to the sea and will run,
>   And the stones in that tower are utterly
>   Satisfied still with their weight.

In these the lines flow easily toward their conclusions, released from the compulsion to make their points with the rhyme. Occasional rhymes and half-rhymes weave loosely from stanza to stanza (as, in the first poem, "cosmopolitan cooking" – "weapon-making"); or inside the lines and connecting them (as, in the second, "Love" – "heaven" – "Alive" – "over" – "weave"; "beating" – "meet"); and the texture is enriched by alliterative reversals (as, in the third, "college" – "agile"). These contribute undercurrents of tension to the steady, river-like progression of the emotion, beautifully exemplified in the song beginning:

Look, stranger, on this island now
The leaping light for your delight discovers,
Stand stable here
And silent be,
That through the channels of the ear
May wander like a river
The swaying sound of the sea.

Of his many poems and songs written, as he says, "About heart, / By heart, for heart," I can cite only a few: his "What's in your mind, my dove, my coney"; "Lay your sleeping head, my love, / Human on my faithless arm"; "Fish in the unruffled lakes" and

That night when joy began
Our narrowest veins to flush,
We waited for the flash
Of morning's levelled gun.

He is unsurpassed in his ability to write very simply about the complex fears of love as it presents itself to the modern consciousness:

Dear, though the night is gone,
The dream still haunts to-day
That brought us to a room,
Cavernous, lofty as
A railroad terminus,
And crowded in that gloom
Were beds, and we in one
In a far corner lay.

The world's ominous note sounds in many of these poems. Its events intrude on the private delights of the lovers:

Easily, my dear, you move, easily your head,
And easily as through leaves of a photograph album I'm led
Through the night's delights and the day's impressions,
Past the tall tenements and the trees in the wood,
Though sombre the sixteen skies of Europe
        And the Danube flood.

Looking and loving our behaviours pass
The stones, the steels, and the polished glass;
Lucky to love the strategic railway,
The sterile farms where his looks are fed,
And in the policed unlucky city
        Lucky his bed.

Whether or not from retrospective discouragement, there is a belittling quality to some of the titles Auden has added, in the collected edition, to his prewar poems. Generally I follow his original first-line usage. Perhaps some day they will be arranged chronologically, in justice to their growing premonitory urgency during the Thirties:

Doom is dark and deeper than any sea-dingle
Upon what man it fall
In spring, day-wishing flowers appearing,
Avalanche sliding, white snow from rock-face,
That he should leave his house,
No cloud-soft hand can hold him, restraint by women;
But ever that man goes
Through place-keepers, through forest trees,
A stranger to strangers over undried sea,
Houses for fishes, suffocating water,
Or lonely on fell as chat,
By pot-holed becks
A bird stone-haunting, an unquiet bird.

"Paysage Moralisé" gains its hypnotic effect by an inspired use of Arnaut Daniel's sestina, a favorite form with Auden. The six unrhymed end-words of the first stanza regularly rotate through the succeeding five stanzas, and reappear at the middles and ends of the three-line concluding stanza. Gradually "valleys," "mountains," "water," "islands" and "cities" come to rhyme, in feeling, with the last word of the first stanza:

Hearing of harvests rotting in the valleys,
Seeing at end of street the barren mountains,
Round corners coming suddenly on water,
Knowing them shipwrecked who were launched for islands,
We honour founders of these starving cities
Whose honour is the image of our sorrow . . .

The doom becomes specific. In his great ballad, "O what is that sound which so thrills the ear," it marches into the room:

O what is that sound which so thrills the ear
  Down in the valley drumming, drumming?
Only the scarlet soldiers, dear,
  The soldiers coming.

O what is that light I see flashing so clear
  Over the distance brightly brightly?
Only the sun on their weapons, dear,
  As they step lightly.

O what are they doing with all that gear,
  What are they doing this morning, this morning?
Only their usual manoeuvres, dear,
  Or perhaps a warning.

O why have they left the road down there,
  Why are they suddenly wheeling, wheeling?
Perhaps a change in their orders, dear.
  Why are you kneeling?

O haven't they stopped for the doctor's care,
  Haven't they reined their horses, their horses?
Why, they are none of them wounded, dear,
  None of these forces.

. . . .

O it's broken the lock and splintered the door,
  O it's the gate where they're turning, turning;
Their boots are heavy on the floor
  And their eyes are burning.

No one else has so fully extracted the latent horror of such words as "weapons," "gear," "manoeuvres," "orders" and "forces." Here, and in his song to the German Jews –

Say this city has ten million souls,
Some are living in mansions, some are living in holes:
Yet there's no place for us, my dear, yet there's no place for us.

– and in "It's farewell to the drawing-room's civilised cry," his light-verse technique and mastery of the cadences of popular song apply thumbscrews to the bitterness of his theme:

Saw a poodle in a jacket fastened with a pin,
Saw a door opened and a cat let in:
But they weren't German Jews, my dear, but they weren't
    German Jews.

Went down the harbour and stood upon the quay,
Saw the fish swimming as if they were free:
Only ten feet away, my dear, only ten feet away.

"Yesterday all the past," he said in "Spain 1937":

The stars are dead; the animals will not look:
We are left alone with our day . . .

If the hope implied in that poem of a conclusive defeat of the forces of evil by military means proved abortive, as it always has, the beginning of the second world war found him, in "September 1, 1939," rededicating his energies:

I sit in one of the dives
On Fifty-second Street
Uncertain and afraid

As the clever hopes expire
Of a low dishonest decade:
Waves of anger and fear
Circulate over the bright
And darkened lands of the earth,
Obsessing our private lives;
The unmentionable odour of death
Offends the September night.

. . . .

Defenceless under the night
Our world in stupor lies;
Yet, dotted everywhere,
Ironic points of light
Flash out wherever the Just
Exchange their messages:
May I, composed like them
Of Eros and of dust,
Beleaguered by the same
Negation and despair,
Show an affirming flame.

2

The most affirming work so far, to my mind, is "New Year Letter," probably the finest long purely didactic poem of our time. A poem of ideas, its ideas have the dramatic force of action. For they are the paired ideas, the false alternatives "left and right" that have been "consonant with History." Auden's attempt is to "Unearth the whole offence / From Luther until now / That has driven a culture mad." The poem might be called his Terrestrial Comedy, occurring, not from Good Friday to Easter, 1300, but from December 31, 1939, to January 1, 1940. Its goal is not Dante's Heaven of the Saints, but a possible Purgatory; an order on earth to replace our ever-recurring Hell.

Taking a "middle flight" between lyric and prose statement, Auden's poem routes its ideas through the susceptibilities. He wants it to be, as he says,

. . . under Flying Seal to all
Who wish to read it anywhere,
And, if they open it, *En Clair.*

It is written in simple Swiftian metre, four-foot rhymed couplets, with occasional triplets. His technical mastery is displayed in the way he keeps his rhymes from "ringing a bell" except when he wants them to. They never degenerate into the epigrammatic monotony of many heroic couplets, whose five-foot metre tends to enforce a pause at the end of each line. Besides this initial wisdom of choice, Auden keeps his lines moving by a play of internal rhymes and assonances that anticipate or follow the end-rhymes, controlling their effect; as in the passage on the approach of war:

All formulas were tried to still
The scratching on the window-sill,
All bolts of custom made secure
Against the pressure on the door,
But up the staircase of events
Carrying his special instruments,
To every bedside all the same
The dreadful figure swiftly came.

The *l* and short-*i* sounds play from "All formulas" and "still" to "scratching," "window-sill," "all bolts." "Secure" fades away into "pressure," "door," "staircase," "carrying." "Pressure" itself leads into "events," "special instruments," "every bedside" and "dreadful." And the various *a* sounds that have been planted throughout the passage now culminate in the ringing "same-came," driving the horror home.

Auden proposes as the central problem of the time: "To set in order." The sun that everywhere saw disorders –

A ship abruptly change her course,
A train make an unwonted stop,
A little crowd smash up a shop,

– shone too on a cottage where Buxtehude's music made "a *civitas* of sound":

For art had set in order sense
And feeling and intelligence,
And from its ideal order grew
Our local understanding too.

Art, then, although it cannot be "A midwife to society," offers examples of order. An example of order for our time is what Auden proposes with his poem, pleading his case before those "Great masters who have shown mankind / An order it has yet to find": the poets of the past who are both his models and his judges. Among these he places Dante, Blake, Rimbaud, Dryden ("The master of the middle style"), Catullus, Tennyson, Baudelaire, Hardy and Rilke.

The modern situation is presented in terms of a detective story:

The situation of our time
Surrounds us like a baffling crime.
There lies the body half-undressed,
We all had reason to detest,
And all are suspects and involved
Until the mystery is solved
And under lock and key the cause
That makes a nonsense of our laws.
O Who is trying to shield Whom?
Who left a hairpin in the room?
Who was the distant figure seen
Behaving oddly on the green?
Why did the watchdog never bark?
Why did the footsteps leave no mark?
Where were the servants at that hour?
How did a snake get in the tower?
Delayed in the democracies
By departmental vanities,
The rival sergeants run about
But more to squabble than find out,
Yet where the Force has been cut down
To one inspector dressed in brown,
He makes the murderer whom he pleases
And all investigation ceases.

When all feel guilty, the clues multiply; yet simplify. All signs point to the present as the Inferno, a region delineated by scientists; and to the Inferno as situated in the human heart, a region delineated by Mephistopheles, the arch-scientist, if a scientist *malgré lui-même.* Mephistopheles is our own desire for a fixed reality. Assuring us that our "knowledge of good and evil" is an absolute knowledge of "which is good, which is evil," he continually proposes false alternatives. Auden cites a number of historical opposites. In religion it is the quarrel between predestination and the doctrine of free will. In politics it is the conservative, who wants the *status quo* no matter what, against the radical, who wants change no matter how. It is Plato's ideal of the Philosopher-King – the rule of the "good," which degenerates into tyranny – against Rousseau's ideal of the Natural Man – a notion of spontaneous democracy, which degenerates into chaos. And again it is the Haves against the Have-nots.

Our devil never lies to us outright. He presents us with half-truths as if they were The Truth. Adhering to either side of his argument, we make of it an evil; until its fallacy is forced upon our attention, usually violently. Then we switch to the opposite half-truth. So Wordsworth, a "fellow-traveler" of the French Revolution until revolted by its bloody excesses, ended by supporting the Congress of Vienna.

This process of action and reaction, historically necessary to free us of our self-imposed bonds (although usually we exchange one for another) ; this nightmare of contradiction in ourselves and in the world we create, will be interminable or will destroy us, unless we take the third step of Hegelian dialectic, by synthesizing our faiths and doubts. We can reach, not The Truth, but a continuing process, the "double focus" of the Double Man.

My quick summary over-simplifies Auden's exposition of his theme. His poem does not reach conclusions, but points directions. He offers no universal panacea; our future depends on our personal choices, on "personal confederation":

. . . O
Three quarters of these people know
Instinctively what ought to be
The nature of society
And how they'd live there if they could.

If it were easy to be good,
And cheap, and plain as evil how,
We all would be its members now.
How readily would we become
The seamless live continuum
Of supple and coherent stuff,
Whose form is truth, whose content love,
Its pluralistic interstices
The homes of happiness and peace,
Where in a unity of praise
The largest *publicum's* a *res,*
And the least *res* a *publicum;*
How grandly would our virtues bloom
In a more conscionable dust
Where Freedom dwells because it must,
Necessity because it can,
And men confederate in Man.

. . . .

O every day in sleep and labour
Our life and death are with our neighbour,
And love illuminates again
The city and the lion's den,
The world's great rage, the travel of young men.

"The Sea and the Mirror" Auden calls "A Commentary on Shakespeare's *The Tempest.*" A series of speeches and songs by the characters after the action of the play has ended, it asks what happens to them when they have left the hands of their creator. What is the relation between art and life? Does art, reflecting the patterns of life, change those patterns? The poem concludes with a restatement of the duality between Caliban, the sea of actuality, and Ariel, the mirror of art.

"For the Time Being, A Christmas Oratorio," might have been called a commentary on Eliot's plays and *Four Quartets:*

If the muscle can feel repugnance, there is still a false move
    to be made;

If the mind can imagine tomorrow, there is still a defeat to
remember;
As long as the self can say "I," it is impossible not to rebel;
As long as there is an accidental virtue, there is a necessary vice:
And the garden cannot exist, the miracle cannot occur.

. . . .

Oh where is that immortal and nameless Centre from which
our points of
Definition and death are all equi-distant? . . .

The "Four Faculties" – Intuition, Feeling, Sensation and Thought – which preside over "The Annunciation" resemble Eliot's four levels of response in his plays, and the four levels of intensity in the *Quartets.* They reappear in *The Age of Anxiety* (Random House, 1947) as the characters Quant, a shipping clerk, whose first speech begins, looking in a mirror:

My deuce, my double, my dear image
Is it lively there, that land of glass
Where song is a grimace, sound logic
A suite of gestures? . . .

Emble, a college sophomore, enlisted in the Navy:

Estranged, aloof,
They brood over being till the bars close . . .

Rosetta, a department-store-buyer:

From Seager's Folly
We beheld what was ours. Undulant land
Rose layer by layer till at last the sea
Far away flashed . . .

and Malin, a professor, now in Medical Intelligence:

No chimpanzee
Thinks it thinks. . . .

They symbolize man's division, quadruple rather than double. Their chance meeting in a bar and mutual introspective recapitulations of the Seven Ages and Seven Stages of Man foreshadow a hope for their eventual reconciliation in the individual. In a state of intoxication, the four "establish a rapport in which communication of thoughts and feelings is so accurate and instantaneous, that they appear to function as a single organism."

The excessive neatness of the scheme is deliberately emphasized by an alliterative Euphuistic verse. Skillfully handled as it is, this sometimes reproduces the accidental effect of headlines — "Fort Forecasts Disaster Unless Rail Rates Rise" — and its rather lulling rhythms, for a poem of such length, may make us slip past its particular excellences: Emble's reflection on the dead soldiers:

> They are nothing now but names assigned to
> Anguish in others, areas of grief.

and Quant, the intuitive, reflecting on an all but incommunicable anxiety:

> As, far from furniture and formal gardens
>   The desperate spirit
> Thinks of its end in the third person,
>   As a speck drowning
> In those wanton mansions where the whales take
>   Their huge fruitions.

Analysis, the reduction of personality or poetry to its component elements, is perhaps more peculiar to our time than to any other in history. Every age has its particular fragmentations; our own seems to split very fine. Auden's reassemblage in *The Age of Anxiety* achieves a synthesis he himself calls "baroque." It is a symbol, as all his poetry is, of the disharmonies of our age, and a search for their resolution.

V

Dylan Thomas

THE INTUITIVE FACULTY that Eliot and Auden have tried aesthetically to isolate is related to a quality that has always appeared, in varying proportions, in poetry. Their attempt to separate it as an element may seem unduly pedagogic; but does help us sense more actively the degree of its presence in other poets. Poetry that moves in the direction of pure intuition, that seems to be possessed by forces outside its control, has a long tradition, from the "Dionysian frenzy" to Æ and surrealism; with considerable dispute in each case as to whether the forces tapped are angelic or demonic. Yet even the sober system-loving Aristotle conceded "madness" as a necessary ingredient of poetry.

"When I am commanded by the Spirits," William Blake told Crabb Robinson, "then I write, and the moment I have written, I see the words fly about the room in all directions. It is then published. The Spirits can read and my MS. is of no further use. I have been tempted to burn my MS., but my wife won't let me."

With Blake it was as if technique could not keep pace with insight.

Brought up in a civilization of crewel-work mottoes whose meanings were slowly fading, he cast many of his countering insights in their form: reversals of GOD IS LOVE. "Everything that is is Holy!" he cried, and called for Minute Particulars, the literal documentation of his vision. But it was as if, in his later poems, he had cast the surface meanings of his words to the winds in order to reach the speech of spirits, a "speaking with tongues." Only spirited readers, themselves flying about the room of his poems, could read his meanings as they flew.

Without Blake's triumphant failure a great epic of modern times might not have been written. James Joyce, speaking literally with all tongues, supplied the details of imagery, the inflections of speech, the Minute Particulars to Blake's inordinate vision.

Blake and the early Joyce are predominant influences on the work of the Welsh poet Dylan Thomas. Fortunate, like Joyce, in possessing the background of a folklore and folk rhythms that provide a natural outlet to the expression of vehement fantasy, Thomas modeled his *Portrait of the Artist as a Young Dog* on Joyce's self-examining first novel. For both, self-examination includes precise observation of the world and people about them. In "The Peaches," a section of the novel included in his *Selected Writings* (New Directions, 1946), Thomas describes two cardplayers seen through the window of a public house: "One man was huge and swarthy, with a handlebar moustache and a love-curl on his forehead; seated by his side was a thin, bald, pale old man with his cheeks in his mouth . . . " Even in such a straightforward description there is a quality of translation; not translation *from* another language, but a translation *of* its rhythms. This is brought out especially in the speech of the characters; as when Gwilym, studying to be a preacher, preaches to the young Dylan from a broken haycart: "O God, Thou art everywhere all the time, in the dew of the morning, in the frost of the evening, in the field and the town, in the preacher and the sinner, in the sparrow and the big buzzard. . . . Thou canst see everything we do, in the night and the day, in the day and the night, everything, everything; Thou canst see all the time. O God mun, you're like a bloody cat."

People who are born with a second tongue seem to possess more easily the gift of second sight. For Thomas this is a pervading fantasy that, like the rhythm of another language, supervenes on what he sees. In "The Burning Baby" it settles down over the story. In others, it alternates with reality; they flicker together; as in "A Prospect of the Sea." Filled with fear and desire being kissed by a girl on a hill, "This is a story, he said to himself, about a boy on a holiday kissed by a broom-rider; she flew from a tree onto a hill that changes its size like a frog that loses its temper . . . " He observes his romantic attachment, in "One Warm Saturday," for a young tart: "He saw her as a wise, soft girl whom no hard company could spoil, for her soft self, bare to the heart, broke through every defence of her sensual falsifiers. As he thought this, phrasing her gentleness, faithlessly running to words away from the real room and his love in the middle . . ."

His poetry too is concerned mainly with the ins and outs of fantasy. This he approaches in three ways. The first is a writing *about* it; in the second, reality and fantasy alternate; in the third, he is writing more purely *in* or *from* it. The divisions are not clear-cut, but matters of degree, shifts of emphasis. When, in the first manner, he is making statements about fantasy, the statements include its alternations with reality:

> The force that through the green fuse drives the flower
> Drives my green age; that blasts the roots of trees
> Is my destroyer.
> And I am dumb to tell the crooked rose
> My youth is bent by the same wintry fever.

"The force" is the fantasy; "the flower," reality. In his statement of their connection — which involves thinking of them separately — they flicker together. The intervening "green fuse" combines the abstraction of "force" and the visible "green" through which the flower has been driven. By a no doubt intentional pun, it "fuses" them. The formal balance of the five-line stanza turns like a rose about its center. Alternating half-rhymes, drawn together in the word "fever," whirl about the central conception, "destroyer." The force that creates is in the same act destroying. This formal organization corresponds to the poet's emotional logic. In the instant of experiencing a total rapport with all created beings, the poet is conscious of his complete isolation. He has the rapport but cannot communicate it. This paradox is central to Thomas' poetry.

In the second manner, he writes more deliberately in and out of fantasy:

> Shut, too, in a tower of words, I mark
> On the horizon walking like the trees
> The wordy shapes of women, and the rows
> Of the star-gestured children in the park.
> Some let me make you of the vowelled beeches,
> Some of the oaken voices, from the roots
> Of many a thorny shire tell you notes,
> Some let me make you of the water's speeches.

Being wrapped in fantasy, he sees others as similarly wrapped: women, children, beeches, oaks and water. Are they containers or contained? Wrapped by his syllables, or he by theirs? Translate me, says the poem, as I am trying to translate. "Some let me make you of the vowelled beeches."

His story "The Orchards" begins with Marlais' dream of the love of two scarecrows. Is it a transition from fantasy when he wakes to find his lips still wet from a kiss? The successive films that pass across the story include rejected fantasies of the writer writing it:

> He sharpened his pencil and shut the sky out, shook back his untidy hair, arranged the papers of a devilish story on his desk, and broke the pencil-point with a too-hard scribble of 'sea' and 'fire' on a clean page. Fire would not set the ruled lines alight, adventure, burning, through the heartless characters, nor water close over the bogy heads and the unwritten words. The story was dead from the devil up; there was a white-hot tree with apples where a frozen tower with owls should have rocked in a wind from Antarctica; there were naked girls, with nipples like berries, on the sand in the sun, where a cold and unholy woman should be wailing by the Kara Sea or the Sea of Azov. The morning was against him. He struggled with his words like a man with the sun, and the sun stood victoriously at high noon over the dead story.

Progressive unfoldings of himself and his imaginary self — his "ghost" — in a real and a phantom world form the action of the poem beginning:

I, in my intricate image, stride on two levels,
Forged in man's minerals, the brassy orator
Laying my ghost in metal,
The scales of this twin world tread on the double,
My half ghost in armour hold hard in death's corridor,
To my man-iron sidle.

Beginning with doom in the bulb, the spring unravels,
Bright as her spinning-wheels, the colic season
Worked on a world of petals;
She threads off the sap and needles, blood and bubble
Casts to the pine roots, raising man like a mountain
Out of the naked entrail.

Beginning with doom in the ghost, and the springing marvels,
Image of images, my metal phantom
Forcing forth through the harebell,
My man of leaves and the bronze root, mortal, unmortal,
I, in my fusion of rose and male notion,
Create this twin miracle.

An increasing impatience with literal meanings leads toward the third approach, a more immediate fantasy. To this style belongs his "Ballad of the Long-Legged Bait," telling of the girl hooked and flung into the sea, who drew all the sea to her.

Whales in the wake like capes and Alps
Quaked the sick sea and snouted deep,
Deep the great bushed bait with raining lips
Slipped the fins of those humpbacked tons

And fled their love in a weaving dip.
Oh, Jericho was falling in their lungs!
She nipped and dived in the nick of love,
Spun on a spout like a long-legged ball

Till every beast blared down in a swerve
Till every turtle crushed from his shell
Till every bone in the scuttle grave
Rose and crowed and fell!

Good luck to the hand on the rod,
There is thunder under its thumbs;
Gold gut is a lightning thread,
His fiery reel sings off its flames . . .

In "A Winter's Tale" his symbols emerge through rhythmic returns in a changing context. The action of the poem corresponds to the action of the symbols forming and changing in the poet's mind. It begins with a snowfall in "the snowblind twilight":

And the stars falling cold,
And the smell of hay in the snow, and the far owl
Warning among the folds, and the frozen hold
Flocked with the sheep white smoke of the farm house cowl
In the river wended vales where the tale was told.

The setting for the tale is perfect in the clarity of its description. Then a veil is drawn across, like a sudden gust of snow, or the effect of snowblindness:

Once when the world turned old
On a star of faith pure on the drifting bread,
As the food and flames of the snow, a man unrolled
The scrolls of fire that burned in his heart and head,
Torn and alone in a farm house in a fold

Of fields. . . .

Has the purity of the snow suggested manna, the drifting bread of faith; therefore a miracle; therefore flame? The transition from surface clarity to symbolic depth causes us to question its meanings and to that extent enter the action of the poem. Is the man with miracles in his heart praying for their appearance on earth? He kneels, weeps and prays — "At the point of love, forsaken and afraid" — until the cock crows and "the morning men"

> Stumble out with their spades,
> The cattle stirring, the mousing cat stepping shy,
> The puffed birds hopping and hunting, the milk maids
> Gentle in their clogs over the fallen sky,
> And all the woken farm at its white trades . . .

We see that the poem is consistently plain in its language about the outer world; veiled when alluding to the inner life of the man. The point of contact between them is the falling and fallen snow: "stars falling cold," "fallen sky"; two metaphors in an unfigurative description. From these the symbols of the inner life take off.

> He knelt on the cold stones,
> He wept from the crest of grief, he prayed to the made sky
> May his hunger go howling on bare white bones
> Past the statues of the stables and the sky roofed styes
> And the duck pond glass and the blinding byres alone
>
> Into the home of prayers
> And fires where he should prowl down the cloud
> Of his snow blind love and rush in the white lairs. . . .

Now the poem leaves the literal snowstorm behind. We follow the "naked need" of the man through an inner storm of symbols, "bread of water," "desiring center," "bride bed," "she bird." They whirl, disappear and are blown together. "Time sings through the intricately dead snow drop. Listen." "For love, the long ago she bird rises. Look." "The sky, the bird, the bride . . ." The poem ends in ecstasy:

> . . . he was brought low
> Burning in the bride bed of love, in the whirl
> Pool at the wanting center, in the folds
> Of paradise, in the spun bud of the world.
> And she rose with him flowering in her melting snow.

The flight of a lark describes the course of the poem. In "Vision and Prayer" diamonds and hourglasses, inspired by George Herbert's "Easter Wings," make the shapes of the stanzas. These rhetorical and visual devices of immediacy are parts of a central paradox: poetry's recapture, by deliberate means, of spontaneity; its plotted exaltation.

VI

Robert Lowell

ROBERT LOWELL'S *Lord Weary's Castle* (Harcourt, Brace, 1946) is unusual in its combination of the devotional and the declamatory. They lie together in an uneasy balance; the balance evidenced in the formal structure of his poems, the uneasiness in the violent urgency of their symbols. As Wilfred Owen strove to overmaster the terror of the first world war and to contain his overwhelming indignation in a resolving music, so one feels Lowell's poems pulling themselves up to oppose the modern corruption by which they are appalled. "The Dead in Europe" recognizes the total involvement of total war:

> After the planes unloaded, we fell down
> Buried together, unmarried men and women;
> Not crown of thorns, not iron, not Lombard crown,
> Not grilled and spindle spires pointing to heaven
> Could save us. Raise us, Mother, we fell down
> Here hugger-mugger in the jellied fire:
> Our sacred earth in our day was our curse.

Wars are not the cause of evil, but its most visible and awful signs. In his symbolic search for the underlying causes Lowell is led in conflicting directions. He is led to question the self-righteous Calvinism that is part of his own New England tradition, and as a result driven in Protestant fury into devotional Catholicism. His impulse is still strong to celebrate what he must most denounce. His sonnet "Salem" ends:

> Remember, seaman, Salem fishermen
> Once hung their nimble fleets on the Great Banks.
> Where was it that New England bred the men
> Who quartered the Leviathan's fat flanks
> And fought the British Lion to his knees?

Part of him still wants to write rousing patriotic verse, and feels cheated by the ignominy of modern warfare: a puny pushing of destructive buttons, a dropping of fearful waterbombs on the children in the street. His predicament recalls that of Herman Melville in "A Utilitarian View of the Monitor's Fight":

> War yet shall be, and to the end;
>   But war-paint shows the streaks of weather;
> War yet shall be, but warriors
> Are now but operatives; War's made
>   Less grand than Peace,
>   And a singe runs through lace and feather.

In trying to trace the streak of yellow that runs through modern war Lowell, who has inherited more than one of Melville's searching ambiguities, may have taken a cue from *Moby-Dick.* The symbolic vessel in which the mad one-legged Quaker, Captain Ahab, hunted the White Whale was named after a tribe of Indians, the Pequots, half-exterminated by Puritan settlers. D. H. Lawrence, in his *Studies in Classic American Literature* (London: William Heinemann, 1924) – especially those dealing with Melville and Hawthorne – speaks of America as a land haunted by the spirits of its murdered Indians. That Lowell shares this feeling is suggested by several allusions in his poems; in "Concord":

> The death-dance of King Philip and his scream
> Whose echo girdled this imperfect globe.

in "Children of Light":

> Our fathers wrung their bread from stocks and stones
> And fenced their gardens with the Redman's bones . . .

and in his poem "At the Indian Killer's Grave," introduced by a quotation from Hawthorne: "Here, also, are the veterans of King Philip's War, who burned villages and slaughtered young and old, with pious fierceness, while the godly souls throughout the land were helping them with prayer." The Calvinist could cheat, pillage villages and decimate Indian families without compunction because they were scarcely human, while he was of the elect. Such a motivation, Lowell implies, accounts for Hiroshima and subsequent preparations. What was once a conviction that right ends justify any means is now found purely in totalitarian political philosophies. But it has had its share in forming our own popular opinions of practical expediency. These commonsense views are contrary to the evidence of practice and sense.

As the observation of our own experience and of history testifies, means and ends are reciprocal. Violence leads to violence, which in turn fosters violence. Only human decision can break the chain of this logic, whose terrible links seem to bind inexorably past and future, as if they grew like a curse of their own volition.

> . . . Fall
> And winter, spring and summer, guns unlimber
> And lumber down the narrow gabled street

says Lowell in "The Exile's Return." Our decisions so slowly learn from our experience that we come to seem to ourselves incorrigible, fulfilling the requirements of original sin. Convinced by a fatalism we cannot accept, we look for the intervention of a suprarational, suprahuman agency.

Fatalism motivates the doom-treading measures of "The Quaker Graveyard in Nantucket":

Sailors, who pitch this portent at the sea
Where dreadnaughts shall confess
Its hell-bent deity,
When you are powerless
To sand-bag this Atlantic bulwark, faced
By the earth-shaker, green, unwearied, chaste
In his steel scales: ask for no Orphean lute
To pluck life back. . . .

The prevailing dread is relieved by the contrast of a devotional sixth section, "Our Lady of Walsingham":

There once the penitents took off their shoes
And then walked barefoot the remaining mile;
And the small trees, a stream and hedgerows file
Slowly along the munching English lane,
Like cows to the old shrine, until you lose
Track of your dragging pain.

In "The Soldier," "Two angels fought with bill-hooks for his soul." And in "The First Sunday in Lent":

On Troy's last day, alas, the populous
Shrines held carnival, and girls and boys
Flung garlands to the wooden horse; so we
Burrow into the lion's mouth to die.
Lord, from the lust and dust thy will destroys
Raise an unblemished Adam who will see
The limbs of the tormented chestnut tree
Tingle, and hear the March-winds lift and cry:
"The Lord of Hosts will overshadow us."

Lowell's declamatory eloquence calls upon a variety of resources to project his emotion with depth and immediacy. In "New Year's Day" it is an accomplished rhetoric of direct statement: "While we live, we live / To snuff the smoke of victims." In "The Holy Innocents" it is a plain symbol derived from the lovingly observed details of a scene:

Listen, the hay-bells tinkle as the cart
Wavers on rubber tires along the tar
And cindered ice below the burlap mill
And ale-wife run. The oxen drool and start
In wonder at the fenders of a car,
And blunder hugely up St. Peter's hill.
These are the undefiled by woman — their
Sorrow is not the sorrow of this world:
King Herod shrieking vengeance at the curled
Up knees of Jesus choking in the air,

A king of speechless clods and infants. Still
The world out-Herods Herod; and the year,
The nineteen-hundred forty-fifth of grace,
Lumbers with losses up the clinkered hill
Of our purgation; and the oxen near
The worn foundations of their resting-place,
The holy manger where their bed is corn
And holly torn for Christmas. If they die,
As Jesus, in the harness, who will mourn?
Lamb of the shepherds, Child, how still you lie.

In "The Ferris Wheel," Part II of "The First Sunday in Lent," it is the dream-real image of the world as a rundown amusement device, from which a "townsman" strains to warn us of our peril. The action develops like a mere anxiety dream; the eagle of war places the wheel in the devil's tent, the man works loose,

. . . drags and zigzags through the circus hoops,
And lion-taming Satan bows and loops
His cracking tail into a hangman's noose;
He is the only happy man in Lent.
He laughs into my face until I cry.

All are brought together in "The Quaker Graveyard," the most fully orchestrated of his poems, which begins with the phosphorescent vision of the drowned sailor:

. . . Light
Flashed from his matted head and marble feet,
He grappled at the net
With the coiled, hurdling muscles of his thighs:
The corpse was bloodless, a botch of reds and whites,
Its open, staring eyes
Were lustreless dead-lights
Or cabin-windows on a stranded hulk
Heavy with sand. . . .

Some of the harsh, sea-revolving rhythms of Melville are heard in the lament that follows:

. . . The winds' wings beat upon the stones,
Cousin, and scream for you and the claws rush
At the sea's throat and wring it in the slush
Of this old Quaker graveyard where the bones
Cry out in the long night for the hurt beast
Bobbing by Ahab's whaleboats in the East.

And Melville's prodigious double symbol of the White Whale – god or devil? hunted or hunter? the evil of existence, its mystery, its terror or its meaning? prophet-swallower, home of Jonas? or fulfiller of prophecy and symbol of Christ, the swallower of his own prophets, who walked on the water? – is reflected and resolved in the magnificent fifth section:

When the whale's viscera go and the roll
Of its corruption overruns this world
Beyond tree-swept Nantucket and Wood's Hole
And Martha's Vineyard, Sailor, will your sword
Whistle and fall and sink into the fat?
In the great ash-pit of Jehoshaphat
The bones cry for the blood of the white whale,
The fat flukes arch and whack about its ears,
The death-lance churns into the sanctuary, tears
The gun-blue swingle, heaving like a flail,
And hacks the coiling life out: it works and drags

And rips the sperm-whale's midriff into rags,
Gobbets of blubber spill to wind and weather,
Sailor, and gulls go round the stoven timbers
Where the morning stars sing out together
And thunder shakes the white surf and dismembers
The red flag hammered in the mast-head. Hide,
Our steel, Jonas Messias, in Thy side.

VII

Elizabeth Bishop

ELIZABETH BISHOP'S "The Map," the first poem in her book *North & South* (Houghton Mifflin, 1946), is a good reference to consult in beginning the exploration of her world. For hers is a clearly delineated world:

> Land lies in water; it is shadowed green.
> Shadows, or are they shallows, at its edges
> showing the line of long sea-weeded ledges
> where weeds hang to the simple blue from green.

This surface clarity is deceptive. Its effect is so natural, we are hardly aware how much is being described: the map itself, the seacoast it suggests, and a particular way of seeing and relating both.

> Or does the land lean down to lift the sea from under,
> drawing it unperturbed around itself?
> Along the fine tan sandy shelf
> is the land tugging at the sea from under?

The method is direct, reticent and gracious. Without preamble we are presented with the poet's observations and reflections as if they were our own.

The map has its mysterious regions:

> The shadow of Newfoundland lies flat and still.

It has aptnesses that seem more than accidental:

> Labrador's yellow, where the moony Eskimo
> has oiled it. . . .

It gives us new experiences:

> . . . We can stroke these lovely bays,
> under a glass as if they were expected to blossom,
> or as if to provide a clean cage for invisible fish.

Its compressions liberate spontaneity:

> The names of seashore towns run out to sea,
> the names of cities cross the neighboring mountains
> — the printer here experiencing the same excitement
> as when emotion too far exceeds its cause.

It extends familiar observation to the unfamiliar:

> These peninsulas take the water between thumb and finger
> like women feeling for the smoothness of yard-goods.

It alters some of our perceptions, and adds others:

> Mapped waters are more quiet than the land is,
> lending the land their waves' own conformation:
> and Norway's hare runs south in agitation,
> profiles investigate the sea, where land is.

How many of these qualities have been put in by the map-maker? How many originated in the world he is representing?

Are they assigned, or can the countries pick their colors?
—What suits the character or the native waters best.
Topography displays no favorites; North's as near as West.
More delicate than the historians' are the map-makers' colors.

Perception, precision, compression: these are some of the qualities of a good map, and of "The Map." It dawns on us that a number of discreet comments on the art of poetry have been implied. They are not stated; we experience them directly in the action of the poem. One of its witty implications lies in its choice of comparison. The exact craft of the cartographer is perhaps least associated, customarily, with our ideas of poetry. By showing us how human the map-maker's decisions have to be, and how imaginative our reading of a literal map, the poem prepares us for poetry's exactitudes. It demolishes a prejudice without alluding to it.

Following the generally southern course of these poems, from "The Imaginary Iceberg" toward the "state with the prettiest name," we are exploring a style supple, versatile and idiomatic. Unpretentiously sophisticated, it has easily assimilated contemporary and traditional techniques. Its rhythms are as natural as breathing. Its images and ideas seem to be crossing our minds. This effect of effortlessness, of great naturalness, conceals its premeditations. Her poems seem to have sought their shapes like water.

"The Imaginary Iceberg," her magnetic north, is that goal we would rather have than the ship, the means of reaching it:

We'd rather have the iceberg than the ship;
we'd rather own this breathing plain of snow
though the ships' sails were laid upon the sea
as the snow lies undissolved upon the water.

Having arrived there, "the ship ignored"—like Keats' "viewless wings"—we inspect our secret wish:

. . . The iceberg rises
and sinks again; its glassy pinnacles
correct elliptics in the sky.

This is a scene where he who treads the boards
is artlessly rhetorical. The curtain
is light enough to rise on finest ropes
that airy twists of snow provide.
The wits of these white peaks
spar with the sun. . . .

Brilliant spontaneity is peculiarly the artist's iceberg; that "artless rhetoric" toward which all techniques are pointed. We may view it only for a moment:

Good-bye, we say, good-bye, the ship steers off
where waves give in to one another's waves
and clouds run in a warmer sky.
Icebergs behoove the soul
(Both being self-made from elements least visible)
to see them so: fleshed, fair, erected indivisible.

In "Wading at Wellfleet" the sea, like an Assyrian chariot, is, in George Herbert's phrase, "all a case of knives."

Lying so close, they catch the sun,
the spokes directed at the shin.
The chariot front is blue and great.

The war rests wholly with the waves:
they try revolving, but the wheels
give way, they will not bear the weight.

How beautifully she has used the simple words "blue" and "great" to emphasize the sea's perpetually foundering menace.

Water images give their fluctuations to the form and rhythms of "Quai d'Orleans":

Each barge on the river easily tows
 a mighty wake,
a giant oak-leaf of gray lights
 on duller gray;

and behind it real leaves are floating by,
    down to the sea.
Mercury-veins on the giant leaves,
    the ripples, make
for the sides of the quai, to extinguish themselves
    against the walls
as softly as falling-stars come to their ends
    at a point in the sky.

Contained in a formal metre and regular rhyme, as a river is contained by its banks, the poem holds within it interlocking devices of sound and rhythm. Alternately towing lines confirm the barges towing their wakes, the giant imaginary oak-leaf trailing its little literal leaves. Whole rhymes ("wake" – "make") interplay glitteringly with their surrounding ripples of assonance, "tows" and "wake" merging into "oak" and recalling her line "where waves give in to one another's waves." Staring into the poem as we would into water, we are aware that its resurgent imagery, its washing rhythms breaking, lengthening and circling, create modulations various and repetitive as the memory it symbolizes:

'If what we see could forget us half as easily,'
    I want to tell you,
'as it does itself – but for life we'll not be rid
    of the leaves' fossils.'

"The Gentleman of Shalott" exemplifies man's duality by his physical symmetry:

. . . this arrangement
of leg and leg and
arm and so on.

Unlike Tennyson's heroine, he doesn't have to look in a glass. His shape is his mirror, divided

somewhere along the line
of what we call the spine.

Which side is which? Where does introspection leave off and solid animal begin? Resigned to imperfection,

> . . . the uncertainty
> he says he
> finds exhilarating. He loves
> that sense of constant re-adjustment.
> He wishes to be quoted as saying at present:
> 'Half is enough.'

Fantasy reflecting reality is beautifully developed in "The Man-Moth." We are prepared for the nocturnal sidewalk emergence of this distinctly urban chimera by the ordinary effects of moonlight:

> The whole shadow of Man is only as big as his hat.
> It lies at his feet like a circle for a doll to stand on,
> and he makes an inverted pin, the point magnetized to the moon.
> He does not see the moon; he observes only her vast properties,
> feeling the queer light on his hands, neither warm nor cold,
> of a temperature impossible to record in thermometers.

The Man-Moth "nervously begins to scale the faces of buildings." He believes the moon is a hole in the sky, toward which he climbs, "his shadow dragging like a photographer's cloth behind him," fearing and hoping to be "forced through, as from a tube, in black scrolls on the light." Failing as usual, he descends to a high-speed subway, which he rides backwards, with his fears in his pockets. In the last stanza we are given the proof of his existence:

> If you catch him,
> hold up a flashlight to his eye. It's all dark pupil,
> an entire night itself, whose haired horizon tightens
> as he stares back, and closes up the eye. Then from the lids
> one tear, his only possession, like the bee's sting, slips.
> Slyly he palms it, and if you're not paying attention
> he'll swallow it. However, if you watch, he'll hand it over,
> cool as from underground springs and pure enough to drink.

There is no general rhetorical effect to be isolated to summarize Elizabeth Bishop's poems. Each poem discovers and is true to its own method. Among many fine ones – "Love Lies Sleeping," which re-creates a waking city; "The Monument," with its intricately clear description of a fabricated and changing object; the Cuban and Negro folksong qualities of "Jerónimo's House" and "Songs for a Colored Singer"; "Anaphora"; "The Weed" – perhaps the finest is the long magnificently incantatory "Roosters":

> At four o'clock
> in the gun-metal blue dark
> we hear the first crow of the first cock
>
> just below
> the gun-metal blue window
> and immediately there is an echo
>
> off in the distance,
> then one from the back-yard fence,
> then one, with horrible insistence,
>
> grates like a wet match
> from the broccoli patch,
> flares, and all over town begins to catch.

Sustained and accelerating, its three-line form constantly suggesting the rooster's triple blast, the poem moves from a country morning to the morning of Christianity. The symbolic triple rebuke of Peter becomes the sign of his forgiveness. In a forgiving mood the poem closes, "old holy sculpture" and "medieval relic" blending now in

> . . . lines of pink cloud in the sky,
>
> the day's preamble
> like wandering lines in marble.
> The cocks are now almost inaudible.
>
> The sun climbs in,
> following 'to see the end,'
> faithful as enemy, or friend.

Or is it "The Fish"? whose captured features —

battered and venerable
and homely. Here and there
his brown skin hung in strips
like ancient wall-paper,
and its pattern of darker brown
was like wall-paper:
shapes like full-blown roses
stained and lost through age . . .

— combine with his history —

. . . five old pieces of fish-line,
or four and a wire leader
with the swivel still attached,
with all their five big hooks
grown firmly in his mouth . . .

— to provide an exultant symbol radiating triumph:

I stared and stared
and victory filled up
the little rented boat,
from the pool of bilge
where oil had spread a rainbow
around the rusted engine
to the bailer rusted orange,
the sun-cracked thwarts,
the oarlocks on their strings,
the gunnels — until everything
was rainbow, rainbow, rainbow!
And I let the fish go.

ORIGINALITY AND TRADITION

Originality and Tradition

THE POETS we have been reading were chosen as examples of originality. We have seen some of their individual qualities in action. Now that we gain perspective, what is it that is common to them all? What is originality?

I hope the question vaporizes in your mind as it does in mine. No blithe generalization is going to be just to such a diversity of method and attitude. Is originality a departure from tradition? Many of these poets, even the most inventive, draw heavily on forms and ideas of the past; while those most concerned with tradition and their place in it do not simply repeat its patterns. Eliot, dedicated as he is to an apprehension of the timeless moment, considers it primarily in its intersection with the temporal present. He has chosen those elements of tradition that he feels contribute to an understanding of contemporary life.

Originality includes but is not innovation. It neither opposes tradition nor is bound by it. If we can think of tradition at all comprehensively and comprehendingly, it is due largely to the action of original minds exploring the past. Tradition itself is another vaporizing conception. It thins out the more it is considered apart from specific action. Customary appeals in its name are appeals to a particular tradition; as if one should call upon the bird to consider the dinosaur.

Originality is not the new and tradition is not the old. But as originality tends to become confused in our minds with its novelties, so tradition tends to become confused with its residues. Poetic conventions, like the dinosaur's bones, are useful to study for their principles. Unless these principles are related to action they are useless. No more spontaneously generated than life, poetry evolves and renews itself.

The life of poetry and the life of lives are of different sorts. In life the individual dies, while the form of life continues. In poetry the individual persists after the form has altered. Homer's *Odyssey* continues to be original. At each return we discover new meanings in it. We may use its form as a model, as Joyce did in *Ulysses,* but only as the model for a new form; we cannot reproduce it.

Forms in poetry alter with the kinds of life they symbolize. Folksong and ballad are natural to a life that is relatively simple. When we use them today, either we write imitations of them – reconstructions of the dinosaur's bones – or we include in them some of the complexities of our own life, and thus alter the form.

In evolving out of the past, in inventing new forms, modern poetry does not thereby exceed the great poetry of the past. It comes into an equivalent condition, a timeless present. Aware of its age and of the conflicts of that age, it shares with the poetry of all ages the common quality of delight, a delight which is a conscious achievement.

In the arts, the ordinary sense of time is a delusion. We live only now, but our imaginations go backward and forward in time. A poem new to us now is new whether it was written yesterday or three thousand years ago. The "time" in the older poem is other people's time. The fact of survival contributes a delusive sense of appreciation. Other people, even generations of them, even generations of the literary critics among them, are no more infallible than we are. All their opinions can give us are hints to our own judgment. If we take the hint for the judgment, we can no more comprehend and evaluate the sonnets of Shakespeare than we can the latest poem in the latest little magazine.

The present is a period that cannot be formulated until it is gone, and cannot be completely formulated then. In poetry the "present moment" is a continuously shifting battleground. Today or in 1798 when Wordsworth's *Lyrical Ballads* were published, it is the scene of a struggle between conventionalism – an excessive appeal to authority – and its opposite number, the espousal of innovation for its own sake. Originality is the quality of mind which throws light both ways: on the conventions, discovering their principles and purposes; on the innovations, discovering their meaningful uses.

Even to reverse the findings of the past is to continue tradition. For tradition, unlike the conventions, depends not on the fostering of rigidities, but on ever greater varieties of flexibility. It does not establish unity by ruling out diversity. Its unity is discovered in and through experience.

The qualities of immediacy and simultaneity characterizing modern poetry have always characterized poetry of "the present moment." Rimbaud worked out a series of color-equivalents for the various vowels. Dante, in "una lunga striga," conveyed the motion of flight – "a long streak" of birds – in the sound of his phrase.

These acts of translation between the senses may thin out into vapidity, like any translation. The search for the elusive may all but elude experience. But in the arts discoveries only come from pushing things too far. Art is like that Eastern potentate who ate and ate and ate. When they asked him if he'd had enough, he replied, "Yes. Too much. Too much is just enough for me."

Immediacy and simultaneity, intensified today as they were by Chaucer and Aristophanes, are related to new attitudes of man toward himself and his world. The tendency is in the direction of observing, without the intervention of authority, custom, or preconceived idea.

When we approach modern poetry with the attention we give developments in mechanics and physics we discover that conceptions similar to those that have revolutionized thinking in the sciences are also at work in the arts; that there are basic connections between some of the time-space formulations of physics, "faceted Cubism," modern harmonics, and the composite symbols of *Finnegans Wake.*

In his great work Joyce achieved complex immediacies and simultaneities never before dreamed of. The title alone is a spiral pun, the equivalent of the reclining 8, the mathematical symbol for infinity. Both words of his title suggest both death and life. "Finnegan," by a pun on the French *fin,* suggests "end again." Yet from the rhyme of the ballad from which it is taken, it immediately recalls "begin again." And "Wake" is both a death-watch and an awakening. Like the book, the title leads continuously into itself.

In expressing modern life, its speed, its incongruities, poets have discovered new relationships, symbolic puns, devices of association and juxtaposition, half-rhymes and broken rhythms. Sometimes these devices are expressive, sometimes merely intricate. It is always pertinent to indicate which one thinks they are, and why. New forms are just as much in danger of becoming clichés as the forms cherished by academicians. This too is legitimate grounds for criticism, just as it is always to the point to spot the influences under which any poet, young or old, is working. And conversely, if one can, to recognize his idiom.

Even those experiments which we may come to regard as unsuccessful in themselves will have sharpened our perceptions and our appreciations. Not only will we be more knowledgeably aware of the more fortunate productions of our time, but we will have gained additional insight into the great works of the past.

The timelessness of the arts has a temporal qualification. If we lose the immediate significance of a work of art, we are less likely to grasp its universal application. An inability to comprehend the relationship of modern work to the age in which we live atrophies our capacity for understanding past masterpieces, related as they are to ages in which we do not, except vicariously, participate.

What is usable in the past is not preserved by repetition. Conventions tend to deny tradition. Originality — the exploration of new forms, the discovery of new relationships — becomes tradition. By it the past, reinterpreted, is revivified. And the present, too, is seen to be, not a collection of relics, but a continuing evolution.

Bibliographies

Bibliography of Principal American Editions

JAMES STEPHENS (1882)

PROSE

The Charwoman's Daughter (Mary, Mary). The Macmillan Co., 1912.
The Crock of Gold. The Macmillan Co., 1912.
Here Are Ladies. The Macmillan Co., 1913.
* *The Demi-Gods.* The Macmillan Co., 1914.
* *The Insurrection in Dublin.* The Macmillan Co., 1916.
Irish Fairy Tales. The Macmillan Co., 1920; listed as a juvenile.
* *Deirdre.* The Macmillan Co., 1923.
In the Land of Youth. The Macmillan Co., 1924.
* *Etched in Moonlight.* The Macmillan Co., 1928.
* *On Prose and Verse.* The Bowling Green Press, 1928.

POETRY

*†‡ *Insurrections.* Dublin: Maunsel & Co., 1909.
*† *The Hill of Vision.* The Macmillan Co., 1912.
*† *Songs from the Clay.* The Macmillan Co., 1915.
*† *The Rocky Road to Dublin.* The Macmillan Co., 1915.
*† *Green Branches.* The Macmillan Co., 1916.
*† *Reincarnations.* The Macmillan Co., 1918.
*† *A Poetry Recital.* The Macmillan Co., 1925.
* *Collected Poems.* The Macmillan Co., 1926.
* *Strict Joy.* The Macmillan Co., 1931.
Kings & the Moon. The Macmillan Co., 1938.

T. S. ELIOT (1888)

PROSE

*† *The Sacred Wood.* Alfred A. Knopf, Inc., 1920.
*† *For Lancelot Andrewes.* Doubleday, Doran and Co., 1929.
Selected Essays 1917–1932. Harcourt, Brace & Co., Inc., 1932.
* *The Use of Poetry and the Use of Criticism.* Harvard University Press, 1933.
* *After Strange Gods.* Harcourt, Brace & Co., Inc., 1933.
Essays Ancient and Modern. Harcourt, Brace & Co., Inc., 1936.
* *The Idea of a Christian Society.* Harcourt, Brace & Co., Inc., 1940.
Notes Towards the Definition of Culture. Harcourt, Brace & Co., Inc., 1949.

* Out of print, as of May, 1949.
† All or mostly included in later volume.
‡ Published abroad.

POETRY

*† *Poems.* Alfred A. Knopf, Inc., 1920.
*† *The Waste Land.* Boni & Liveright, 1922.
*† *Ash-Wednesday.* G. P. Putnam's Sons, 1930.
*† *Poems 1909–1925.* Harcourt, Brace & Co., Inc., 1932
* *The Rock.* Harcourt, Brace & Co., Inc., 1934.
Murder in the Cathedral. Harcourt, Brace & Co., Inc., 1935.
Collected Poems 1909–1935. Harcourt, Brace & Co., Inc., 1936.
The Family Reunion. Harcourt, Brace & Co., Inc., 1939.
Old Possum's Book of Practical Cats. Harcourt, Brace & Co., Inc., 1940.
Four Quartets. Harcourt, Brace & Co., Inc., 1943.

MARIANNE MOORE (1887)

*†‡ *Poems.* London: The Egoist Press, 1921.
*† *Observations.* The Dial Press, 1924.
* *Selected Poems.* The Macmillan Co., 1935.
‡ *Selected Poems.* London: Faber and Faber Ltd., 1935.
* *What Are Years.* The Macmillan Co., 1941.
Nevertheless. The Macmillan Co., 1944.

E. E. CUMMINGS (1894)

PROSE AND REPRODUCTIONS

The Enormous Room. H. Liveright, 1922. Modern Library edition, 1934.
Him. Boni & Liveright, 1927.
* *CIOPW.* Covici Friede, Inc., 1931.
Eimi. Covici Friede, Inc., 1933. Reissued by William Sloane Associates, Inc., 1948.
* *Tom.* Arrow Editions, 1935.
* *Anthropos — the Future of Art.* The Golden Eagle Press, 1945.

POETRY

*† *Tulips and Chimneys.* T. Seltzer, 1923.
*† *XLI Poems.* Dial Press, 1925.
*† *&.* Privately Printed, 1925.
† *Is 5.* Boni & Liveright, 1926.
*† *Christmas Tree.* American Book Bindery, Inc., 1928.
*† (No Title). Covici Friede, Inc., 1930.
*† *W (ViVa).* H. Liveright, 1931.
*† *No Thanks.* The Golden Eagle Press, 1935.
*†‡ *1/20.* London: Roger Roughton, 1936.

Collected Poems. Harcourt, Brace & Co., Inc., 1938.
50 Poems. Duell, Sloan and Pearce, 1940.
1X1. Henry Holt & Co., Inc., 1944.
Santa Claus. Henry Holt & Co., Inc., 1946.

WALLACE STEVENS (1879)

Harmonium. Alfred A. Knopf, Inc., 1923, 1931.
Ideas of Order. Alfred A. Knopf, Inc., 1936.
The Man with the Blue Guitar. Alfred A. Knopf, Inc., 1937.
Parts of a World. Alfred A. Knopf, Inc., 1942.
Transport to Summer. Alfred A. Knopf, Inc., 1947.

EZRA POUND (1885)

PROSE

*‡ *The Spirit of Romance.* London: J. M. Dent & Sons, Ltd., 1910.
* *Pavannes and Divisions,* Alfred A. Knopf, Inc., 1918.
* *Instigations,* Boni & Liveright, 1920.
* *Antheil and the Treatise on Harmony.* P. Covici, 1927.
* *ABC of Reading.* Yale University Press, 1934.
* *Make It New.* Yale University Press, 1935.
Polite Essays. New Directions, 1937.
* *Culture.* New Directions, 1938.
* *ABC of Economics.* New Directions, 1939.
The Tao Hio of Confucius. New Directions, 1939.
The Unwobbling Pivot of Confucius. New Directions, 1947.

POETRY

*† *Ripostes.* Small, Maynard & Co., 1913.
*† *Lustrae.* Alfred A. Knopf, Inc., 1917.
*† *Poems 1918–21.* Boni & Liveright, 1921.
†‡ *A Draft of XVI Cantos.* Three Mountains Press, 1925.
Personae: The Collected Poems of Ezra Pound. Boni & Liveright 1926; reissued by New Directions.
†‡ *A Draft of 17–27 Cantos.* London: John Rodker, 1928.
‡ *Guido Cavalcanti, Rime.* Genoa: Marsano, 1932.
*† *A Draft of XXX Cantos.* Farrar & Rinehart, Inc., 1933.
*† *Eleven New Cantos.* Farrar & Rinehart, Inc., 1934.
*† *The Fifth Decad of Cantos.* Farrar & Rinehart, Inc., 1937.
*† *Cantos LII–LXXI.* New Directions, 1940.
† *The Pisan Cantos.* New Directions, 1948.
The Cantos of Ezra Pound. New Directions, 1948.
Selected Poems. New Directions, 1949.

WILLIAM CARLOS WILLIAMS (1883)

PROSE

* *Kora in Hell; Improvisations.* Four Seas Co., 1920.
* *The Great American Novel.* Three Mountains Press, 1923.
In the American Grain. A. & C. Boni, 1925. New Directions edition, 1939.
* *A Voyage to Pagany.* The Macaulay Co., 1928.
* *The Knife of the Times, and Other Stories.* The Dragon Press, 1932.
* *Novelette and Other Prose,* 1921–1931. Bruce Humphries, Inc., 1932.
*† *White Mule.* New Directions, 1937.
Life Along the Passaic River. New Directions, 1938.
† *In the Money.* New Directions, 1940.
First Act (White Mule and *In the Money* combined). New Directions, 1947.
A Dream of Love (play). New Directions, 1948.

POETRY

*† *A Book of Poems, Al que quiere!* The Four Seas Co., 1917.
*† *Sour Grapes; a Book of Poems.* The Four Seas Co., 1921.
*† *Collected Poems: 1921–1931.* The Objective Press, 1934.
*† *An Early Martyr, and Other Poems.* The Alcestis Press, 1935.
*† *Adam & Eve & The City.* The Alcestis Press, 1935.
* *The Complete Collected Poems: 1906–1938.* New Directions, 1938.
* *The Broken Span.* New Directions, 1941.
* *The Wedge.* The Cummington Press, 1944.
Paterson (Book I). New Directions, 1946.
Paterson (Book II). New Directions, 1948.
The Clouds, Aigeltinger, Russia, Etc. Wells College Press and the Cummington Press, 1948.
Selected Poems. New Directions, 1949.

OGDEN NASH (1902)

*† *Hard Lines.* Simon and Schuster, Inc., 1931.
*† *Free Wheeling.* Simon and Schuster, Inc., 1931.
*† *Happy Days.* Simon and Schuster, Inc., 1933.
*† *The Primrose Path.* Simon and Schuster, Inc., 1935.
*† *The Bad Parents' Garden of Verse.* Simon and Schuster, Inc., 1936.
I'm a Stranger Here Myself. Little, Brown and Co., 1938.
* *The Face Is Familiar.* Little, Brown and Co., 1940.
Good Intentions. Little, Brown and Co., 1942.
Many Long Years Ago. Little, Brown and Co., 1945.
The Selected Verse. Modern Library, 1946.

Versus. Little, Brown and Co., 1949.
In collaboration with S. J. Perelman:
One Touch of Venus. Little, Brown and Co., 1944.

In collaboration with Vernon Duke:
Ogden Nash's Musical Zoo. Little, Brown and Co., 1947.

W. H. AUDEN (1907)

*† *Poems.* Random House, Inc., 1934.
*† *On This Island.* Random House, Inc., 1937.
*† *Another Time.* Random House, Inc., 1940.
*† *The Double Man.* Random House, Inc., 1941.
*† *For the Time Being.* Random House, Inc., 1944.
The Collected Poetry. Random House, Inc., 1945.
The Age of Anxiety. Random House, Inc., 1947.

In collaboration with Christopher Isherwood:
* *The Dog Beneath the Skin.* Random House, Inc., 1935.
* *The Ascent of F–6.* Random House, Inc., 1937.
* *On the Frontier.* Random House, Inc., 1938.
* *Journey to a War.* Random House, Inc., 1939.

In collaboration with Louis MacNeice:
* *Letters from Iceland.* Random House, Inc., 1937.

DYLAN THOMAS (1914)

PROSE

Portrait of the Artist as a Young Dog. New Directions, 1940.

POETRY

* *The World I Breath.* New Directions, 1939.
* *New Poems.* New Directions, 1942.
*‡ *Deaths and Entrances.* London: J. M. Dent & Sons, 1946.
The Selected Writings. New Directions, 1946.

ROBERT LOWELL (1917)

*† *Land of Unlikeness.* The Cummington Press, 1944.
Lord Weary's Castle. Harcourt, Brace & Co., Inc., 1946.

ELIZABETH BISHOP (1911)

North & South. Houghton Mifflin Co., 1946.

Bibliography of Recordings*

JAMES STEPHENS

London Library of Recorded English: (Book I, Record 5, Side 2) The County Mayo; The Fifteen Acres.

T. S. ELIOT

Columbia Records: Pleasure Dome Album: The Waste Land. II, A Game of Chess (by permission of *Library of Congress*).

Harvard Vocarium: (SS–5052, 53) Gerontion; The Hollow Men.
(*P–1202, 03) Journey of the Magi; A Song for Simeon.
(*P–1206, 07) Fragment of an Agon.
(P–1200, 01) The Love Song of J. Alfred Prufrock.
(P–1204, 05) Triumphal March; Difficulties of a Statesman.

Library of Congress: (P11A–B) The Waste Land. I, The Burial of the Dead. II, A Game of Chess.
(P12A–B) The Waste Land. III, The Fire Sermon. IV, Death by Water.
(P13A–B) The Waste Land. V, What the Thunder Said.
(P14A–B) Ash Wednesday. I, "Because I do not hope to turn again." II, "Lady, three white leopards sat under a juniper tree." III, "At the first turning of the second stair." IV, "Who walked between the violet and the violet."
(P15A–B) Ash Wednesday. V, "If the lost word is lost." VI, "Although I do not hope to turn again." Landscapes: I, New Hampshire. II, Virginia. Sweeney Among the Nightingales.

London: HMV: Four Quartets.

* *Note*: My list includes only commercially produced or purchasable records. For information about these and other recordings of modern poetry, address the following:

Harvard Vocarium Discs, edited by Associate Professor F. C. Packard, Jr., Harvard College Library, care of the Business Office, Cambridge 38, Massachusetts.

London Library of Recorded Music, edited by V. C. Clinton-Baddeley, United Programmes, Ltd., 8 Waterloo Place, London, S.W. 1, England. (At present, mostly traditional poetry recited by such readers as Dylan Thomas, V. C. Clinton-Baddeley, James Stephens, etc. An album of modern poetry is in preparation.)

National Council of Teachers of English, Walter C. Garwick, Harrison, N.Y.

Twentieth Century Poetry in English, Recording Laboratory, Division of Music, Library of Congress, Washington 25, D.C. (Catalogue 5¢).

MARIANNE MOORE

Columbia Records: Pleasure Dome Album: In Distrust of Merits.

Library of Congress: (P7A & B) Rigorists, Spenser's Ireland, Selections from Virginia Britannia.

National Council of Teachers of English: He Digesteth Harde Yron, See in the Midst of Leaves, What Are Years, The Buffalo.

E. E. CUMMINGS

Columbia Records: Pleasure Dome Album: "Spring is like a perhaps hand," "this little bride & groom," "pity this busy monster,manunkind," "rain or hail."

***Decca*: "Poem, or Beauty Hurts Mr. Vinal," "Item," "Buffalo Bill," "In Just Spring," "Oh Sweet Spontaneous Earth," "Since Feeling is First," "Somewhere I Have Never Traveled."

Library of Congress: (P18A & B) "plato told him," "my father moved through dooms of love."

The National Council of Teachers of English: Numbers 13, 29, 33 and 42 from *50 Poems.*

WILLIAM CARLOS WILLIAMS

Columbia Records: Pleasure Dome Album: The Young Housewife, The Bull, Poem ("As the cat"), Lear, The Dance, El Hombre.

Library of Congress: (P16A–B) Peace on Earth, Light Hearted William, Spring and All ("By the road to the contagious hospital"), It is a Living Coral, Queen-Ann's-Lace, The Yachts.

National Council of Teachers of English: The Red Wheelbarrow, Trace, A Coronal, The Defective Record, To an Old Woman, To Elsie, The Wind Increases, Classic Scene.

OGDEN NASH

Columbia Records: Pleasure Dome Album: Allow Me, Madam, But it Won't Help; The Hunter; The Perfect Husband; The Outcome of Mr. McLeod's Gratitude; Introspective Reflections; So Penseroso.

Decca: (Album) Two and One Are a Problem, The Individualist, Traveler's Rest, The Husband's Lament, Bankers Are Like Anybody Else Only Richer, Seven Miles to Joe's Place, I Have It on Good Authority, Seaside Serenade, The Drop of a Hat, Just Be Quiet and Nobody Will Notice, One Third of a Calendar, The Common Cold, Isn't Nature Wonderful.

** Out of print.

W. H. AUDEN

Columbia Records: Pleasure Dome Album: Ballad, Prime.

Harvard Vocarium: (P–1052, 53) The Traveller, and Sonnets XVII, XXI, XXVII, etc.

Library of Congress: (P3A & B) Alonso to Ferdinand, Musée des Beaux Arts, Refugee Blues.

National Council of Teachers of English: In Memory of W. B. Yeats, Casino, Law Like Love.

DYLAN THOMAS

Columbia Records: Pleasure Dome Album: Poem in October, In My Craft Or Sullen Art.

ROBERT LOWELL

Harvard Vocarium: (P–1128, 29) Yankee Graveyard in Nantucket.

ELIZABETH BISHOP

Columbia Records: Pleasure Dome Album: Anaphora, Late Air, The Fish.

Index

Index